VOICES
from
VIETNAM

★

MICHAEL E. STEVENS
Editor

A. KRISTEN FOSTER
ELLEN D. GOLDLUST-GINGRICH
REGAN RHEA
Assistant Editors

Center for Documentary History
STATE HISTORICAL SOCIETY OF WISCONSIN
Madison: 1996

For those who died in Vietnam

Front cover: Co. B, 2nd 506th Infantry, Airmobile 101st Airborne CP (Command Post),
March 21, 1971. On the ridgeline overlooking FSB (Fire Support Base) Vandegrift with
land formations "The Rockpile" (center - see map page iv) and "Razorback" in the
background are (l to r) Sgt. Patrick Bailey, Artillery Forward Observer Radio RTO (Radio
Telephone Operator); Lt. Don Speet, Artillery Forward Observer; SP4 Steve Commo,
CP Medic; Capt. Carl Jensen, Company Commander; and SP4 Donald Thies, Battalion
Radio RTO. In front is SP4 Buford Byers, Company Radio RTO.
Photo by SP4 Mark Wissel, Secure Set Radio RTO. WHi Image ID 87338.

Back cover: WHi Image ID 87337.
Cover design by Andrew J. Brozyna

LIBRARY OF CONGRESS CATALOGING-IN-PUBLICATION DATA
Voices from Vietnam. (Voices of the Wisconsin Past.)
Michael E. Stevens, editor.
A. Kristen Foster, Ellen D. Goldlust-Gingrich, Regan Rhea, assistant editors.
Includes glossary, bibliographical references, and index.

ISBN 0-87020-285-5 [clothbound]   0-87020-287-1 [paperbound]

1. Vietnamese Conflict, 1961–1975—Personal narratives, American.
2. Vietnamese Conflict, 1961–1975—Veterans—Wisconsin—Diaries.
3. Veterans—Wisconsin—Correspondence.
4. Veterans—Wisconsin—Diaries.
I. Stevens, Michael E. II. Foster, A. Kristen. III. Goldlust-Gingrich, Ellen D.
IV. Rhea, Regan. V. State Historical Society of Wisconsin. VI. Series.

DS559.V65 1996
959.704'38—dc20   96-5333
                                                                  CIP

Contents

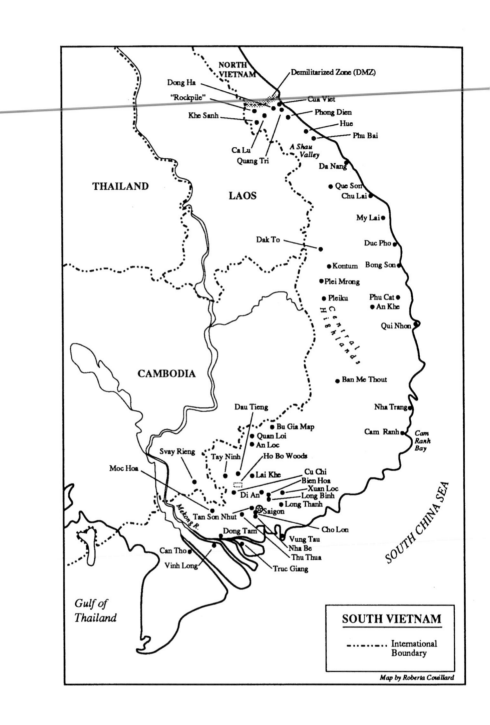

NORTH
VIETNAM

Demilitarized Zone (DMZ)

Dong Ha
"Rockpile"
Khe Sanh
Cua Viet
Phong Dien
Hue
Phu Bai

Ca Lu
Quang Tri
A Shau
Valley
Da Nang

THAILAND

LAOS

Que Son
Chu Lai

My Lai

Dak To

Duc Pho

Kontum   Bong Son
Plei Mrong
Pleiku   Phu Cat
An Khe

Qui Nhon

Central Highlands

CAMBODIA

Ban Me Thout

Dau Tieng

Nha Trang

Bu Gia Map
Quan Loi
An Loc
Ho Bo Woods

Cam Ranh   Cam
Ranh
Bay

Svay Rieng
Tay Ninh
Moc Hoa
Lai Khe
Bien Hoa
Di An

Cu Chi
Xuan Loc
Long Binh
Long Thanh

Tan Son Nhut
Saigon

Mekong R.

Dong Tam

Cho Lon

Can Tho
Vinh Long
Nha Be
Thu Thua
Truc Giang

Vung Tau

SOUTH CHINA SEA

Gulf of
Thailand

SOUTH VIETNAM

·-·-·-·-·-· International
Boundary

Map by Roberta Couillard

Introduction

We can go without food, or luxury, but not without the support of our country, in spirit.
—ROGER BOEKER, 1966

Damn this war and everything that's put us here. If I'm to die here, I only wish it were for something I believed in.
—STEVE PLUE, 1970

Each generation shares a common, defining experience that distinguishes it from preceding generations. For the children of those who fought World War II, the war in Vietnam became that pivotal event. Since March, 1965, when the first U.S. ground troops landed at Da Nang, Americans have struggled to come to terms with Vietnam, and the scars of the war still remain on the national psyche. The war brought massive changes in the ways Americans viewed themselves, their government, and the world. As the nation divided between prowar "hawks" and antiwar "doves," it tore apart the social fabric and accelerated social and cultural change. The war intensified generational conflict, turning children against parents and students against teachers. It alienated many citizens from their government, laying the groundwork for a cynical rejection of authority.

The media—principally television—gave the war an unprecedented immediacy, bringing the fighting into American homes and underscoring the human cost. At the same time, television provided a vehicle for debate over the nation's Vietnam policy, reminding viewers of the national fissures over the war. Afterward, the very term "Vietnam" became a reference point for public policy debates, just as "Munich and appeasement" had served as a ready-made analogy for those who remembered World War II.

Although the United States as a whole bore the wounds of Vietnam, the young men (and all but 7,500 of the 2.5 million U.S. military personnel in Vietnam were male) who fought the war shouldered the heaviest burden. Unlike World War II, Vietnam often divided those who fought from the many at home who opposed the war. Younger than their fathers who had fought in World War II (the average age of GIs in Vietnam was nineteen, compared to twenty-six in World War II), American soldiers in Vietnam came disproportionately from rural areas and urban working-class backgrounds. GIs knew they were risking their lives in a war not of their making and opposed by many of their peers. Understandably, many soldiers resented the situation. However, as the war dragged on, the GIs themselves became deeply divided, and many, though not all, came to share the views of antiwar protesters back in the States. Because of the army's policy of rotating servicemen into Vietnam for a year at a time, GIs had difficulty developing the cohesiveness found in their fathers' wartime units. Vietnam veterans also returned home individually rather than as members of a military unit. While this policy gave GIs some modicum of certainty about their time of service, it also made "short-timers" wary of taking risks during their final months, weeks, and days in Vietnam. The end result was the gradual dissolution of morale and cohesion in the military.

Upon returning home, Vietnam veterans encountered a different reception than did their fathers. Fighting in the jungles of Southeast Asia one day and then returning to the United States on a jet airliner the next provided little time for emotional decompression and transition. More troubling, many Vietnam veterans found themselves blamed for a war that they had not wanted and had themselves grown to hate. Without the homecoming parades and honors that had feted their fathers in World War II, Vietnam veterans remained in the background, forgotten.

In recent years, however, Americans, regardless of their views on the conflict, have been able to disassociate the war from the warrior and have recognized the burden borne by many veterans. The expressions of support for returning American hostages from Iran (1981) and for Gulf War veterans (1991) and the building of the Vietnam Veterans Memorial in Washington, D.C., focused attention on Vietnam veterans. Reflection on the meaning of the war also has spurred an outpouring of memoirs, novels, and films recounting the story of the war through the filters of memory. Nearly twenty-five years after the guns fell silent, Americans at last seem ready to deal with the dark emotions generated by Vietnam.

Voices from Vietnam offers a different perspective. This book tells the story of the war as it unfolded from the point of view of the ninety-two Wisconsin men and women whose Vietnam letters and diaries appear here. Part of the *Voices of the Wisconsin Past* series, which presents first-person narratives about our common past from the vantage point of the participants, the texts emphasize the ordinary citizens of the state and offer an account unmediated by the historian's narrative. They provide the reader with a sense of the authentic voice of the participants.

More than 57,000 Wisconsin residents served in southeast Asia; 1,239 of them lost their lives. The letters and diaries printed here were written by men and women who either lived in the state when they joined the military or moved to Wisconsin after their discharges. The book also includes letters from a Red Cross worker and two civilian Army Special Services workers who served in Vietnam. Although the letters were collected from Wisconsin veterans, the stories they tell could no doubt be repeated by many of the more than 2.5 million Americans who served in Vietnam.

The letters and diaries cover a wide range of experiences and a broad sampling of opinions and attitudes. The book opens with accounts of basic training, feelings about the trip to Vietnam, and first impressions upon arrival. Chapter 2 offers slices of daily life, ranging from accounts of "humping the boonies" to descriptions of life in the rear. Vivid accounts of combat appear in chapter 3, while chapter 4 reveals GIs' opinions on the war and shows how they were affected and divided by the debate at home. Chapter 5 looks at two events during the pivotal year of 1968—the Tet Offensive and the siege of Khe Sanh—that influenced attitudes back in the States. Fredric Flom's powerful diary in chapter 6 gives a harrowing look into his more than six years of captivity and torture by the North Vietnamese. Chapter 7 examines the effect of the war on the GIs' relationships with their parents, younger brothers, spouses and girlfriends, children, and friends as well as with the Vietnamese people. The book's final chapter contains accounts of the heavy physical and emotional costs of the war.

Although the attitudes of individual servicemen varied widely, the themes of adaptability, courage, and deep feeling run throughout these writings. American soldiers struggled to put into words their powerful emotions about being caught in an impossible situation while wanting to do their best for themselves and their buddies. Yet how to describe the indescribable to an uncomprehending world? Ed Beauchamp put it well when he wrote home from Vietnam about a dream in which he returned to Milwaukee from the war but was greeted by his friends as if he had only been away on a vacation: "And then I wanted to tell them about this place but I saw it was no use." His listeners didn't care: "To them it was only news."

The letters of Vietnam GIs often included good-natured banter as they tried to reassure their friends and loved ones at home of their safety. After lugging sixty or seventy pounds of gear throughout the jungles and rice paddies of Vietnam, George Godfrey told his father that family vacations would have to "undergo drastic changes" after his return; he had had more than enough of camping. Other GIs told about lighter moments, such as watching the ubiquitous Bob Hope shows. Yet the letters also tell tales of anguish and of men trying to make sense of terrifying conditions in a time of upheaval and uncertainty. John Abrams, a helicopter pilot, expressed frustration at fighting a guerrilla war in which he couldn't "decide which ones are the bad guys and which ones are the good guys." George Kulas became outraged at characterizations of his generation as "a bunch of hippies, draft card burners & bums." He asked, "But who's dying over here every day!" GIs included both supporters of the war who despised antiwar demonstrators as well as opponents of the war who put McGovern-for-president bumper stickers on jeeps and helicopters.

Soldiers struggled to explain the war to their families at home. Mike Jeffords wrote to his younger brother that "Fighting out here isn't like the movies, Francis. I wish there was some way I could make you understand that. When a man goes down it isn't 'tricky' or exciting or 'sharp' the way he looks. . . . Someone has to win; someone lose. And in the end no one wins." Joseph Pilon worried that his young daughter, Anne, would not understand why he had gone away. "How could I have explained war to her so that she could understand why other little girls' daddies got together to fight other little girls' daddies and after it was all over a lot of little girls would be without daddies."

The most poignant letters were written by young men who saw their friends die. They come from men such as Jeff Fields, who witnessed his company commander killed by friendly fire, or R. Patrick Bourget, who wondered about fate when the man who took his place one night died, or Steve Plue, who told of how he and his colleagues watched a buddy "dying and we couldn't do a damn thing to help." There is John Marshall's haunting account of "a dream last night that some VC were coming towards me and I got shot pretty bad"—written three days before he died. To carry on, Tony Paulson had to suppress feelings about the death of men in his unit: "I can't show it or everybody will feel bad and nobody will work. When I get home I think I am going to let go with a whole year's worth of emotions." Others, like Darrel Lulling, wrote letters as a way of purging themselves of bad memories. After being wounded in action, he wrote to his girlfriend, "I am going to write you this letter and then I am going to try to forget it all."

Yet despite all efforts to put the war behind them, GIs knew that the memories of Vietnam would not fade and that the war would leave its mark. Mike Jeffords reported that GIs became "old men before their time. I feel ten years older myself." Howard Sherpe concurred, noting, "It doesn't take long to age a boy in Vietnam." Images of lost youth and innocence, of course, are not unique to Vietnam. They appear in writings about other wars, though rarely with the same level of cynicism and despair. Doug Bradley put it eloquently when he wrote that "the effect Vietnam has had on our youth has been most devastating. It is they that have lost their spirits & their souls. . . . We have denied our sons the laughter of their youth—a youth that is not confined to the adolescent years—but an aura of youth—of a brightness & a glow—that remains with a man until his own children take it up for him. . . . There is a vast emptiness here—no love, no compassion, no peace, no brotherhood, no beauty—& no tomorrow."

For those who served in Vietnam, that lost youth could not be recaptured, any more than the nation as a whole could return to a more innocent time. But we can, and should, remember.

*   *   *   *   *

This book began with a conversation with Bob Jauch, a state senator from Poplar, Wisconsin, and a Vietnam veteran himself. After reading an earlier volume in this series, *Letters from the Front, 1898–1945,* Senator Jauch pointed out the need for a similar book on the state's Vietnam veterans. The problem, however, was that this type of documentation remained in the hands of the veterans themselves or their families rather than in libraries or archives. With the help of Senator Jauch and others, the state generously provided funding for a project to gather the necessary documents and assemble the text.

Beginning in the summer of 1994, the project staff appealed to the public to loan or donate enough material for the book. The response exceeded most optimistic expectations and forced some difficult choices. More than 230 Wisconsin Vietnam veterans and their families donated more than 12,000 items, and the problem quickly became one of selection from an abundance of riches. The staff reviewed every donated letter, diary, and journal entry and from them gradually distilled a sampling that illustrates the full range of experience of the state's Vietnam veterans. Many powerful stories and documents had to be omitted for lack of space.

In editing the volume, we have tried to preserve the sense of immediacy in letters often written under trying wartime conditions. We have not corrected grammar or capitalization, although we have silently corrected spelling and have standardized date and place lines. Editorial insertions of words or letters needed to clarify meaning appear in brackets. Slips of the pen (e.g., repeated words as in "the the" or errors in typing) have been silently corrected. Minor changes in punctuation have been made only when necessary for clarity. Because these letters are often quite long and include references to family and private matters, we have excerpted many of them to include material from as many writers and on as many themes as possible. In addition, several of the letter writers have asked that we delete an occasional sentence for personal reasons. All omissions, for whatever reason, are noted with spaced ellipses marks (. . .). A number of writers used ellipses to indicate a thought that trails off; these ellipses are retained and are printed without spaces (...). According to one GI, "Hell can't be as bad as war." Readers are warned that the language and descriptions in the letters printed here are sometimes raw and shocking, even though they are by no means the most graphic to be found in the war correspondence of the state's veterans. But the editors believed that to sanitize the GIs' language would dishonor their deeply held feelings and distort their experiences.

All texts appearing in this volume are taken from the original manuscripts, with the exception of the following: the letters of Marvin Acker and Joseph Pilon, as well as Howard Sherpe's letter of August 16, 1966, were taken from transcripts; George Godfrey's letter was typed by his wife in 1970 for distribution to his family and friends. Terri Vining dictated her letter of March, 1971, on audiotape, as John Abrams did with his letters of May 6 and June 6, 1968. These texts were transcribed directly from the recordings.

Because of space considerations, the overwhelming majority of letters submitted to the project could not be included, but many of the originals or photocopies were donated to the Archives of the State Historical Society of Wisconsin and are available as part of the Wisconsin Vietnam Veterans Collection. Additional collections can be found at the Wisconsin Veterans Museum in Madison.

The State Historical Society has been working to preserve the record of Wisconsin history since 1846. Volumes in the *Voices of the Wisconsin Past* series would not have been possible without the donation of letters and diaries written by the state's citizens. The Society continues to collect the letters of Wisconsin's veterans, from the territorial period to the present. Persons wishing to discuss the donation of manuscript material are invited to contact the Archives Division at the State Historical Society of Wisconsin, 816 State Street, Madison, WI 53706.

Acknowledgments

Voices from Vietnam truly has been a collaborative project, and its completion is due to the hard work and dedication of the staff. Kathy Borkowski helped develop the project during its initial days and laid the groundwork for the collection of material. Kristen Foster and Regan Rhea, who succeeded Kathy, worked closely with veterans and other donors of materials; their careful efforts ensured the gathering of a valuable collection of materials for review. Kristen, Regan, and Ellen Goldlust-Gingrich reviewed the donated manuscripts, proofread texts, researched and drafted notes, and closely participated in every stage of the book's creation. Their dedication and commitment were vital to the project's success. Steve Burg helped with the research and drafting of notes and, along with Sean Adams, provided additional assistance with the proofreading. Kari Benson and Charmaine Harbort made the initial transcriptions of the materials that appear here. Kari also ensured that the project operated smoothly by maintaining the files, preparing mailings, and handling a multiplicity of other tasks. Paul Hass offered useful advice and his always fine editorial hand. Chris Kolenda provided assistance with military terminology, and Vince Demma of the U.S. Army Center for Military History patiently answered numerous questions.

The book never would have been produced without the interest of Senator Bob Jauch, who initiated and led efforts to furnish funding for the project. H. Nicholas Muller III and Bob Thomasgard, the Society's director and associate director, continued to provide support for the Voices of the Wisconsin Past series. Thanks are owed to Colonel Raymond Boland of the Wisconsin Department of Veterans Affairs, who offered his support while this project was still in the planning stages, and Richard Zeitlin and his staff at the Wisconsin Veterans Museum, especially Mark Van Ells and Bill Brewster, who gave us access to Vietnam-era materials in the museum's collections. We are grateful to Stanley Kutler and Stephen Wagley, who let us use an advance copy of the *Encyclopedia of the Vietnam War,* which will be published by Charles Scribner's Sons.

Finally, this volume would not have been possible without the generosity of the veterans whose letters appear here and their families. The project's staff has been moved by their support, enthusiasm, and encouragement. In offering their letters, diaries, and photographs, they not only provided a piece of history but also shared a part of themselves. We deeply appreciate the generosity of the following individuals who served in Vietnam and their families for loaning materials to the project. They are listed in alphabetical order, with the name of the donor following in parentheses if different from the letter writer.

John L. Abrams (Ellen Abrams Blankenship); Marvin S. Acker; Charles Alger (Judith James); Scott R. Alwin (Wally Alwin and Teresa Alwin-Nguyen); Gregory Amato (Joyce N. Amato); Kenneth L. Anderson; Kenneth M. Anderson (Mabel Panek); William R. Anderson; Ronald Augustine (Chris Renard); Kenneth H. Baas (Audrey Baas); Terry D. Babler; Richard L. Bachmann; Roger Backes; Fred E. Baewer; Micheal L. Baldwin (Mary Baldwin); Edward J. Beauchamp; Andrew R. Beiler; Dennis M. Belonger (Mrs. V. Ehlinger); Arlen H. Bliefernicht; Kris Blumer (Virginia Blumer); Roger S. Boeker; Darlene and Michael Borchardt; Robert Patrick Bourget (Truman and Donna Bourget); Michael J. Bovre; Dennis L. Boyer; Douglas J. Bradley; Joel H. Bradtke; Dennis Bries; David E. Brott (David and Alice Brott); Hugh Brown (Mrs. Hugh Brown); John M. Brown (Lois J. Brown); Lawrence A. Bueter (Ruth M. Bueter); Michael A. Burke; Charles E. Campbell; Gregg M. Carlson; Jim Carlson; William D. Carlson; John F. Caruso (Lillian Caruso and Virginia Knobeck); Michael J. Chamberlain; Jeanne M. Christie; Brian L. Ciriacks; Margaret M. Ciurlik; David Clark; Lynn F. Columbia; Thomas E. Cook; James E. Cooper (Barbara M. Cooper); Tom J. Cress (Barbara M. Krumrai); Glen Cruikshank; William L. Cunningham (Dawn DeBruin); Gregory E. Custer; Dennis M. Daane (Donna J. Klosterman); David D. Daley; Dennis Darmek; Robert L. Dean; Wayne L. Dehne; Jeffrey M. Dentice; Gilbert L. Docken (Betty M. Docken); Ronald J. Doering (Nancy L. Doering); Jerry Doll, Jr. (Margaret Miller); Thomas J. Downs (Sandy Tyson); Teddy Lynn Duckworth; Ron Dudek; Alan A. Ehrhardt; Jeffrey M. Fields; Orval Fisher (Patricia Fisher); John J. Flaherty; Fredric R. Flom; Skipper W. Ford (Alice Ford); James R. Foti; Wayne P. Frank; Judith Jenkins Gaudino; William D. Gilmore; John R. Gmack (Robert and Gertrude Gmack); George Godfrey (Lowell F. Jevens); Dennis L. Goetz (Dorothea Quam); Ronald D. Golden (Ruth M. Golden); Susan Haack-Huskey; Joseph Hajny; Roger D. Hallingstad; Anthony L. Hamelink; Mary Ann (Lemieux) Hartl; James Hathaway (Nancy Hathaway); Paul Hegge (Sandy Tyson); Donald L. Heiliger; Thomas Hekkers (Victoria Hekkers); Richard H. Heming; Kate Hephner; Thomas E. Hoffmann; Thomas M. Hounsell; Steve House; Steven Hovel; Ross T. Jabs; Todd R. Jackson (Ray and Olive Jackson); Robert A. Jacky (Suzanne F. Jacky); Judy A. Jacque; Michael Jeffords; Darryl E. Johnson; Norma Roska Johnson; William C. Jung; Philip A. Kalhagen (Rita McGrath); Phil Kallas; Larry P. Kammholz; Frank Kanaskie (Sally

Litka); Roger E. Kaschner; Michael E. Kastern; James A. Kempf; Robert L. Kintz; Leander F. Knight; Roy M. Knutson; John R. Koeppen; Lynn C. Kohl; Michael Koshenina (Alice Koshenina); Michael J. Kowalkowski (Victoria Hekkers); David T. Kramarczyk; Ronald Krasinski (Lee Ann Koch); John W. Kreckel (Janet Brantzeg and Bernice Kreckel); George S. Kulas; James Kurkowski (Frances Kurkowski); Donald R. Last (Jo Ann Last); William B. Leppert; Ronald D. Lewis; James A. Long; Darrel R. Lulling; Arthur E. Lunde (Pat Lunde and Donald Gerczak); Don T. Lutz; Kenneth E. Marine; John K. Marshall (John E. and Helen A. Marshall); Thomas R. McCabe (Marie McCabe); A.J. McCaskey; Larry A. McDowell (Gloria J. Wolff); Richard C. McKee, Jr. (Maxine L. Nichols); Paul T. McMahon; Dennis McQuade; William W. Maves; Lloyd C. Mertens; Terry F. Mezera (Frank and Betty Mezera and Pam Nesbit); John R. Miller, Jr. (John and Elaine Miller); Paul F. Miller; Thomas Miller; Michael Miotke; Brian Murray; Robert S. Muth; Robert J. Norder (Robert and Alice Norder); Steven E. Novotny (Hattie and Henry Novotny); Michael B. O'Meara (Marguerite S. O'Meara); Donald Ohme; Marvin B. Olsen; David R. Olson; Jay L. Olson (Sally C. Olson); Robert G. Olson; Thomas P. Olson (Rose Olson); Erik P. Opsahl; Gerald L. Paul; Tyrone M. Paulson; Frederick T. Pennell; Dennis J. Peters; Larry D. Peterson (Rachel Tabor); Stanley Robert Peterson (Joni Peterson); Mark R. Pfaff (Sylvia Pfaff Bryhn); Jim Pick; Joseph E. Pilon; Alan Piotrowski (Stephen J. Piotrowski); Stephen J. Piotrowski; Gary A. Plath (Kirsten N. Plath); Steven E. Plue; Larry M. Podoll; Peter Ponti; Charles E. Queen; Leland E. Radley (Darlene Lawrence); David Ramseier (Beverly and Paul Ramseier); Dennis Ramseier (Beverly and Paul Ramseier); Ronald Ray (Irene Ray); Gloria Redlin (Janis Eberhart); Jay Reed (Christine Reed); Thomas A. Reneau; Jerry A. Rieck; Roger Ritschard (Susan Wild); Bob Rock; Bruce E. Rodland; Mark K. Rowan; Justin Runcie; Brian L. Rupnow (Denis Rupnow); Harve W. Saal; David L. Sartori (Edward Peterson); Daniel W. E. Schacht; Michael Scharfman; Jerry Schmidt (Melanie Reynolds); James Schroud; Kristopher Schultz (Victoria Hekkers); Michael A. Scott; Richard J. Shafel; Howard M. Sherpe; Lance P. Sijan (Jane A. Sijan); David Terrence Smith (Donna L. Murphy and Marion Smith); William W. Sommers; Timothy B. Staats; Steven M. Staffeil; Gerry Stiemsma; Ray W. Stubbe; Anthony Suminski (Josephine Suminski); Wilbur A. Sundt (Jean and Wilbur Sundt); Charles N. Sweetman; Larry W. Swiggum (Diane L. Cody); Steven L. Tabor (Rachel Tabor); Gary J. Tenpas (Marjorie Tenpas); Bruce Thibodeau; Donald E. Thies; John Thoemke; Gary Thoms (Carrie Thoms); Dale M. Vanderfin; Allen P. Van Dyke; Thressa and Bill Vining;

Richard D. Voltz; John R. Waldeck; Donald N. Warnke; Helen E. Weidner; Fred J. Wenger (Rachelle Wenger); Gary G. Wetzel; Charmaine Whitburn; John Willems, Jr. (Anita Willems); Les F. Willems; Dennis Wolf (Victoria Hekkers); Alfred F. Wolff (Gloria Wolff); Richard P. Wolff; Richard K. Yazzie; Ralph O. Zahnow; David A. Zien; and James N. Zitzelsberger.

The following individuals also generously donated material related to the war or provided assistance in preparing this book: Louella J. Arnold; Vicki Buschman; Edward M. Coffman; James Randy Ebert; Marie Gaedjin; Paul Gartzke; Don Malin; Peg Olson; Laraine Post; and Shirley Swenson.

VOICES
from
VIETNAM

1

From Basic Training to Vietnam

Training for Vietnam

During the Vietnam War era, registration for the draft became a rite of passage for young men on their eighteenth birthdays. As a result of the post–World War II baby boom, 27 million men reached that age between 1963 and 1974. Approximately 2 million of these men were drafted, 9 million enlisted, and 16 million received deferments or never served. Ultimately, about 2.5 million men served in Vietnam. Whether drafted or enlisted, all who served experienced basic training before embarking on their yearlong tour of duty in Vietnam. For eight weeks, new recruits underwent rigorous training that transformed them from civilians into soldiers. The following letters describe these men's reactions to the physical and psychological pressures they encountered while preparing for Vietnam.

LAWRENCE A. BUETER (b. 1944) was born in Antigo, grew up in Sheboygan, and lived in Minneapolis, Minnesota, prior to enlisting in the Marine Corps in June, 1966. Sergeant Bueter served as a draftsman (1st Mar. Div.) near Da Nang from July, 1967, to May, 1969, when he was discharged. He returned to Wisconsin for a short time before moving back to Minneapolis, where he continues to work as a draftsman. Bueter sent the following letter to his parents while he was in basic training at Camp Pendleton in San Diego, California.

[July 20, 1966]

Hi All,

. . . We usually get up at 5:00 A.M. every morning & get 8 minutes to make our rack & get dressed. Sack time at night is 9:00 P.M., just after mail call.

Then we got to take off those ugly yellow sweat shirts and the white gym shoes that identify a new recruit. Boy were we ever glad! The second week we went to a lot of classes on various subjects: first aid, history, bayonet training, M-14 rifle, interior guard, religion, .45 automatic pistol, & hand-to-hand combat. We had at least 2 or 3 hours of classes for each one. (More on some)

We did more physical exercises and went to the obstacle course a few times the second & third weeks. Then we were given our initial P.T. (physical training) test. A score of 140 or more was needed to qualify. We were graded according to the number of pull-ups, push-ups, sit-ups, & squat thrusts we could do. And there was only about a 5 minute rest period between each test. Then after all that we had a 300 yd. run for time (I did that in 37 sec.). My total score was 259 so I was pretty glad to get that. Our drill instructor said that if we didn't get over 300 we weren't in our best shape. I knew I wasn't yet—beer belly & all considered—but I'm getting there fast.

We have a set of rifle exercises we do quite often that are designed to strengthen our arms. Also just last week we started running 2 or 3 miles about every 3rd day.

If ever anyone screws up or makes a mistake he has to do a few exercises to help him remember. That's the way most guys get their exercise before they learn—I've been lucky so far & escaped unexercised. A few times we've loused up as a platoon so we've made a few trips to a nearby sand pit where we play games until the D.I. is satisfied we've learned our lesson. They always use that threat when we get a little out of hand— "Keep it up and we'll go to the pits tonight instead of taking showers." It usually works too!

We have to wear these stupid covers everywhere we go—except indoors. So, when I get back, the bottom half of my "gourd" will be tan and the top half will be white. Oh, yeah, we got our "gourds" shaved again yesterday and they let the top alone. All the guys look like Indians now—sure is funny. We also got to make a PX call yesterday, our second one since we've been here. They don't have much in it except the bare necessities. I got more writing paper, soap, a flashlite, socks & stamps. The prices sure are reasonable—comparatively speaking.

A few general things we can and can't do—we don't do anything without being told first; we get 2 or 3 minutes for a head call except at night; 15–20 minutes for shower & shave at night; we can smoke only when told (and that's only when the D.I. feels good) and then only one; we change our clothes when told; we very seldom get free time (before this week) and then we use that for writing letters.

This week has really been nice for a change—we finish our detail by about 7:00 and come back here. We have 3 drill instructors who take turns being boss for 2 days each. Sometimes they let us just sit in our billets all day—other times we have to sit outside and clean our rifles and polish our boots or do laundry. Oh, yes—that's another thing, we do our own laundry too & by hand yet. I just changed my uniform today for the first time in 3 weeks—I almost feel clean again.

I don't know if I told you about our inspection last week, but we got to wear a starched pair of clothes with our spit-shined boots. Oh, and we also got our pictures taken for our yearbook last week. We changed into a dress blue uniform with white hat & all for the picture. Boy, did that ever feel & look good. I can hardly wait until I get my own. I'll bet there are a lot of things I haven't told you yet that I can't remember, but I'd better sign or I'll be writing all day. . . .

So love to all,
Larry

THOMAS R. MCCABE (b. 1947) grew up in Madison and attended the Madison campus of the University of Wisconsin until he was drafted in the late summer, 1968. He served with the army as an infantryman (A Co., 1–5th Cav., 1st Bde., 1st Cav. Div. [Airmobile]) near An Duc from March, 1969, until he was wounded in June of that year. McCabe then spent a year at Fort Lewis in Seattle, Washington, before being discharged in the fall of 1970. He now lives in Fairbanks, Alaska, where he does wildlife work. McCabe wrote the following letter to his parents from Fort Campbell, Kentucky.

November 10, [1968]
Howdy—
. . . First of all, basic training consists of getting up at 3:30 AM, cleaning the barracks and oneself until 5:15 AM; then running a couple of miles; then breakfast and then off into the schedule of the day. The daily routine varies considerably. There is of course D. & C. & P.T., (Drill & ceremony which is marching & Physical Training which naturally is exercises), but also classes in other subjects such as UCMJ (uniform code of Military Justice), driver's ed, military courtesy, health and a few other miscellaneous ideas.

We have also been shooting the M-14 and playing "kill" with our bayonets. You know it's really hard to believe from the outside, but once you're in the army it isn't, that America really has an effective war machine. Everything we do is directly orientated to killing people effectively. Even the cadence we chant says "I want to go to Vietnam, I want to kill some Charlie Cong." Bayonet practice is done to the chant of "Kill" while assimilating a thrust with the bayonet into someone's chest and withdrawing it ready to attack again.

Well for the most part that is what we do day after day 6 days a week 3:30 AM to 9:00 PM. Fortunately the army does feed us a good meal three times a day, the only annoying factor is that is the same meal every day, with only slight variations. Breakfast is always two pieces of French toast, two eggs, two pieces of bacon, 1½ slices of cold toast, & hot or

Soldiers training at Fort Benning, Georgia.
Courtesy Michael Chamberlain.

dry cereal—milk & juice. Like I said it's good and it's filling, but I certainly get tired of the menu. Lunch and dinner are primarily the same with a meat dish (usually hamburger or chicken), a vegetable, cake, rolls, salad and milk. Again filling but lousy variety.

My biggest gripe about this training, is the way clothing is regimented, in other words everyone has to wear the same am't. and style. The perturbing factor here is that on a cold day if someone should forget his gloves, then we all have to go without gloves. The same goes for long-johns. The weather here has been quite cold and not being able to adapt one's own clothing situation can become very uncomfortable. Also they have a bad habit of running us to death then making us stand in formation and freezing as the cold wind blows through your sweat-soaked clothing. Needless to say I have had a constant head cold which is very troublesome, especially when I get up in the morning with my lungs, throat & sinuses congested. . . .

Your loving Son
Tom

JAMES R. FOTI (b. 1949) was born in Milwaukee and was working in West Allis as a carpenter when he enlisted in the army in July, 1970. Foti served as a door gunner and as a ham radio operator (A Troop, 7-1st Cav. [Air Cav.], 164th Avn. Grp., 1st Avn. Bde.) near Vinh Long from December, 1970, to December, 1971. Discharged in January, 1972, he now lives in New Berlin and works as a carpenter. He wrote the following letter to his girlfriend, Beverly Ann Pelnar, who is now his wife, while at Fort Campbell, Kentucky.

August 6, 1970

Dear Bev,

Hi! Guess what Bev, my luck just ran out today again. Today at the rifle range everything was going good until my second time to shoot. I was in a kneeling position when one of the empty shells hit me in my neck, and stayed in my collar causing my neck to burn. Now, on the rifle range you are never suppose to move because you might shoot somebody. So, when the shell hit me I moved to shake the shell off my neck. Well, the guys in the tower didn't go for that at all and proceed to scream at me for doing that. Well, the thing is, that the shell was burning my neck, kept this in mind. They said that I could have shot someone dead because of my actions. But I knew what I was doing. So my buddy, the second lieutenant came charging over by me and pro-ceed to *chew* me out. He first hit me over my head with his helmet and told me that I could have killed somebody. After he chew me out I was so shook that I couldn't hit my targets. So he came up by me once again and told me not to worry about it anymore. After 8 rounds I began to shoot like I was before. (pretty damn good) Well, after I got done shooting the lieutenant walk up to me *again* and grab me by the collars and shook me vigorously. Then he ask me if I went into the infantry what would I be. I told him that I probably would be a foot soldier. Then he said that I would be in Vietnam and that I wouldn't worry about a hot shell down my neck. So after all this my morale was -20 below *zero*. Then I got your letter and my morale rose to 100%. Ha! Ha! Ha! (I got the army this time). . . .

God Bless
With all my love,
James

DARRYL E. JOHNSON (b. 1945) was raised in Illinois and was drafted into the army in March, 1968. He served as a forward observer (E Co., 1-22d Inf., 2d Bde., 4th Inf. Div.) in Pleiku, Ban Me Thuot, Kontum, and Suoi Doi from August, 1968, to August, 1969. Sergeant Johnson received an early release in January, 1970, and attended St. Norbert's College. He now teaches eighth-grade social studies in Green Bay. In this letter to Judith Ann

Kaeseberg, who later became his wife, Johnson describes bivouac during
basic training at Fort Benning, Georgia, in which recruits camped out in the
field and participated in war games.

April 15, 1968

Honey,

. . . From Tues until Friday night we were on bivouac. Indeed we
were busy learning combat techniques and survival in a combat zone.
Every minute was occupied with some little task. I pitched my tent with
Lorne Kovich, our platoon guide. I mentioned him earlier. He's a great
guy & we look almost like twins. We centered our tent in the middle
of our platoon so we could keep an eye on the activities of all our men.
We made sure all their tents were squared away and properly camouflaged. The next three days were spent in outdoor classes. We covered
tactical marches, camouflage, methods of attack, sanitation, infiltration
of enemy lines, and all and all how to kill and stay alive. . . . All our
training is basically centered in the light of Vietnam. Most of our instructors have seen combat in Vietnam and the stories they tell are almost
unbelievable. When I get time, I'll tell you all about "Charlie" (the Viet
Cong). But all our time wasn't spent sitting and listening. Every morning we awoke and fell in formation with our rifles. Then we would run
for about 2 or 3 miles with them in front of us, over our heads, or at
port arms (a position for carrying the rifle). We'd run through sand,
over hills, down hills, everywhere. Many of the guys would fall out but
by and far the 2nd platoon showed more muscle & endurance than the
rest. By the end of the week we led the company whenever we marched
or ran. This was really an honor for our hard work. When we would
get back from running, we would eat chow. Sweat rolled down our faces
and got into our food. Some guys got blisters on their feet, but we made
it all the way. We did the same running every night after supper. I lost
10 lbs, but I know & have confidence that if I ever have to run or crawl
or dig or whatever, I can go & go until whoever is making me do it
drops. I have never dropped out of PT or ever said "can't" (a word not
recognized by the Army) and I never will. I'm the world's best trained
soldier and there's not a man alive, other than my fellow soldiers, that
can out-perform my buddies and me. I'm not bragging but just believing what has been worked, worked, and worked into me down to my
very fibers. All this might seem unusual to you and you may not even
like it, but you must know your abilities, realize them, put them to use.
Otherwise, just count yourself *dead* if you happen to meet Charlie. I'm
not scared because I know I can do my job. Enough of that. I guess
I got a little carried away, huh?

Dennis McQuade firing a .50-caliber machine gun during basic training. Courtesy Dennis McQuade.

Anyway, Wednesday the weather became really hot. Guys were drinking water like it was going out of style. Our drill sergeants, in order to make it a little tougher on us, rationed out our water to discipline us as a consequence. We really began to overheat and it was a real effort to even move. But the running continued & soon tempers became on edge and morale was dropping. That's where Kovich & I came in. We had to keep our men from fighting & keep telling them it would be over soon and those that didn't fall out now would be rewarded with passes on the weekend. They listened and did a great job. Blisters became larger and more numerous, we wore the finish off our rifles because of the sweating from our hands. Our bodies smelled so bad because we were too tired to wash our underclothes. They wouldn't dry overnight anyway. There were gas attacks at night and people tried to infiltrate our camp. We could only get about 6 hrs. of sleep. Some guys gave up when it came to running in the morning and fell out but the others pushed harder and made it. As I said earlier, the 2nd plt did pretty good. Then came the infiltration course, the hardest and most trying of them all. For 150 meters you climb over a wall with full combat pack on & weapon. Then you crawl with bullets whizzing over your head. Your knees get scraped against stones & pieces of cement. The same happens to your elbows. You concentrate on not letting dirt get into the muzzle of your M-16. Your belt buckle digs into your stomach, you scrape your knuckles. Your first obstacle is a barbed wire fence. Roll over and under you go with your rifle resting on your stomach. I touch the wire and see how

taut it is. I've got to get low to get under. Boy I wish I was 4 ft tall
and weighed 75 lbs. I draw my legs up and thrust out. The dirt scratches
my neck and works its way down my back. My pants catch on the wire.
I lo[o]se myself and thrust again. This time my rifle falls off my stomach.
I slide it back on my stomach and thrust again. I'm past the wire and
I roll over on my stomach. I continue to crawl until a flare lights the
sky. Damn! Someone tripped a wire and set it off. Clumsy idiot. I freeze
until the flare burns out because with my camouflage, I blend with the
terrain and the outline of my body is broken. I start crawling again, feeling
the ground in front of me, searching for trip wires and booby traps. I
feel another barbed wire fence in front of me. Again I go under it but
about halfway through something explodes. Dirt flies in the air with
water from the demolition pit where the TNT went off. Of course, it
comes straight down on me. I continue until I get to a large log. I crawl
over it. My knees hit hard against the solid earth. The machine gun
is getting louder and louder. I must be only about 10 meters from it.
I crawl closer and closer. The ground shakes from the explosion of each
bullet. The percussion is so great that my head vibrates. I crawl faster
until I'm past the machine gun and reach a trench. It might be deep
so I jump into it feet first. I stand against the wall & wait for the rest
of my squad to reach the trench. Some are here already. I give the signal;
we're going to rush. We fix bayonets and all together we jump out of
the trench and rush the enemy. Each of us thrust our bayonets into a
dummy target. We continue our rush until we get to the zone we're supposed to occupy. We hit the dirt behind cover and assume a good prone
firing position. A whistle blows and we're through. Breathing heavily
and with a sigh of relief we walk to the break area. Soaking in sweat
and dirt we clean each other off. We talk and laugh about the whole
thing and we're happy it's over because we know bivouac is over. A hot
shower and soft bunk is waiting for us all back at the barracks. Sounds
like Hell doesn't it? It was. . . .

All my love & more,
Darryl

BRUCE THIBODEAU (b. 1947) lived in Algoma and Sheboygan prior to being
drafted into the army in January, 1967. He served with the infantry (B Co.,
1–22d Inf., 2d Bde., 4th Inf. Div.) near Pleiku and Dak To from July, 1967,
to July, 1968. The army discharged Thibodeau in July, 1968, and he now
lives in Green Bay, where he is a self-employed taxidermist. In this letter,
Thibodeau discusses the death of his cousin, Steve Perlewitz of Algoma, who
had recently extended his tour in Vietnam for an additional six months.
Perlewitz was killed in action on February 26, 1967, near Thua Thien.

February 27, 1967

Dear Grandma,

Thanks for the box of goodies! The timing was great. Tonight they really short-handed us in chow line and I couldn't wait to get back to the billet and fill up!

You really know how [to] make a hungry GI happy! The selection was great. I split the cookies up with the rest of the fellows. Some of the fellows said to give you a big kiss for them when I get home, the cookies really hit the spot. I owe you quite a few kisses too. So pucker up when I get home!

I got an emergency phone call from Mom & Dad last night about Steve, I can't believe it. I've felt so depressed since then and that's all I think of too when my mind's not on my training. I feel so sorry ... I'd like to send June & Howie a card, but I don't even know what I could say. I wish you would say something to them for me, I get a lump in my throat here now just thinking about it. I just can't believe it. But then I guess there isn't much we can do when the Good Lord wants us, as he does all loved ones. We'll all be together again someday. I am waiting for announcement of funeral arrangements, so that I can see my company officer about an emergency leave. I don't know if I can, I hope so. By the time you get this letter we'll probably both know if I'll be coming or not, as phones are much faster than mail. But just had to write and tell you how grieved I am to hear of this, in case I can not come home. . . .

Your 3 lb. 12 oz. Grandson,
Bruce

STEVEN E. PLUE (b. 1950) was raised in Fort Atkinson and lived in Madison prior to being drafted into the army in July, 1969. He served as an infantryman in Cu Chi and Tay Ninh (A Co., 2–18th Inf., 2d Bde., 1st Inf. Div. [Big Red One]; C Co., 4–9th Inf., 1st Bde., 25th Inf. Div.; 15th Admin. Co., 1st Cav. Div. [Airmobile]) from November, 1969, to February, 1971, when he was discharged. He attended the Stevens Point and Whitewater campuses of the University of Wisconsin, and he currently lives in Fort Atkinson and works in the landscaping business. In his letter, Plue notes the declining morale among some Vietnam recruits as a result of casualties and public attitudes toward the war. He also describes the draftees' resentment of the 1 million enlisted men in the National Guard and reserves. With a waiting list of nearly a hundred thousand men in 1968, service in the National Guard and reserves permitted most of their members to fulfill their military duty while remaining stateside.

August 24, 1969

Dear Mom & Dad:

. . . Things are looking bad my way I'm afraid. My name was one

*Steven Plue. Courtesy
Steven Plue.*

out of 47 others that was called to go and practice fire the M-16, the
type rifle they're using in Nam today. And to add to that, our orders
came in as to where we'll be going next. And my name appeared on
the list for Fort Polk Louisiana. Which means I'll have extra training
in infantry. And then from Ft. Polk is Nam. So I'll probably be sent
over in Dec. sometime. I guess that's what I get for being one of the
top firers in our Co.

If Nixon needs so many men, they divide it amongst the divisions
here and keep breaking it down and take only the top men from each
platoon.

I have only one other hope, and that's that they may be sending me
to cook school. All the cooks go to Polk for their training. But with
all likelihood, I'll probably be in the infantry and end up being just another
GI over in Nam fighting this ridiculous war.

So I had better get use to this type of life we're having in basic, because
our infantry men won't have one easy moment for 2 yrs. If you want

to survive over there you had better learn and learn fast what they teach you around here. It'll be nothing but training til Dec. and then when I get sent over, I had just better remember what they taught me here. Sometimes I sit around and listen to the boys here that have gone over already and just what it's like there. How it feels to fight an enemy when you can't even see them. A great number of our boys are killed by the Cong's booby traps. Traps you wouldn't imagine. But they're there and there's not a thing one can do about it but just hope it's the guy in front of you that gets it first.

For once now, I'm actually getting nervous about this war. One keeps putting it off in his mind about going and then finally when you realize it's all for real, you get scared.

It's really a funny type of feeling I have about what's going to happen to me. A type I can't really explain. I'm really not afraid of being killed because if it's to happen, it's going to happen. But I don't want to come back crippled like some of these fellas I've seen.

And I'm not exaggerating, some of these guys would be better off dead then to look like they do. Facial scars from Fire and scars that are just horrible. People never hear about these guys. At least I never did. I could never imagine how deformed some of them are.

And who really cares. The news comes on at 6 every night and old Walter Cronkite rattles off a few Vietnam casualties and no one pays attention. Big Deal, no one cares if John Doe gave his life. Hasn't affected their life any. But it sure meant a hell of a lot to him. People just don't think about the boys there.

And the same here. You walk down the street in your uniform, and people look at you like you're a monkey. If only they'd stop and think what we really stand for.

I was the same way before I came in, I could care less if some guy got drafted, wasn't affecting my immediate life any. Big joke, Uncle Sam grabbed your ass for 2 years. But now I'm here and I look at it a lot differently now. If I make it through I'll have respect for each individual I meet that's in our armed forces. Man the American attitude toward the soldier is really hurtin. They really don't wake up til they have a family casualty. . . .

Another type of guy I can't stand here is the National Guard fellas. They make smart remarks about those that are going over and they complain constantly about how homesick they are and how ungodly long it's taking them to get out. Four months of active training and they can go home. Like to punch them in the nose than to talk to one. But so much on our little war. . . .

Love,
Steve

Advanced Individual Training

After undergoing basic training, recruits spent between two months and a
year in advanced individual training (AIT), which was based on one's
military occupational specialty (MOS), assigned at the end of basic. Those
assigned with an 11B MOS in the army or 0311 in the marines were
virtually guaranteed to find themselves fighting on the ground in Vietnam,
and their training reflected this likelihood and focused on advanced weapons
use. Many veterans reported that little of the training addressed the
particular conditions of the war in Vietnam or the culture of its people. In
the following letters, TOM MCCABE and JIM FOTI describe their experiences
in AIT. (For biographical sketches of McCabe and Foti, see earlier in this
chapter.) McCabe compares AIT to basic training and expresses his concern
about his assignment to the infantry. Foti's letter reflects the racial tensions
and divisions in the military.

February 2, 1969

Dear Mom, Dad & Kevin—

Sorry I haven't written sooner, but time for writing has been limited.
We don't do a lot of strenuous training but we spend a lot of time doing
extra details. Last week we were up 'til ten or later cleaning the M-60
machine guns we were firing during the day. Nite tactics also cuts down
on letter writing time among other things. Sleep here is a scarce commodity; we have lites out at 10:00 PM & are up at 4:00 AM 6 days
a week. This AIT is worse than basics because the hours are longer,
the training redundant and unnecessary and the Mickey Mouse harass-
ment ridiculous. There is absolutely no military organization within the
company. The young NCO's run the individual platoons but are very
unsatisfactory & unfit for their positions. The senior DI is a fine soldier
no doubt, but unaware of human nature and forever killing morale in
the company. We have been on restriction since we got here, which is
something that is unheard of in AIT normally. Time seems to go a little
faster than it did in basics, but I'm considerably more unhappy here than
I was at Ft. Campbell. I am subject to days of severe depression due
to this situation I'm in. I was just straightening myself out & getting
a grip on my future; life was turning itself out correctly for me, when
the dilemma of 11B10 stepped in. I must admit that I'm afraid as any
individual can be. The idea that I might not return haunts me, not because
of life itself, but because I have so much I want to accomplish; an education and position similar to Dad's, a happy married life & children with
Nicki, & just plain experiencing life as I have never been able to do
before. The army has changed my opinions & way of thinking a great
deal, but unfortunately it doesn't help me identify with this way of life;

Jim Foti in Vietnam. Courtesy Jim Foti.

instead it makes me feel that America's policies are weak and in dire need of change both internally & abroad. One thing is very evident since having more contact with returning troops & that is that no one really feels like he is a great patriot or that he has fought for any apparent justifiable reason. Going to Nam, for the soldier, is simply an unavoidable obligation that one has to fight to stay alive to finish. It rather makes the whole affair more frustrating.

The squad I'm in is made up of college students or graduates, which makes life a little more bearable since the conversations are diverse and intelligent. Getting enough food & sleep is my major concern at the moment, both are a rare commodity in this company. . . .

Your loving son
T Mc

October 2, 1970

Dear Beverly,

Hi!!! How ya doing? I sure hope everything is turning out ok for you at school and at work. You're just "super great."

. . . I'm kinda glad that Mike has it easy, because he would never made it in infantry. Not that I'm saying that I'm better than Mike but after what I saw at basic training, I'm glad that he got artillery. The training down here is pretty rough and you can ask Linda to ask Mike about Fort Polk and he will tell her that this place is the worst. Guys down here take dope and smoke pot to get through the training. And now we have in *our* barracks a war between the whites and blacks, and Mexicans. The blacks and Mexicans are against the whites all the way. When we first got here there was no trouble but now we have all kinds of trouble, fights and gang wars down here. I got to admit that I'm scare[d] to go places. Right now there's a fight going on right at the end of the bay area. But I sit in my area and write letters to the most wonderfulest girl in the world. And all these I forget because the army or anyone else is not going to mess my mind up. Right! Right now we got about 10 guys fighting and someone went to get the lieutenant and the MP's. I sure hope *we* don't get into any trouble because of this. It's really bad here. I can't wait until I get home to *ya*. . . .

Well, Bev the MP's are here so I got to stop for now. I wish I could continue to write but there's so much noise and yelling going on that I'm making too many mistakes. So, I'll get another letter off to ya this weekend. ok! . . .

Love & Kisses 4 ever
Jimmy

On to Vietnam

Following AIT, recruits often received leave to travel home prior to departing for Vietnam. In 1965 and 1966, most major units arrived in Vietnam by ship, although by 1967 replacement troops typically arrived by commercial airliner. Once on the ground, the new soldiers were greeted by veterans in shoddy worn-out uniforms who jeered at them before boarding the same planes headed back to the United States. These "newbies" or "cherries" now had 365 days "in country." The "Date of Expected Return from Overseas" (DEROS) marked the end of a tour of duty and the return to "the World."

MICHAEL A. JEFFORDS (b. 1943) was raised in Milwaukee and enlisted in the Marine Corps in November, 1962. He arrived at Da Nang on March 8, 1965, as one of the first 3,500 U.S. combat troops deployed to Vietnam. Corporal Jeffords served as an infantryman and a squad leader (B Co., 1/3d Mar., 3d Mar. Div.) in rural Da Nang from March to November, 1965. Following his discharge in March, 1966, Jeffords held a number of positions before settling into a career in finance, and he now lives in Boyceville.

March [8], 1965

Dear Folks—

I'm writing this on some transportation (I can't say what) and I have a while to write. I plan on mailing it as soon as I can. I know you will be worried by the news broadcasts at home. I didn't have time to write sooner. We've been very very busy.

I want you not to worry. I am all right!!

I am going to *Vietnam.* By the time you read this I will already be there. I can't say it won't be dangerous, because the possibility exists and you wouldn't believe me if I did, however, at the moment I am in no more danger than the marines that landed [at Guantánamo Bay Naval Base] in Cuba in 1962. If you remember nothing happened there.

The men in my battalion and myself are, right now, ready and willing to go. I trust them without any reservations and I think they trust me. I'm glad we're going in a way because it is what we've been trained for all these sweating, blistering months. It is the job the Marine Corps is paying us to do. Maybe now it will feel more like we're getting paid for our job.

I will do my job. I'm no hero. The marine corps has no use for heroes; just steady workers. One thing nice I know I won't get laid off! I know you'll be asking yourselves, "Why him?" I asked myself that many times before this happened. I realize now, finally why it has to be us (the Battalion), and myself. Who should come over here? Tom? Ken? Tim? Ronny? Or in a few years Francis? No, I'd rather it was this way.

Funny, I always thought I'd be scared to death but I'm not. It is like breathing a deep sigh of relief. There will be no more wondering. The waiting is the damnedest part. It's over now.

God, this sounds morbid. I'm trying to make you realize how calm everyone is, that there isn't that much to worry about (believe me from the bottom of my heart there isn't), and instead I'm afraid I'm scaring the hell out of you. I can't put it down on paper. The simplest I can put it is: We are going in to be a show of force and protect an installation. It is a proven fact the Viet Cong will not attack such a large force and supporting arms. So, there isn't anything to sweat, hummm?

It is funny for me to think of Tim being 21 years old. I had a drink for him. How is he? Wait till I get back, he and I will really celebrate it. Right? Dad too.

Dad, I hope you can make ma realize what I'm trying to say. You're a man, you understand better than she does. You know how nervous she gets. I have the luck of the Irish and the courage of a mouse. Make her realize there's no sweat!

God, I hope you all understand? . . .

Sincerely,
Mike

P.S. If it helps any, I believe President Johnson is doing the right thing. He should be—I voted for him. See you soon!!! Don't worry!!

JOHN L. ABRAMS (1940-1968) was raised in the Milwaukee area and enlisted
in the navy prior to his graduation from Stout State College in 1962. He
was commissioned in January, 1962, and served at bases in Virginia,
Florida, and Bermuda before volunteering for Vietnam. Lieutenant Abrams
acted as a helicopter fire team leader in the Mekong Delta, serving on the
USS *Harnett County* (Helicopter Attack [Light] Sqdn. 3, Detachment 1). On
July 13, 1968, four months after his arrival in Vietnam, he was killed when
his helicopter was brought down by enemy fire on Cu Lao Island. The
following two entries are taken from his journal and were written just before
he departed the United States for Vietnam.

March 18, 1968

. . . Tomorrow we leave the States headed for Vietnam; for combat
and the unknown. Now, though, everyone is spending his last night in
his own way. Some with their wives, others finding love with a different
woman, still others looking into a glass of scotch whiskey watching the
ice melt. The bantering and joviality is over for awhile; no more kidding each other about "getting your butt shot off." It's almost here, that
time of leaving. And until 1900 tomorrow, when we again join together
at Travis AFB for our flight to Saigon, each of us will be encapsulated
in his own little shell, reminiscing in his own world before the reality
of tomorrow crashes in.

March 19-20, 1968

This morning we walked around San Francisco—looking. Looking
in stores, at people; mingling with the crowds; inhaling Americana: smog
and flowers, perfume and diesel exhaust—the wonderful, beautiful com-
binations we take for granted (perhaps even dislike) but will soon miss.
Union Square—flower stalls and free livers—how lucky they are.

Now at Travis; wives and lovers holding onto their men until the last
moment. Those of us here alone have said our goodbyes in different
airports and again on the telephone. That last goodbye, not knowing
if you will ever hear that voice again, is strange and stilted. So many
things unsaid, so many things undone. . . .

ROBERT M. ROCK (b. 1946) grew up in Dodgeville and joined ROTC while
attending St. Norbert's College in De Pere. He was commissioned in June,
1968, and served as an infantry platoon leader and executive officer (A Co.,
3-506th Inf., 101st Abn. Div. [Airmobile]) in Bien Hoa, Hue, and Phu Bai
from June, 1969, to June, 1970. Lieutenant Rock was discharged in June,
1970, and returned to Dodgeville to work in his family's retail agricultural
business. He remained in the Army Reserve until 1981, when he retired as a
major, and he currently works in the travel business in Minneapolis. Rock
wrote this journal entry shortly after arriving in Vietnam.

[June 30, 1969]
I think everyone was experiencing what is known as "delusion of reprieve." What the military calls it I couldn't say. We stood around the terminal at Travis AFB in Fairfield, Cal. for about 3 hours before the boarding call came for flight 2B3A for Bien Hoa. By this time, most had convinced themselves that they were in fact going to Vietnam and were tired of waiting. When they announced there would be a slight delay in our flight there were threats of protesting and engaging in a sit down strike. It became evident that at heart this is what most really would've liked to do as the discussion on the plane during the 20 hr. flight ranged from the good old days at Armor School and at Ft. Leonard Wood and Finally Jungle School in Panama to a serious discussion about the morality of the War and the possibility of ever succeeding. These latter problems were only discussed from what we knew about war from hearing about it. The real problem we were about to face was the control of men and self survival.

I sat on the plane with Tom Powell of Gainesville, Florida and Rick Pickett of Kansas City, Kansas. Ahead of me were Nick Bangert of Green Bay, Wisc whom I had been on orders with since our ROTC days at college. Next to him there were 2 enlisted men who for 20 hours seemed to do nothing but think. Sometimes that's all you have to do when you feel you're all alone though. Most of the thoughts I'm sure were of loved ones at home while others talked of their 428 Charger that's sitting home depreciating. . . .

After 4½ we touched down in Hawaii for refueling. Some headed for the souvenir counter and some for that much needed glass of beer while still others were busy sending postcards home.

We were in the air 7½ hours en route to Guam where we again stopped for refueling. We were in Guam for 4½ hrs with nothing to do and with thoughts of Vietnam only 5 hours away nerves began to manifest themselves. Many were too nervous to eat while others had lost their appetite from an ungodly amount of cigarettes that clouded the small terminal with a smoke that burned your eyes. Spilled coke & coffee from jittery hands were not at all uncommon in the crowded cafeteria; while others' kidneys were being punished only as a pregnant woman's would. We boarded shortly after the sun had set and were seeing darkness for the first time as we were no longer moving faster than the earth.

The flight to Bien Hoa was one of restless sleep for all. Some time ago men had to unboard their DC 8 under ground fire from the enemy and many a treacherous landing had been made with only the use of flares to light the runway.

As we were making our approach we could see numerous villages lit up with fires, some small American base camps, a few scattered flares probably lit to search for the enemy around a base camp perimeter. A few small firefights and scattered rifle flashes could be seen from our window. A Lt. behind us says, "Well, it looks like we here" and sighed as our wheels touched the ground. "Unmistakably profound," pipes up another. As we were walking toward the terminal we could see and hear the helicopters overhead keeping the airfield secure while the planes landed and the soldiers were unloaded. After stomping both feet on the ground Frank Gooding, another armor expert who admits he doesn't remember a tinker's Damn about a tank, said "They finally did it, they sent me to Vietnam."

Early Impressions

The first impressions many veterans recount is that of the heat and pungent smells that assaulted them as they exited their transport. They had entered unfamiliar territory where tropical temperatures soared, and the people, sights, and sounds were often frighteningly different. The following letters address many of the questions, issues, and concerns confronting newbies as they adjusted to their new environment. While attempting to reassure their loved ones of their safety, the writers discuss their initial impressions of the Vietnamese people and culture, their heightened senses, and their thoughts on the U.S. role in Vietnam. The following two letters from MIKE JEFFORDS describe the first week of American combat in Vietnam in March, 1965. (For a biographical sketch of Jeffords, see earlier in this chapter.)

[ca. March 10, 1965]

Dear Folks,

I'm writing this on top of a c-ration box so if it's difficult to read you'll know why. The Air Force is making a hell of a racket outside and me trying to write. They are not very considerate. Neither is the weatherman—it must be 90° outside. My shelter-half is ten degrees hotter. You either are soaking wet from rain or broiling in the sun. I'm laying on my bullet-proof vest and wondering how to break the news to you. I wrote a note on the way down here that explains a lot of the way I feel but it comes out morbid when I read it. Anyway, if you haven't thought of it from seeing the newspapers and television my battalion was moved some. I'm at Da Nang Airfield in South Vietnam. It makes me laugh. Everything I told you wouldn't happen—has happened. It makes me look like a liar.

Funny, I used to watch movies, see television and read books about combat in war zones and get excited. The funny part is I'm not excited but calm—even bored from the heat! It isn't anything like I thought it would be. The excitement just isn't there.

One thing I've found is that all the days, months, and years that went before the last two days seem like a dream—unreal. Here, my senses of sound, sight, and touch have sharpened. And my awareness of reality. Every second—every minute I breathe I'm very aware of it. I'm enjoying life like I had never lived before. Maybe it is the purpose—feeling that you're doing something besides marking time. Doing what you've trained for. I wouldn't want to be anywhere else.

I just read over what I wrote and I'm afraid you'll get the impression that we're engaged in combat. We're only guarding the airfield against a Viet Cong attack. There haven't been any I've seen or anybody else yet. We expect it and we're ready but there isn't any trouble from them.

I'm telling you the facts so you don't get all excited over everything you read in the papers. . . .

Hey, how about telling Pat to change frequencies when she goes to church. Somebody's got their wires crossed. For eight months she's been praying I didn't go to Vietnam. Wha' Hoppen??? It must have been me praying I did.

I can't tell you how much peace of mind I've had since I've been here. The games are over. We know just what's expected of us.

I've been rambling on and on. Listen, this operation isn't any worse than Lebanon in 1958 or Cuba in 1962. If you remember nothing happened in either of those places. Don't you think if there was any *real* immediate danger I would never sound as good and high-spirited as I do. I'd be scared to death and crying to go home. Right? So, don't worry. I'm having something of a vacation. Don't sweat it. . . .

I have to get this done. They only pick up mail once a day. At night we can't move around too much and I want to make *one* trip. There and back. I'm too *lazy* to make more than one, that's why.

See you soon--

Sincerely,
Mike

P.S. I never felt better. DON'T WORRY!!

Da Nang, March 16, 1965

Dear Folks,

. . . Everything is routine here. We've been digging emplacements and sand-bagging them during the day. At night we sit in them alone and count the stars and listen to the brush rustle. You know me, if anything was happening I'd tell everything. Especially if there was any shooting. It's routine! Quiet days!

It's about 95° here during the day. The sun shimmers off the grass and bush. If you come out of the shade to the sun you almost go blind. Most of the area under the grass is sand. We go without shirts most of the day. But you have to wear flak jackets (bullet-proof vests) so it doesn't make much difference. Your head cooks under the helmet.

Vietnam is not backward. Its roads are more urban than Okinawa. The people are as friendly as you let them. We don't mingle with them much. Even the kids. The Cong don't wear signs announcing who they are. Even the kids have been used at times. Rather than have to hurt them we keep them away. Most of their buildings are metal corrugated shacks and concrete. Some grass homes but not many. There is traffic on the roads all the time.

At night it cools down to about 65° until midnight. Then a ground fog about knee-high moves over the deck. It's eerie as hell. Much like a graveyard or a spooky picture—it's that quiet. Not even a bird chirp. Every now and then something stumbles through the brush to keep you alert. One of these nights I'm going to stab one of these farmers' chickens or pigs and eat something besides c-rations. We've been on Cs for two weeks and there's more coming. The silence at night makes you think a lot. You can hear the wheels grind in your brain. About 3 in the morning you can hear your relief coming through the field about sixty feet away. Most of the watch consists of listening rather than seeing.

We're sleeping in tents (2 man type). The weather never gets cold but the dew settles on everything and a small wind blows enough to chill you some even here. In the morning when you wake up you shake out your mosquito net, blanket, poncho, and pack and watch the menagerie take off. First, a cloud about six feet high of mosquitoes takes off, then the frogs hop out to get them, the lizards crawl away to find a cooler spot before the sun comes up, one or two mice vamoose, the snakes head for their holes, the chiggers come out of your skin when you fry them with a cigarette, and finally you knock a 1 inch spider off your rifle who has been indifferent enough to build a web between it and your tent pole. All this happens at different times. They don't all appear at once. The variety keeps you guessing. The mosquitoes get high on the repellant we put on. My face looks like a boulder full of pebbles.

The platoon and squad have never been closer. Even in boot camp I've never been tighter with a bunch of marines. Everyone avoids trouble with each other. We all know our job and try to help the other jarhead do his. These gyrenes are the best. . . .

Three years ago I graduated from high school. A week and a half ago I was in a chapel on base, then to a movie, then the club. All of it has changed in a week. Everything before seems a dream unreal. I realize how good life is and how lucky we are to live in America. To walk down a street without looking over your shoulder or sleeping with a bayonet. Wisconsin Avenue seems like paradise. It will be good to get back. Sometimes I wonder if it or I will ever be the same. I feel about forty years old. It's a lousy feeling.

But—that's only when I really fill up with self-pity. When I try to find the easy way out. I feel good and healthy and alive most of the time. Don't sweat it!! . . .

Have to Run—something came up!

Mike

Don't sweat it!!

MICHAEL E. KASTERN (b. 1947) lived in West Allis prior to volunteering for the draft in August, 1967. Sergeant Kastern served as an infantryman (A Co., 4-3d Inf., 11th Inf. Bde. [Light], 23d Inf. Div. [Americal]) in Chu Lai from January, 1968, to January, 1969. Following his discharge in August, 1969, he attended the University of Wisconsin-Milwaukee. He has worked for the postal service since 1974 and makes his home in East Troy.

In the following letter, Kastern discusses the fragmented nature of the South Vietnamese forces. The Army of the Republic of Vietnam (ARVN) served as the main corps, but local militia units such as the Regional Forces (RF) and Popular Forces (PF) supported the regular troops. The tribal Montagnards, who resided in the strategically crucial central highlands, aided South Vietnam and the United States throughout the war. In addition, men from the Republic of Korea (ROK), Australia, New Zealand, Thailand, the Philippines, and the Republic of China (Taiwan) served alongside American soldiers.

March 9, 1968

Dear Mom & Dad,

. . . They keep fortifying this position here and sending in more troops. They are expecting something pretty big, I guess, but so far not much except a few mortar rounds. We're all bunkered in and we've set out minefields, trip flares, concertina wire etc. so I guess they must be pretty sure of something going to happen. Also working with us are Korean Forces (ROK marines), Vietnamese Popular Forces (PFs), Vietnamese Regular Army Forces (ARVNs), Montagnards (South Vietnamese mountain people) and other American armor and artillery units! Most of those people mentioned above are American uniformed and supplied. The Vietnamese troops (south, that is) carry M1s, M2s, grease guns, B.A.R.s etc. Once I was talking to one of the Pfs who had a B.A.R. and he pointed to his rifle and shook his head and said "Number 10!" (meaning not very good). Then he pointed to my M-16 and smiled and said "Number 1!" (meaning the best). Most of these people are very friendly, especially the kids and the South Vietnamese soldiers, but like I said before they are awfully hard to communicate with.

The other day while on a patrol we came upon a PF village (Popular Forces—usually part time farmers & part time soldiers—our side, that is)! Those type of people are somewhat aided by the Americans as far as tools for their farming (rice) and also seeds and stuff for better crops etc. plus advice and technical know-how. What a difference there was between that village and regular villages we come across. It was real clean and well kept and the young men were working in the fields (you seldom see any activity in other villages) and there were whole families living together. (In other villages you usually just see old women and young children because all the men & some women between the ages of about 16 & 50 are VC and are hiding during the day.) Also in this PF village the people were clean looking with clean clothes on. (Usually they are dirty and diseased with dirty and shabby clothes & especially the children!) The most noticeable thing of all was that the people were industrious and looked happy! It really made me feel good when I saw that place after some of those other ruined villages. I guess the Americans are doing some good after all (or at least trying). . . .

Love,
Michael

DAVID R. OLSON (b. 1943) was born in Madison and attended the Madison campus of the University of Wisconsin before enlisting in the army in February, 1966. He served as a chief warrant officer (B Trp., 7–17th Cav., 17th Avn. Grp.), flying helicopters near Pleiku and Dak To from October, 1967, to October, 1968. Olson was discharged in December, 1969, re-enrolled at the university, and later moved to Texas, where he worked in computer programming from 1973 to 1993. He returned to Madison in March, 1994, and currently is working on an education degree at the university.

November 7, 1967

Dear Mom & Dad & All

We finally made it! We docked at Qui Nhon harbor on _____ Oct. We then loaded on trucks (18 to a truck) and moved the whole 7th SQDN by convoy. We took Highway 19, which runs due west and slightly north from Qui Nhon. We went through An Khe, up through the Mang Yang Pass, and through Pleiku. We are at Camp Enari, which is 12 miles south west of Pleiku. The trip took a little over six hours, for a distance of

120 miles! 90 of the 120 miles was on the worst highway you ever want to see. Any way the trip was uneventful and we hit Camp Enari just before dark. . . .

A few words about Vietnam and the Vietnamese people: the country is for the most part very beautiful. Where I am there are two seasons. Very wet & very dry. The monsoon season just finished and we will have about seven months of dry weather. There is one drawback regarding the dry season—it is dusty as hell! It gets into everything. However one gets used to it very quickly and if you can shower every day it's not bad at all.

The standard of living in Vietnam is just what one would expect—very poor. The housing in general is terrible and the level of sanitation you would not believe. The Vietnamese however, have a great solution to the diaper problem. All the kids who aren't toilet trained run around naked from the waist down, and relieve themselves wherever & whenever they want to. The disadvantages however, are rather obvious. No big thing though, because a good number of people of all ages use latrine facilities anywhere, just about, where they wish.

Most of the people are very friendly and the kids are cute. You really can't help but like them. Dave Peterson and I sat around for about 1½ hours this afternoon with 6 of them trying to learn some Vietnamese. Only two of them knew any English at all and it was mostly pidgin English. The conversations were pretty hilarious and they enjoyed it as much as we did. We did however learn some Vietnamese and I'm willing to bet that in about 2 months I'll be able to speak enough to get by. It's a heck of alot more fun to learn it here than in a classroom. . . .

Don't shovel too much snow

Dave

DARREL R. LULLING (b. 1948), a Madison native, was drafted into the army in August, 1968. He served as an infantry squad leader (B Co., 1-11th Inf., 1st Bde., 5th Inf. Div. [Mech.]) in Quang Tri province from August, 1969, until he was wounded in action on October 1 of that year. Lulling attended the University of Wisconsin-La Crosse after his discharge in June, 1970, and currently works for the U.S. Department of Veterans Affairs as a psychology technician in Oakwood, Illinois.

August 26, 1969

My Dearest Darling Jane,

. . . The Vietnamese people are really something so friendly and carefree just working each day to survive. A very saddening thing is that most of the GIs do not understand the people and try to exploit them or reject them as lesser beings.

Darrel Lulling, Fort Campbell, Kentucky, September, 1968. Courtesy Darrel Lulling.

Their culture is so very different, simple, yet they are beautiful people. The U.S. has come here and all of a sudden tried to make Vietnam a modern western model of a country. In certain ways it is destroying the old way of life which I think is really a crime—We are destroying the countryside, bomb craters all over the place and trash left by the great U.S. war machine, a complete rape of the land yet the people are not in much better shape—still the rich get richer and the poor get poorer. I wish you could meet some of these people who have not been corrupted, they are really nice human beings. So far all I have seen is the harm we have done. I have not seen much good but I am still looking. . . .

Love
Darrel

2

A Year in Country

A soldier's year in country could mean many things, depending on rank, location, skill, or simply luck. Perhaps most important, the nature of a GI's daily existence depended on whether he was assigned to duty in the field or to a relatively safe job in the rear. The letters in this chapter offer a glimpse into the rhythms of daily life for American soldiers in Vietnam.

In the Field

Life for the foot soldiers or "grunts" was not only dangerous but also tedious and frustrating. American forces patrolled the jungles and rice paddies of Vietnam on search-and-destroy missions, stemming from the American strategy of attrition, which dictated that American forces should try to break the will of the communists by killing soldiers and destroying equipment until the north could no longer tolerate the losses. Americans pursued the enemy, trying to draw fire and engage in battles.

Troops moved in platoons of sixteen to twenty-four men and marched in a long column, spaced roughly fifteen to twenty feet apart to avoid a wholesale disaster if someone stepped on mine or booby trap. These men carried packs that weighed about eighty pounds and marched for days wearing thick flak jackets and carrying mines, mortars, machine guns, and ammunition as well as rifles. They carried and consumed C-rations and substantial quantities of water as they slogged through what was often debilitating heat until resupply arrived. Foot soldiers went without showers, enduring jungle rot and leeches and sleeping an average of four hours a night—if they were lucky. After humping a variety of terrain, grunts ended the day by cleaning equipment, placing a claymore mine with the "front toward enemy," applying insect repellent, and stealing what sleep they could before guard duty and eventually another day. The following letters offer descriptions of the daily life, duties, and struggles of foot soldiers in Vietnam.

GEORGE L. GODFREY (b. 1944) was born in Lodi and was teaching high school in Oconomowoc when he was drafted in October, 1969. He served with the army as an infantryman with a mortar squad (A Co., 5–7th Cav., 2d Bde., 1st Cav. Div. [Airmobile]) near Bien Hoa and in Cambodia from June, 1970, until March, 1971. Discharged in July, 1971, Godfrey lives in Lodi, where he owned a bicycle shop and now works as a carpenter.

25

July, 1970

Dear Home:

. . . I was sent to the field to join my squad on the 23rd of June in Cambodia. The action was over and I just joined them for the long walk through the jungle back to Vietnam and to the rear for the rest of three days. I took in the publicity and picture taking like a real veteran. I put down the Verona Press as hometown paper since I'm already receiving papers from Lodi and Oconomowoc.

In the field or to the jungle is called "humping the boonies." The humping means carrying the gear needed on the back. The boonies are the vast areas of dense jungle which I will spend my year in. First, the humping, I hump several things and this is the hardest of the two, adjusting to. I hump my personal gear which includes only the bare necessities as follows: Poncho liner, which is very light down, but warm and is used as a blanket or pillow on the real warm nights. Sheet of plastic which is the floor of the tent or raincoat which I don't use because the rain is our only bath. This all goes on the bottom of my pack along with my air mattress.

Our company is one of the few that let the troops blow up the air mattresses while in the field. This usually isn't allowed due to the noise they make while being blown up. The air mattress is my prize possession, one of the few luxuries I have. The pack I spoke of is called a "Ruck Sack," and each humper has one. It has a steel frame that fits the back with bags, pockets and straps all over it. Inside the large bag, I keep my shaving equipment, pipe tobacco and so forth. Everything of value must be kept in plastic bags. It's hard to believe back in the world (that's USA) that the sweat of a day's travel would soak a man's entire equipment, but it is an almost daily experience. Just the humping of my own sweat or the rain of the Monsoon season adds quite a little weight to the pack. Each pocket has drain holes which help some. That is the extent of the personal gear except maybe one change of socks. Each day I wring out the socks of yesterday and dry them for tomorrow. Along with foot powder, my feet are holding up real good. The clothes are the same ones, just shirt and pants with cads of pockets for a period of at least 3 days or longer with Log Day, which is troop supply day. The set I removed yesterday were on my body since I entered this country June 12. I was lucky midway of my short tour, we came upon a large bomb crater filled with rain water and I enjoyed the greatest swim of all time. Boots and pants still on and tied tightly to protect from leeches, and other little jungle critters. I know that sounds just terrible (jungle critters) and I'm sure you are shivering with the thought of step and a half snakes and crocodiles.

Heavily burdened GIs "humping the boonies."
Courtesy Bruce Thibodeau.

. . . Most all men here carry jungle rot which is the worst of all evil here. Worse than the enemy because the Medevac Chopper is Johnny on the spot when "Charlie" leaves a calling card. The jungle rot, one just bears with it for a year. I plan on some jungle rot, but not from the jungle critters. Nobody worries about it, just itch it occasionally and enjoy the relief. Malaria is common and is good for 2 Mo. sham time in the rear. We pill for it every morning with the little white ones and the big orange one comes on Monday. That's our only identification of the days of the week. When the big orange one comes, I know that I missed church yesterday again. . . .

To continue with my ruck sack, I hump the standard equipment of 2 smoke bombs, 2 hand grenades (handled with loving care and now I'm rid of them), 2 trip flares and sometimes a Claymore mine for night protection or could be used for a boat anchor. 2 gallons of water needed for the 3 days between logs (supply days). Often get a kick-out (chopper drop) of water on the second day. I'm adding another half gallon to my supply, in the field water is better than gold because I wouldn't hump 2½ gallons of pure gold if it was mine just for the humping. Water, for example, is not used to brush teeth, one just spits for awhile. Sweat from the shirt washes the canteen out for dinner use and all water goes to the best of use down the hatch, along with the sand of the last swallow. Humping food for 9 meals is another must. I've really learned the body's needs of food, water, and shelter when it's all on my back. Just glad I don't have to carry the air to breathe also, just a gas mask to purify it in case "Charlie" advances to chemical warfare or a GI screws up with ours.

The food is C rations or "Lurps." The Cs weigh more because they contain fruit. One can of pears or peaches is all I can down for lunch in the heat of the day. The night meal with tents up and time to spare is a real treat. Lurps are dried food like powder. Add water heated with C4 (explosive that just burns in small quantities) inside an ingeniously cut tin can stove, and before the eyes appear the beans, peas, meat, potatoes, and all kinds of good things. The peas taste more like beans and the beans kinda like potatoes, but all food is good over the open fire out-of-doors. After the humping of the day is over, the remainder of the day and night is as a camping trip except for ½ hr. spent on guard duty. Then too, Ginger usually had me pulling at least a ½ hr. guard duty every night of our camping vacations.

I believe after this year, our family vacation plans are going to undergo drastic changes. Dad, you just inherited one Coleman lantern and any other camping equipment presently in my name.

Finishing off my ruck sack with 2 and on the 5th day 3 mortar rounds at a chubby 15 lbs each. Bandoliers of rounds criss cross my chest containing 16 magazines and some 3 or 4 hundred M16 (rifle) bullets. The M16's primary function at present for me is a walking stick.

Under the weight I carry, I think you can see its need. Its other purpose, I don't know if it works, and I pray that I never have to find out. By the look of it, I doubt if the last owner had to use it except for a cane. I believe with the first aid pack and pistol belt, my pack is completely described and weighing in at something I don't like to talk about. Dad and Gram, don't think you're slow at getting up from a sitting position because you're like Jack the Ripper compared to me in full gear. The first day is the worst, and the second is better. Why, simply 3 less meals and a gallon less water. The third day is like air-borne until the Log hits. So that's the humping part and now a little about the Boonies.

Dense—is the best word. Solid and thick fit also, with visibility 5 to 20 meters at best. Often I can smell the man in front of me on the trail before I can see him. Bamboo and vines, and fern, and more bamboo. Overhead is complete shade which is nice. The only open spaces are the bomb craters and just before them the bamboo is all twisted and crossed, making travel very slow. We walk for maybe ten minutes then rest, 5 minutes up to an hour. Up a hill—rest, over top—rest, down the hill—rest. Over and over the cycle continues. Our biggest day was 3½ (1000 meters to a click) all in 13 hours' time. Cambodia's border and North Vietnam's border where I will probably spend my tour has all hills and little or no swamp or rice paddies, just rubber plantations. The hills are hands and knee action, going up from bamboo to bamboo and then on the butt to slide down the other side. Sometimes gaining inches at a time especially if it rains and the red clay holds no friction. During this time we rely strictly on the bamboo. Once in awhile I look to my front and tell the Lord he missed a spot in his planting. Then the M16 becomes a step-ladder and drive on.

During the real heat of the day the feeling can't be described with one word. Sweat runs like I've never seen it before. The humidity clings like smoke and the air is heavy and hard to breathe. The entire body is sore from hours under the weight of the pack. Often blood dripping from the many cuts of the hands from sharp bamboo ends and thorns of the vines. The insect repellent burns every pore of the skin and as the sweat washes away, the mosquitos find the weak spots. Tempers grow short and the body is so weak it trembles under strain and the rest period offers little relief.

Drive on, there are no boys here, all men, some quite young, but they're men now. Human torture describes the feeling, it has really amazed me what the human body is capable of functioning through. My hands heal very quickly and no rot sets in. There is no exaggeration to the heat of the day, tis true only men going through it know the real story. It can't be told and believed in the world. I was at my worst the first bad day when we all took our swim. Money couldn't buy that feeling of cool water. Sometimes the rain comes just at the right time when I think I can't go on. Well that's how it was the first week for me. Getting better by the day now as I'm getting conditioned to the environment. Also learning tricks from the longer term men to ease the situation. A towel pad placed just right on the lower part of the pack, rearranged shoulder straps, shifting the weight, using the M16 as support for the pack whenever possible, continually wiping the heat away with the sweat. All these things really are making the difference for me and I can make it O.K. now. Days are going by fast, June is all gone. There is no place in the Army I would rather be—just where I am—and what I'm doing. One big camping trip and now and then a vacation from that. When our Co. got in last night, some guys for the only time since April, showers flowed constantly, and the beer was cold. GIs were like wild animals set free. Quite a sight to see and good feeling to be a part of.

So that's my version of "humping the Boonies" told like it is so you can understand and live this year out with me. The Army provides quite adequately. Send lots of letters, mail call on Log day is a big thing here.

I won't be able to write often as I'd like, but I'm sure you can understand.

Love,
George

TOM MCCABE, an infantryman near An Duc, described some of the difficulties of life in the field in the following letter to his parents. (For a biographical sketch of McCabe, see chapter 1.)

June 1, 1969

Hello

. . . As for a rundown on our mission last month, let me first summarize it by saying it was very miserable. We started out with a Charlie Alpha into an area just northwest of Dolly. Since I was on one of the first birds in I had to wait out in the open field for the rest of the company to fly in. It was about 120 °F out there so I commenced to inhale my water supply which I had reduced from 5–4 qts since the previous mission. Well that was the beginning of a long dry mission. Supplies never came regularly & when they did they were never adequate and furthermore they would come in the morning so we would have to hump all the excess supplies all day. To say the least it was a miserable set-up. I was usually stuck with a 5 gallon plastic lugger jug of water which was heavy, bulky & very cumbersome. We only stayed in that area for a few days and then CA'd to another area more north of Dolly. Here we continued our crazy supply scheme with much suffering from the troops. We changed from a search and destroy type tactic to one of wait and ambush. This meant that some 20 men would find a likely spot for gooks to walk by & then set up and wait. We stayed on ambush for about 36 hours at a time. For some reason the Company commander figured that since we were just sitting on ambush that we didn't need more than one or two qts of H2O a day. Well we proved him wrong, but we were the ones that suffered the consequences. We were so dry by the third day that we couldn't even sweat. We were finally forced to dig some water out of the bottom of a bomb crater. The water was 70% emulsified clay and didn't taste worth a damn even tho we boiled it, put iodine pills in it & numerous types of artificial flavoring. Although it was wet it didn't quench our thirst one bit, in fact it had a detrimental effect on my system. After about a week and a half of this type of tactic we charlie alphaed again into an area along the Saigon river. We were there just one day & they moved us again; this time into an area that was known to have a large caché of gook supplies. We landed at an abandoned LZ (Phyllis) & moved out about 800 meters. We sent out a few patrols that immediately found several small cachés along a rather large Ho Chi Minh trail, (a foot path about 5'–6' wide). I and about 10 other men from my platoon were sent out to ambush the trail that nite. Surprisingly for all the supplies we eventually found there wasn't any VC in the immediate area. The bad part of the whole thing was that we weren't getting any food or water. The rest of the company did but since we were on ambush we didn't get any. So for two days I lived on a small pecan roll from my remaining C-rations & two quarts of H2O. We did finally get hot chow & our beers & sodas at the end of the second day. The cachés we found were quite something; for instance at one spot we found 45, 250 lb bags of rice. All totaled we destroyed 67 tons of rice and numerous mortars rockets & other ammo. We charlie alphaed again after two days of destroying cachés & went to an area southwest of Dolly. It was here that I flaked out on the trail. The CO pushed us hard thru thick bamboo in the heat of the day. We were all humping heavy since we had two days supplies on us. I was humping the machine gun so was even heavier than most of the troops. We had several people collapse because of the strain & the heat but still the CO wouldn't slow down. I finally hoisted a water container that one of the men dropped because he couldn't hump it any further. My fear of having to go thirsty outweighed the discomfort the added water made. I went some 800 meters thru the bamboo when we reached a small clearing. I was half way across the opening thinking to myself that it was good we were out of the thick stuff when all of a sudden everything blacked out. I came to shortly thereafter to find myself surrounded by medics & my buddies pouring water on me & fanning me with towels. Not being one that likes to be fussed over and being mad at myself for not making it all the way I made an attempt to get to my feet. Well that turned out to be the wrong move for I blacked out again & the next thing I knew I was in a medevac bird with one doc putting plasma in my arm & the other cutting my clothes off. As it turned out I was completely all right & ended up getting a two day vacation in Tay Ninh. From Tay Ninh I came up to Dolly. So that about covers my last mission. . . .

Love to all—your son
T Mc

A radio-telephone operator checks with headquarters while the rest of his company waits in the bush. Courtesy Jim Carlson.

A. J. McCaskey (b. 1947) was born in Mauston and was living in Wautoma when he was drafted in April, 1968. McCaskey served in the army as an infantryman (A Co., 4–47th Inf., 2d Bde., 9th Inf. Div.) near Dong Tam and Truc Giang from September, 1968, to July, 1969. He was discharged in January, 1970, and now lives in Wautoma, where he runs a food service business. In this letter to his mother, McCaskey notes American servicemen's interest in souvenirs.

October 16, 1968

Hi,

Got your goodies a couple days ago. Good to get the reading material and stuff.

We went out on a mission, my first one. It wasn't too bad. Just too much mud to walk through and too much equipment to carry. We had some luck and came across a very big cache of VC equipment. Loudspeakers, piles and piles of documents, weapons, pictures, flags, and lots of propaganda. The CO was quite happy. Then, we had a three star general come out to look it all over. But before he arrived we had to build a bridge for him so he wouldn't get his feet muddy!! He was quite impressed with our find though.

When we got back to the boats for our ride back to the ship I found out we infantrymen have a distinct advantage. The Navy guys heard about our cache and were offering tape recorders for VC flags and any other prizes we had. Well the Captain kept a pretty close eye on all the goodies and made sure it went out on the choppers. Not *all* of it made [it] though. . . .

[A.J.]

RICHARD D. VOLTZ (b. 1948) was born in Amery and was living in Milltown when he was drafted into the army in January, 1968. He served as an infantry rifleman and as a radio operator (D Co., 1–5th Cav., 1st Cav. Div. [Airmobile]) near Hue, Quang Tri, Khe Sanh, Tay Ninh, and An Khe from June, 1968, to June, 1969. Discharged in October, 1969, Voltz currently lives in Baraboo and works for a marketing firm. In the following letter to his parents, he reflects the army's concern with gathering statistics during the Vietnam War. Lacking more conventional means of measuring the progress of the war, the "body count" of enemy dead became the measure of success, despite problems with establishing accurate numbers. Voltz also expresses the relief felt by fighting men after they had been in country long enough to gain experience and the respect of the other men in their platoon. Because servicemen rotated in and out of Vietnam for a one-year tour of duty, new and inexperienced men could be dangerous to themselves and to others. After four months in country, Voltz was no longer a "new guy."

October 5, 1968

Dear Mom & Dad

Well another day in the Nam, well my last letter said we were in the lowlands waiting for a tropical storm to pass over and then back to the mountains, well we are back in the mountains.

I got a few statistics on that sweep that we were involved in. I thought you might be interested. There were 279 NVA killed, 5 POW, 134 small Arms captured and 7 crew manned weapons captured that is such things as mortars and machine guns.

I guess they consider it pretty successful. Yesterday when we were moving down a trail we came into a bunker complex and we found an 82 mm mortar tube and 8 rounds for it, plus all sorts of small arms ammo.

Wow 4 mo are almost behind me, it sure is a great feeling. Now I can start giving all the new guys that are coming in hell. That is what they use to do to me. They use to ask me how many days I had left and things like that. I almost consider myself an old timer now, because we got so many new guys in. . . .

Well not much else new, just thought I would drop you a line, take
it easy on your vacation and don't be lonesome for the cows.

Love
Rick

DAVID D. DALEY (b. 1949) was born in Rochester, Minnesota, and was
attending the University of Minnesota when he was drafted in September,
1969. Daley served with the army (A Co., 1–27th Inf. [Wolfhounds], 25th
Inf. Div.) as an infantry machine gunner near Cu Chi, Xuan Loc, and Dau
Tieng from June, 1970, to March, 1971. Discharged in March, 1972, he now
lives in Wauwatosa and works as a newspaper reporter. In the following
journal entry, Daley conveys the tension between career military personnel
("lifers") and draftees. Daley also touches on the problem of drug use
among soldiers: the availability of marijuana and heroin during the war
raised questions about the combat readiness of troops who used drugs as a
means of escape.

August 24, 1970

Lord save us from lifers! The new E-6 2nd platoon has is a neander-
thalic monstrosity—a drill sergeant in a combat zone. A fucken dud lifer.
He's made our one day out in the field a complete miserable fuck-up.
It's supposed to be his third tour, but he doesn't know his ass from the
proverbial hole in the ground.

I call him Sgt. Swino. He's got a blunt thick lipped face, whitewalled
crew cut, a thick neck, short squat pot-bellied body. He's from Tennessee and talks like it. He favors the word fuck in all its forms when
speaking. He uses his fingers to add and still comes out wrong. He's
a grim faced, threatening middle aged man, stuck in the Army rut and
probably enjoying every mediocre minute of it.

We moved out by choppers yesterday afternoon. Before we did, Sarge
had us line up all our gear in a row outside the hootch and he walked
by inspecting. He brought out three LAWS [Light Antitank Weapons]
from supply. God knows what we're gonna do with them.

Then he gave us a short, sweet pep talk:

"Men, I don't care if you wear beads and headbands out in the field,
and Charlie don't care either. He'll slit your throat and leave you your
beads."

"This platoon is gonna shape up and start functioning the way a platoon is supposed to function. I been watching you guys around here,
and you been dragging your ass."

"When we're in here we're gonna play, but when we're out we're gonna
work."

"I don't mind you smoking pot in here. You can go in that hootch and blow the roof off if you want to, but don't let me catch you doing it in the field. If somebody gets zapped because you were smoking pot, you're not gonna make it back babe."

"I don't care what you are—Airborne, Ranger, Recondo—Charlie don't care whatcha got stitched on you either. He'll still fire up your fucken ass. And there's plenty of dead rangers out there to prove it."

That was the gist of Sarge's welcoming speech to 2nd platoon.

EDWARD J. BEAUCHAMP (b. 1949) was born in Milwaukee and was attending Platteville State University when he was drafted into the army in May, 1969. Beauchamp served in the infantry (E Co., 4–31st Inf., 196th Inf. Bde. [Light], 23d Inf. Div. [Americal]) and performed reconnaissance northwest of Chu Lai from March, 1970, until February, 1971. Beauchamp was discharged in February, 1971, and now lives in Bayside. In this letter to his sister, Beauchamp describes a recon patrol, in which men went out into the jungles and mountains of South Vietnam in small groups to gather information and to find the enemy.

[June, 1970]

Dear Ruthann

Well I received your letter today & I was happy to hear from you. Well you wanted to know why our purpose was in going out. Well the first time was as a blocking force. This time I'm with Recon. because they needed men so I've been drafted. Being with Recon is no picnic. I don't know how long I [will] be with them but I hope it isn't long. For the main reason Recon has 23 men. Sometimes it gets as low as 15 men. Recon's job is to locate the enemy. Not to fight them unless a line company is pinned down. In other words we're usually a reserve unless the enemy finds us first.

Right now we're working with Delta Company. Delta's gone through hell. They have 30 some men now out of an original 130 men. I think this place is the hottest it ever was. I read in the paper there's 10,000 troops & 100s of tanks after 1 regiment of VC in Cambodia. I will tell you this. Our battalion 1st has about 500 men, 250 to 300 are in the field. We have 2 Regiments we're fighting here. (so much for complaining.) About West though—West & Siberia are our fire support bases. Talk about growth the hilltop is barren to give a clear field of fire. The grass down further & in the valley are shoulder high. Also it's double canopy & triple canopy jungle.

Today delta found a booby trap but no one was hurt.

Chow isn't too good because of the c-rations all the time. Put it this way Ruthann, I've never been so miserable in my whole life. I'll be going behind the lines at the end of June for standdown for 3 days. . . .

Love Your Brother
Ed.

DENNIS M. BELONGER (1948–1969) grew up in Manitowoc and enlisted in the army in August, 1968. He served as a long-range reconnaissance patrol (LRRP) member (HHC, 1st Bde., 4th Inf. Div.) in the central highlands northeast of An Khe from May, 1969, until his death on July 19, 1969, during a search for enemy casualties following an ambush. In this letter to his brother, Belonger describes his work as one member of a specially trained, four-man LRRP. Helicopters inserted men on these risky operations into enemy territory for five days to two weeks at a time.

May 28, [1969]

Dear Dan,

. . . I came in off a mission yesterday and go out the day after tomorrow—which is a break. They're only sending out 1 team tomorrow so I get an extra day's rest. It's a well deserved rest I must say. Though I've only had one completed mission (out of three), I know it gets hard and the rest is needed.

The scariest thing about a mission is probably the insertion. The chopper comes down on the LZ (I've had to jump 2 out of 3 times) and the 4 of us get out and head for cover hoping we weren't spotted going in. It's a helpless feeling for the first few hours not knowing if they're coming up on you or not. By the way, I've a price on my head, I'm worth $500 to the Charlie who can kill me. Of course no one will collect on me. They'll have to earn their money some other way.

Maybe you don't even know what I'm doing. I'm a LRRP (Long Range Recon Patrols). A 4-man LRRP team is inserted by helicopter into a 2000 meter square area of operation. Our purpose is to observe everything in the area: troop movements, signs of previous movement, trails, etc. Although there are some "killer" teams sent out to make contact, most try to stay quiet. We've come damn close to being discovered but haven't had any contact yet.

One of the team members is a 14 year old Montagnard. He carries an M-16, frag grenades and everything I do. He'll be fighting here as long as he lives. It's a shame for that to have to happen. . . .

We'll see you soon.

Peace
Dennis

Troops in the field dispensed with formalities, eating and resting when and where they could. Courtesy William Carlson.

MICHAEL J. CHAMBERLAIN (b. 1945) was born and raised in Beaver Dam and enlisted in the army in November, 1965. He was commissioned as a second lieutenant in December, 1966, and served as a platoon leader (B Co., 2–5th Cav., 2d Bde., 1st Cav. Div. [Airmobile]) in An Khe from June, 1967, to January, 1968, when he was wounded. Chamberlain was discharged from the service in December, 1968, and enrolled at Stout State University. He currently works as a carrier for the U.S. Postal Service and lives in Madison. In addition to describing infantry duty, Chamberlain notes the differences he observed between the Viet Cong (VC), an indigenous insurgent force dedicated to overthrowing the South Vietnamese government, and the North Vietnamese army (NVA).

August 4, 1967

Dear Ma & everybody,

. . . Right now we are at a LZ (landing zone) called Two Bits about ½ mile from the Bong Son River. They have permanent type LZ all over VN and the Infantry has to protect these, mainly pull security. It is like a break because they have built up bunkers and you stay in one place. You get hot chow every meal and then have a small PX, get a few cold beers.

Since I've been here it seems to work or their system is set up like this.

You are out in the field humping mountain, rice paddy searching village etc looking for Charlie for about 5–10 days. Then you come back and secure LZ for about 2 to 5 days. It is just a rotation system set up so all the Infantry company stay equal.

About 3 days ago when we were searching a village we capture[d] 20 VC and also 3 NVA without firing a shot. The 3 NVA wouldn't come out of the holes they were in, instead they blew themselves to hell with a grenade. I've been told that the NVA that come down from the north are really "hard core," they fight to the end, never give up. They aren't like the VC who hit and run and they give themselves up all the time. The NVA are the ones well trained and devoted to the cause, they have good discipline and know more about military tactics. . . .

Love
Mike

After spending two weeks to a month in the bush, infantrymen could look forward to a well-deserved albeit short rest, known as standdown. The men returned to a secured base and pulled guard duty while they enjoyed a few hot meals, showers, and much-needed sleep.

JOHN R. KOEPPEN (b. 1950), a Milwaukee native, was working as a machine operator and attending college when he enlisted in the army in September, 1969. Koeppen served in the infantry (A Co., 6–31st Inf., 1st Bde., 9th Inf. Div.; E Co., 2–3d Inf., 199th Inf. Bde. [Light]; E Co., 4–23d Inf. [Mech.], 2d Bde., 25th Inf. Div.; C Co., 1–27th Inf., 3d Bde., 25th Inf. Div.) in a variety of locations, including Long Binh, Xuan Loc, Cu Chi, and Cambodia, from February, 1970, until March, 1971, when he was discharged. He now lives in Racine and works for a telecommunications firm. In this letter to his family, Koeppen describes a standdown cut short by a zealous commanding officer.

January 1, [1971]

Dear Blood

Happy New Year!!

I do hope that your New Year's Eve was under much better conditions than mine. Before I go into that, I'll start a couple days before that.

On the morning, of the 30th, we were picked up by helicopters and flown to firebase Beverly for our two day standdown after ten days in the boonies. Let me tell you that there isn't too many other things that feel as good as walking in a firebase after ten days out in the jungle. It was like Christmas for us, we received three days' back mail, ten days' back packages from home, a little package from the red cross, a cot to sleep on, a tent to sleep under, a shower, hot meal, a cold beer and a couple of great days to do nothing. It was great!

John Koeppen humping through a banana plantation.
Courtesy John Koeppen.

Thanks for the package and games. The games come in more than handy out in the field and nothing beats a package from home. Thanks, again.

Then the sky fell in ... our CO volunteered us to go, after only one day standdown. To impress you more, after 240 hours or more in the field, you usually get a 50 to 72 hour standdown. We ended up with about a 28 hour standdown and are going out for another ten days. I can't describe my feelings!! One of the reasons we went out was because of the New Year's truce—figure it out for yourself.

Then, ... then, they sent us out into a damn swamp. It took us two hours to hack our way into a swamp about 400 meters. We almost lost one after he fell into something similar to quicksand and was up to his neck. After two hours, we figured out we were lost and didn't know where the hell we were going. So at about 5:30 PM we stopped and asked for some arty marking rounds to help us out. After 6:30, we decided to go back and get on dry land because we couldn't even get a couple of marking rounds to help us out. To top it off, we only had about 20 minutes of daylight left.

Well, we made through, the swamp, dark and everything at about 7:30 and everybody was in no mood for playing games. And that's how we spent New Year's Eve!! Half of us, are so mad that we are ready to write the President—himself!! . . .

Take care
Swamp Fox

NORMA "NICKI" ROSKA (JOHNSON) (b. 1945) was born in Milwaukee and was living with her parents in Glendale when she was hired by the Red Cross in December, 1967. She worked with the Red Cross Clubmobile at Phu Loi, Qui Nhon, and Pleiku from February, 1968, until March, 1969. She now lives in Greendale, where she is an educator. As in previous wars, American women did not serve their country in combat as did Vietnamese women. Instead, American women contributed to the war effort in a number of other ways: as nurses, Special Services workers, and Red Cross volunteers. More than 7,500 women served with the military in Vietnam, most of them as nurses. More than 600 civilian women volunteered to serve with the Red Cross in Vietnam, and about 200 women joined the Special Services. In this letter to her parents, Roska describes the role of Red Cross workers in raising the morale of combat troops at a forward base camp.

April 7, 1968

Hi All,

. . . I've had 2 chances so far to get out in the field—one is a place called Thunder 3 (I think I told you about that one) and the other is part of the 4 Cavalry Unit (Quarter Cav. for short) called Dragoon Forward. Virginia and I went out there last Saturday afternoon and had a fabulous time walking around and talking to the men. There were only about 75 men there then but about 5:00 all the rest started coming back from their day's work—riding in tanks hunting "Charlie." I got to ride in one of the tanks, just around the base area, of course, and it was a riot. One young man was so cute—he made me put on his flak jacket and steel helmet and then took a picture of me. Found out one thing though—there is *no* possible way of getting in or out of a tank gracefully while wearing a dress! Also while we were out there I made an acquaintance with an ugly monkey that had been brought up by the VC who doesn't like girls so I ended up with a chomp in my finger and a tetanus shot to go along with it. The finger is convalescing fine—I hope the monkey is suffering!

Red Cross workers Nicki Roska (Johnson) (left) and Lori Clause conduct a clubmobile program for the 1st Division Artillery Battery at Firebase Thunder II near Phu Loi, June, 1968. ARC photo by Mark Stevens. Courtesy Nicki Roska Johnson.

We ended up by serving the men their dinner, which had to be brought in by chopper, and just barely getting out before it started getting dark. I can understand the R.C. policy of having the girls back before dark because dusk is the time when the VC pick to come out and the choppers make good targets especially when they have to fly low-level.

The social life is probably more tiring than the work if you can believe that. It's not that we're so popular, it's just that there are only 4 of us to how many thousands of them. There was a party Fri. night, 2 parties last night, and a BBQ tonight—we don't have to stay long but still it's a drain. We always have our group at the Divarty [division artillery at divisional headquarters] to fall back on which is nice because they're just like our big brothers and they don't expect us to be charming "Belles of the Ball." . . .

Love,
Nicki (yes, I go by Nicki over here)

DARRYL JOHNSON, a forward observer with the army, was stationed at Dak To when he described to his fiancée a much appreciated visit from Red Cross workers. (For a biographical sketch of Johnson, see chapter 1.)

Dak To, December 10, 1968

Hello Doll,

. . . Later this afternoon, a bird came with Donut Dollies. These are Red Cross girls who come to the field to play games & hand out presents to the GIs. It was a nice break. We had teams & played games like identifying states with clues they gave. The presents were wonderful. They came from the Ladies American Legion Auxiliary. Mine had little useful stuff like a soap dish, comb, pen, peanuts etc. What was especially nice was it also had a recording tape. I was able to get three of them by trading other guys for them. I was delighted because now I can send you more tapes and one especially for Christmas instead of a card. Pretty good huh? . . .

I Love You,
Darryl

Move to the Rear

Life in the rear, while replete with its own difficulties, was generally easier and certainly safer than life as a foot soldier. Infantrymen were backed by a huge rear echelon of support personnel. For every man in the field, another five to ten served in the rear, fixing and maintaining equipment, driving trucks, cooking meals, and serving as clerk-typists for officers and the large military bureaucracy. While men on the larger bases enjoyed nightly movies and television, even the men on the smaller bases generally had hot showers, cold beer, warm meals, and electricity. Despite these amenities, men in the rear faced long hours at monotonous jobs. The following letters suggest some of the differences between life in the field and life in the rear. In the following letter to her parents, Red Cross worker NICKI ROSKA (JOHNSON) contrasts the experiences of infantrymen with those of support personnel. (For a biographical sketch of Roska, see earlier in this chapter).

September 27, 1968

Hi—

Decided it was about time to write altho I don't know if I should considering I haven't heard from you for awhile! By the way, what's Mary's address so I can write and bug her. Life is as disorganized as usual here— we're still in the process of getting settled in our rooms and the center we don't even talk about! I suppose I should consider myself lucky, but I get so impatient with the girls when they complain about not having any hot water, or how hard it's raining or how hard they have to work;

or with the guys when they think they've got it really bad—a beautiful library, the beach, clubs & entertainment, the town (when it's on limits) and yes, even the R.C. Center. If they only knew. Sometimes I just want to scream at them all—tell them they don't know how good they have it, but you can't find fault with them because they have nothing to compare their living conditions to. The guys, and girls alike, can only try to imagine what it's like living in a poncho-covered hole that is filled up with water more often than it's not; going for days without a shower; getting excited because it's been so long since you've seen a television set; trying to make a joke of the war because if you don't you may crack under the strain; keeping yourself from getting too attached to your buddies because you never know how long they'll be alive enough to be your buddies. There are men in this area who do know, who live and work in the "boonies" but the majority live a safe, 8 hour workday and these are the men we see and are friends with. I see them as the type of friends I may have back in the States, tho—A light, passing relationship, somewhat superficial even with the best friends because there isn't the need here. Perhaps by not being a novelty I see the whole situation in a different perspective, but whatever it is I no longer have the patience necessary to do a good job here (meaning Qui Nhon).

I've been trying since I got here to figure out why I feel the way I do and the only thing I can think of is that I got so attached to the men we saw in respect to the 1st Division and they were so open and honest with their opinions and feelings because of the intensity that they were living their lives, that I lived just as intently, I felt just as deeply, I wept just as painfully and I cared more than they could ever know. Then I came up here and I had to let go of it all. I can't just discard all the experiences and memories and start all over. They're always going to be with me—so much so that I can't accept the people here with the same closeness and warmth. I think that's what I meant about the relationships here being light and superficial. The others are what are real, and they are the relationships that will always be special. I'm happy here, don't get me wrong, but I'm not a part as I should be because I can't and don't care enough to make myself a part. I wish every girl could experience the joys—and the sorrows—that I did down in Phu Loi because it's something that can only be felt—never explained.

As is probably obvious, I'm going to request another forward area because that is where I feel I'm the most needed, where I'm the most comfortable—I love everything (well, almost everything) about it. Fortunately for this specific program, some girls prefer the atmosphere of a center and some prefer the atmosphere of the more rugged—the field, the chopper rides, the guys at their worst. I just happen to fall into the latter category. As I see it, I should be just about rested up enough by the end of November to forge on to a new area—keep your fingers crossed Saigon will see it the same way!

Must close or Chuck (our driver) will leave without me.

Happiness is being alive!

Write—

Love,
N.

BRUCE E. RODLAND (b. 1950), a native of Buffalo, New York, volunteered for the army in March, 1970. Rodland served as an infantryman and radio operator (B Co., 3-1st Inf., 11th Inf. Bde. [Light], 23d Inf. Div. [Americal]) near Duc Pho and Chu Lai from August, 1970, to August, 1971. After his discharge in December, 1971, he settled in Stoughton, where he is a self-employed woodworker and antique dealer. Having spent his first four months in Vietnam in the field, Rodland clearly appreciated the changes he encountered in the rear.

January 26, 1971

Dear Mom, Dad, & Mary,

Hello, finally, from me again. Sorry I haven't written for so long, I've been kinda busy. Thought you might [like] to hear the good news first. I am no longer splashing around in rice paddies or climbing mountains! I have a "rear" job, mainly, RTO at the Tactical Operations Center in Duc Pho. I have my own room, with a real bed, mattress, sheets, blankets, pillow, electricity, curtains, a Vietnamese woman to wash all my clothes and iron them, and she also cleans the room, polishes my boots, and makes my bed (after I get out of it).

In very close proximity to my hooch is a PX, steam bath, watch repair, engraving shop, Oriental gift shop, EM club, outdoor theater, and even an office where a Dodge salesman sells new dodge products to GIs who have dreams of being greeted at home with their own new car!

I've got a radio on now, listening to Donovan sing Hurdy Gurdy man, one of my favorites. The radio station is AFBN, or Armed Forces Broadcasting Network. So, I'm really not doing too bad now. I don't have to pull guard, so I don't even have a weapon anymore. . . .

Well, I'm sorry to say it, but that's about it, as I must go shave and eat before going to work. It's 4:10 P.M., I go to work at 5:00 P.M., and work till 1:00 A.M. It's a real good shift, as I can sleep as late as I want, goof off the rest of the day till time for work. Well, take it easy, and all that.

Love,
Brucy

GILBERT L. DOCKEN (b. 1943) grew up in Galesville and attended the
Madison campus of the University of Wisconsin before being drafted into
the army in April, 1965. Corporal Docken served as an air traffic controller
(11th Avn. Grp., 1st Cav. Div. [Airmobile]) in An Khe from January, 1966,
to January, 1967, when he was discharged. He returned to the university and
currently is a Madison realtor. In the following letter, Docken describes his
work in the rear and notes how remote he felt from the war itself until the
bodies of dead soldiers arrived at his airfield.

An Khe, February 6, 1966

Dear Folks,

   . . . I'm working tonight in the tower and there is very little traffic.
I'm on the "C" shift from 4:00–midnight. We each work one 8 hr. shift
every 48 or 40 hrs. It's not bad at all. Except when traffic is heavy, on
"B" shift from 8:00 AM until 4:00 P.M. The older guys that have been
working in Air Traf. Control say this is the busiest field they have ever
been on. If so, when I leave here I should be well qualified to control
traffic most anywhere, except I won't be F.A.A. certified. We have maybe
3 or 4 choppers landing and departing every minute at times. They usually
come in "spurts." It gets pretty busy at times. When they slow down
I manage O.K., but if it gets too heavy I give the mike to the other guy
in the tower who is experienced and they don't have a bit of trouble.
It's really amazing the way they do it and I guess I'll be doing it too
shortly. I sure hope so.

I explained to you before what the situation is like here. It doesn't
seem like a war at all, just a big work camp. When you see the Medical
Evacuation choppers unloading men they have carried in from the field
dead or wounded you are reminded of the seriousness of it. I thank God
that I don't have to go to the field and I wish no one did. It must be
hell when they are out there.

Right now I can hear and feel the shock waves from our artillery as
they fire rounds out to keep the VC away from our perimeter and to
keep them dispersed. Now and then you see a flare floating down slowly, lighting the area so the guards can see if there really was something
out there or if it was just their imagination. I haven't heard any small
arms or machine gun fire yet and I don't imagine I will, but some people think the VC may come back in the area and if they do, there will
most likely be quite a commotion when they are spotted. Rockets from
the helicopters, mortar fire, and our guards will all let loose. But I doubt
if the VC will chance it.

Friday a rocket fired accidentally from one of the choppers and came
about 20 feet from our tower just about level with it. It hit a large hill

to our rear and there was no damage done. It could have been catastrophic. Headquarters for the 1st. Cav. Div. is behind us too, and it went right over their tents. . . .

Hope the weather warms up for you soon.

Love to all,
Gib

GARY J. TENPAS (b. 1946) was born in Lima and was a management trainee for a Ripon appliance firm when he was drafted into the army in January, 1969. Tenpas served as a company clerk (Hq. Co., 71st Trans. Bn.) in Long Binh from July, 1969, until July, 1970. He was discharged in December, 1971, and now lives in Menomonee Falls and works in financial equipment sales. Writing to his family, Tenpas details his life at a large base in the rear.

[November, 1969]

Dear Relatives,

Mother suggested that I write a letter to be read to everyone on Thanksgiving. I thought it was a good idea because I've gotten letters from some of you and never got around to answering them. I'll start from the very beginning and try to give you a good picture of everything that has happened here.

When I got to Vietnam, the first place I was sent was the 90th Replacement Battalion. This is one of the places where people are kept when they are coming into or leaving Vietnam. After 2 days I was sent to Bien Hoa and then down to Saigon. I spent one night in Camp Davies, where most of the people that work on the docks in Saigon live. From there I was sent to Long Binh. My orders said I was to be assigned to the 71st Transportation Battalion. When I was at Fort Eustis I was trained to be a Movement Specialist. They do all the paperwork in the movement of cargo. But when I got to Battalion Headquarters, The Headquarters Company was looking for a clerk. The other company clerk had just come back from Saigon where he had been AWOL for 2 weeks. (He eventually got a dishonorable discharge.) I didn't think too much of the idea at first. For one thing, I didn't know anything about the job. And secondly, I wanted to work in a job I was trained for. But in the Army you really don't have much choice. You go where they want you to go. . . .

I usually get up at 6:15 in the morning, eat breakfast, and get to the office at about 6:50. I work till 6:30 at night but quite often it runs later than that. I get 1½ hours off at noon to eat and take a nap. My work seems to come in bunches. Some days I have very little to do and then all of a sudden I have so much to do I don't know where to turn. We have 25 officers and 105 enlisted men in our company which is quite a few for one clerk to handle. The first sergeant says we should have 2 clerks but I think I would get pretty bored on some days. I really enjoy the work. I know everybody in the company and they all know me. Everybody calls me Head and Head or First Sergeant.

We have a real good group of guys in our company. Most of them are pretty intelligent and mature. However, we have 4 other companies in our Battalion area that have a lot of duds in them. Our Battalion's main job is unloading the ships that come into the Saigon and Newport dock area. . . .

There isn't much to do in your spare time around here but we really don't have a lot of spare time anyway. We only get 1 day off every 2 weeks. We have an air conditioned day room. In the day room we have books and magazines, TV, ping pong table, popcorn machine, and a game called Fussball. The Armed Forces operates a TV station 12 hours a day. The shows are the same as over in the States but somewhat older. Across the street we have an Enlisted Men's Club. Here you can get sandwiches or something to drink. They have a band about every other night. Most of them are pretty bad and they get pretty sickening. We also have a theater. All it really is is a white wall. It used to have a roof on it but it got blown off in the windstorm we had a couple of months ago. They show movies about 5 nights a week. We have Chapel services every Sunday but the Chaplain is lousy. He never really says anything and he's pretty weird. Chapel attendance is never very good.

Our barracks are better than the average here in Vietnam. They are made of sheet metal. We have 2 fans on the ceiling which circulate the air. Some of us also have fans that we put at the foot of our beds to keep the bugs off of us at night. (The First Sergeant gave me a fan.) All our water is trucked in and stored in tanks. This doesn't provide much water pressure for showers. We have no water heater so getting really clean in the shower is difficult. Our latrines are also without running water. Two Vietnamese men come in every day and burn the stuff.

The chow here is pretty good but we get roast beef every day and it gets sickening. I don't trust our Mess Sergeant. I've known guys who worked for him. He owns half interest in a lumber yard over here and I think he pays the help with our food. The NCOs seem to be eating steak every night. The officers and NCOs really have it made over here. Most of them have private rooms. . . .

Long Binh is a pretty safe place. Our company hasn't gotten hit since August 15. I guess they caught it pretty hard last February during the Tet Offensive. A little ways from here they have an artillery battery

which is usually busy at night. About ¼ mile from us on the hill is the
US Army Vietnam Headquarters. Charlie likes to throw rockets at that
puzzle palace. On the other side is a petroleum storage area which is
also a good target. We have plenty of helicopters in the area if they decide
to attack on the ground. They killed 150 VC on our perimeter last
February.

The protest about this war seems to be growing in the States. A lot
of people think it hurts the morale over here. I think it's the other way
around. Most of the guys hate it here and they are glad somebody is
trying to get them out. I really haven't heard anybody complain about
the war protestors.

Well, I think I've told you about everything that goes on around here.
I'm looking forward to next July (224 days) when I'll be able to see you
all again. Until then, I hope everyone has a happy Thanksgiving and
God bless you.

Love
Gary

DAVID L. SARTORI (b. 1942) was born in Fond du Lac and attended River
Falls State University. He was living in Pittsburgh, Pennsylvania, and
working as a juvenile probation officer when he was drafted into the army
in August, 1967. Sartori served as a cook and psychiatric aide, hospital
liaison, and prison social worker (C Co., 7th Spt. Bn., 199th Inf. Bde.
[Light]) in Phu Bai, Da Nang, and Long Binh from May, 1968, to May,
1969, when he was discharged. He currently lives in Fond du Lac and
works as a probation and parole agent for the Wisconsin Department of
Corrections.

Although life in the rear was generally easier than life in the field, danger
threatened those serving in noncombat positions too. In this sense, Vietnam
differed from other wars, in which support troops could count on relative
security. Americans had a difficult time discerning friend from foe because
the Viet Cong in particular waged a guerrilla war throughout the south. In
the following letter to Edward Peterson, a history professor at River Falls,
Sartori describes the VC's potential threat to those in the rear.

July 3, 1968

Dear Pete,

    . . . While in Da Nang I had a most unusual & interesting experience.
A nine year old youth, or there abouts, approached me while I was waiting
for the navy bus & begged me to have my boots polished. I resisted but
finally gave in after he started to polish 'em. Initially the fee agreed upon
was 25¢ which is enough to support one Vietnamese for approximately
three days. Midway thru, he changed his price to one dollar & later to
two & five dollars. When I handed the youth a 25¢ note, he screamed

& demanded five dollars. After this I became stubborn & insisted on paying him only 25¢. He took the bill & picked-up two large rocks & approached me in a most threatening manner, especially for a youth of his age. As I began to board the bus, he threw both rocks at me hitting me in the knee & leg. I chased him & naturally caught him. A strong verbal admonishment was being administered by me when a US army truck pulled-up & three South Vietnamese military policemen approached me. They demanded that the youth be paid the full five dollars & that they would accept it since it had "to be registered" at the police station. To me this was nothing but "highway robbery." Suddenly, I saw a shore patrol jeep appear & I dashed onto the highway for help. I attempted to explain the situation to the sailors but the Vietnamese police attempted to interfere. One sailor stopped a truck loaded with armed Marines & then the senior sailor abruptly advised everyone to "shut up." My story was told & the Vietnamese police suddenly remembered that they "needed gas" & suddenly disappeared. The youth's shoe shine box was found by a Marine & contained a small plastic bomb. I was told to "move out" & to keep my mouth shut. Certainly, I moved out in a very fast hurry. What became of the youth I'll never know. Also, how he gained entry into the post is hard to understand. . . .

dls

GARY A. PLATH (b. 1947) grew up in Madison, where he attended the University of Wisconsin before enlisting in the air force in January, 1967. Plath served as a clerk and an English-language instructor for the Vietnamese Air Force (37th TFW) at Phu Cat and the Cho Lon area of Saigon from February, 1968, until November, 1969. Since his discharge in September, 1970, Plath has lived in Madison and worked for the U.S. Postal Service and the Wisconsin State Patrol. An assignment in Saigon did not necessarily guarantee one's safety, as Plath reveals in this letter to Kirsten Nielsen, who later became his wife, describing a Viet Cong car bomb attack.

Saigon, August 8, 1969

My Dearest Kirsten,

It's rather early to be writing a letter but I just can't sleep and I had to write to you and tell you what happened at school yesterday. You may have read or heard about it already on television but I want to tell you so you have no misunderstanding.

At 1605 on the 7th of August our school was seriously bombed and many people were hurt, eight (8) killed. I happened to be one of 60 instructors that was injured, a deep cut on my left hand. You don't need to worry Honey because I'm fine now, scared but alright. I went to the

The aftermath of a car bomb attack on the building that housed Gary Plath's school in Saigon, August 7, 1969. Courtesy Gary Plath.

hospital in Saigon and the doctor took care of my hand cut and remove[d] some glass from my back.

This is how it all happened, what I remember anyway. I got somewhat drunk afterwards so I could try to forget about what happened but I can't eat, sleep or sit still. It's really an awful feeling Honey, I want to be near you but I can't.

Yesterday at 1600 hrs I heard a terrible explosion, I was in the office when this happened. Moments later I saw smoke and broken glass all around. I then ran out of the office and there was another explosion that came from behind me. The door blew off and knocked me to the floor. I got up and ran to the weapons room but when I got there the door was locked so I broke the door down. I then passed out the weapons and began to help those who were seriously wounded. Then another explosion came and glass, fire and smoke was all over the building. I noticed blood coming from my left hand so I took off my shirt and covered the wound.

I then remembered that there were two American women in the building and tried to find them to see if they needed help. I could only find one of them so I stay[ed] with her, making her lie on the floor near the wall so she wouldn't get injured if more bombs would explode. She was uninjured but scared like everyone else. Another explosion followed and then there was rifle fire for 10 minutes. The Viet Cong were killed and as mentioned before 8 students, no instructors were killed thank God. Fifteen minutes later another explosion was heard and I then grabbed the woman's hand (Miss French) and told her to follow me. We ran downstairs and outside, for ¼ of a mile we ran to safety. I took her into a hotel and told the manager to take care of her. I then went to my room, put on a shirt and went to the hospital.

It was terrible Kirsten, I prayed that no one would get killed and I was real scared. The guys called me a Hero but I couldn't remember what happened until an hour ago. I risked my life to save that woman, we both could have been killed but I had to get her to a safe place.

I will receive two medals for what happened yesterday, the Purple Heart medal for getting wounded and the Bronze Star medal for helping the wounded and protecting Miss French. I don't care about the medals Kirsten, I'm just happy to be alive, God am I. If I would have stayed in our office I would have been killed, there was nothing left of it. I did the right thing because I'm still alive but I never want to re-live yesterday.

You would have been proud of Your Gary yesterday. I tried to act like a man and to keep my "Cool." I was scared, really scared but I did what was right.

It's all over now. I'm going to leave Saigon as soon as possible, no more war games for me. I'll go to jail before I stay another day here.

I love you Kirsten, I wasn't going to tell you because I didn't want you to worry. I knew you might hear it on the news or read about it so I thought it would be best to tell you.

Honey, I'm OK and please don't worry. I'll be with you very soon and soon there will be no war for me.

Take good care.

I really love only Kirsten
Love,
Gary

CHARLES E. QUEEN (b. 1929) lived in Chicago until he enlisted in the army in 1947. Queen was a weather service specialist (HHB, 6–27th Arty., 23d Arty. Grp.) near Saigon from August, 1965, to September, 1966, and near Qui Nhon and An Khe (HHB, 8–26th Arty., 41st Arty. Grp.) from August, 1968, to July, 1969. He retired from the service in February, 1970, and now lives in Mequon. In a letter to his wife, Queen notes the dangers of Saigon and expresses his appreciation for foot soldiers and the job they did in Vietnam.

Charles Queen with a photograph of his wife, Faye.
Courtesy Charles Queen.

June 14, 1966

Hi Pretty,

. . . Since I am the club manager I can go to Tan Son Nhut AFB almost any time. I don't go to Saigon anymore, and I can't get anyone here to go. We all agree, that we are much safer up here in war zone D than you are in Saigon. TSN AFB has anything you want, it's like any AFB in the states. Those guys down there don't even know there is a war going on. I take that back, they did get hit *one* night, and got tore up pretty bad, but what did they do, call in more infantry to protect them. Dear, any soldier you see who is wearing the CIB and he has been to Vietnam, he deserves to have you take your hat off to him. The CIB is the Combat Infantry Badge. Whoever he is, he has earned it. Well my sweet, I know you know I love you, but I will say it anyway. I love you. Until tomorrow.

Your Lover
Poopie

Bringing Home to Vietnam

Those who served in Vietnam tried to remind themselves of home through various means, including football games, USO shows, holiday celebrations, and even bragging about their home states. The following letters describe some of the ways that GIs tried to alleviate tension and reminded themselves of life back in America.

LARRY P. KAMMHOLZ (b. 1938) was born in Rib Lake and was working as a medical intern in Milwaukee when he was drafted in July, 1965. He served as the commander of the 736th Medical Detachment at Moc Hoa from July, 1966, until his discharge in June, 1967. He now lives in Oshkosh, where he is a physician. In the following letter to his wife, Bonnie, and his infant daughter, Jodi, Kammholz describes a party that stemmed from a friendly rivalry between men from Illinois and Wisconsin. Unfortunately, the beer that Kammholz requested could not be sent through the mail, and the food was barely edible by the time it finally arrived in Vietnam.

September 18, [1966]

Dear Bonnie, Jodi & Everyone,

. . . Higgins & I were arguing about Illinois & Wisconsin & decided to throw a party for Larry & Rick as a return favor for Larry's parties. We'd like to have a contest to see which state makes the better beer & sausage so a favor please. Would you mail—2 cans Schlitz, 2 cans Blatz, 2 cans Miller High Life, 2 cans Pabst, 2 cans Gettelman's 1,000 beer, 2 cans Schlitz Malt Liquor. Also some selected Wisconsin cheeses— American & cheddar & enough for 8 people also 2 or 3 sausages. I know this will cost a good deal of money to mail but we really owe them a party. You'll have to mail it in several different packages because air mail limit is 5 lbs. Would you please do this Bonnie. . . .

Love much
Larry

PETER M. PONTI (b. 1943) was born in Madison and was working as a bricklayer there until he was drafted into the army in September, 1966. Ponti drove trucks and did construction work (B Co., 25th Supply and Trans. Bn., 25th Inf. Div.) near Cu Chi from February, 1967, to February, 1968. Discharged in September, 1968, Ponti now lives in Marshall and works as a bricklayer. In the following letter, Ponti describes his time at a USO show.

December 28, 1967

Dear Aunt Agnes.

Well I saw the Bob Hope show today. I went down there at 9:30 this morning and the show did not start until 3:00 in the afternoon. It was really a good show and that Raquel Welch is just as beautiful in person

The Bob Hope show at Cu Chi, December, 1969. Courtesy Dennis Bries.

as she is in the movies. It only lasted for about 1½ hours but it really made me feel homesick again. That Barbara McNair is really a beautiful Negro and she can really sing. Boy they sure aren't taking any chances with him getting shot by the VC. They have been staying in Bangkok and flying in for each show. We did not know what day he was going to be here until this morning. They had a couple of armored personnel carriers alongside of the stages and had day guards in all the bunkers on the perimeter also. I guess the VC have really got a price tag on his head and they were not taking any chances. I forgot to tell you I got a seat in the 7th row behind the wounded men. I was about 50 feet from the stage so I don't think any of the pictures I took will come out too good. I bet there was at least 15,000 men there today. What a target for Charlie. . . .

See ya in 55 days.
Love
Pete

HELEN E. WEIDNER (b. 1945) was born in Milwaukee and was living there when she joined the Red Cross in 1968. As a Red Cross recreation aide in 1968–1969, she flew to bases and landing zones and organized recreational activities for the troops near Chu Lai and Cam Ranh Bay. After leaving the Red Cross, Weidner joined the Department of the Army Special Services Agency and worked at a variety of locales, including Long Thanh North, Long Binh, and Tan Son Nhut, as a service club program director from November, 1971, to February, 1973. She now lives in Houston, Texas, where she works as an attorney. In the next letter, Weidner describes her behind-the-scenes vantage point at a USO Christmas show. Her discussion of the problem caused by Jimi Hendrix's music also shows that the cultural divide so prominent on the home front also made its way to Vietnam.

January 2, 1973

. . . The Bob Hope show was fun. It was Christmas Eve Day. Marynoel & I and one WAC were in the girls dressing room, a trailer. We passed out iced washcloths, helped them get in & out of costumes, poured cokes, ironed the long white evening dresses they wore for the "Silent Night" that always ends the show. The girls were fun to work with, pleasant & cheerful in spite of the heat they are not used to. We overheard one of the girls say "You just can't wear makeup in this heat," and we 3 "locals" looked at each other and laughed. Few of us even try anymore.

. . . We saw snatches of [the show] from backstage. Rose & Marynoel & I talked about the war during one number when all the girls were on stage. The whole show had expected the trip to be a peace celebration, so were bitterly disappointed that the war continued. They passed out POW bracelets to everyone backstage—both Marynoel & I were glad, as we had planned to send out for them. The girls were nervous about being in Nam, glad they were flying to Bangkok for the night. Rose asked how life near Saigon is, and we told her like we tell anyone, that Saigon is just another big city. We go to the zoo, to art exhibitions, eat out in the restaurants, go to movies, shop, have clothes made. No problem, just hop in a taxi & tell him where you want to go. When a plane flew overhead, the girls were nervous, & we told them not to worry, only *we* have planes down here.

The show was a pleasant lull in the busy day. Back at the club, we set up the elves workshop, 4 Vietnamese girls wrapping 100 pks of cigarettes, 100 wash & dry, 100 puzzles, 100 other little toys, for filling stockings. They sat on the floor with piles of wrapped & unwrapped gifts around them. Meanwhile, in the kitchen, other Vietnamese & GIs were stuffing the stocking toes with candies and candy bars. We stuffed 100 stockings.

We started the guys on a game at 730, & Gail & I snuck off to church for the 8 pm candlelight service, which was great fun, and a very full church.

. . . A band came Sunday [December 31], CBC, the best band in Nam. We asked them please not to play [the] Jimi Hendrix version of the Star Spangled Banner. They said OK. The girl said she was glad to be told, that many of the guys like it, but they played it at an NCO club & the manager stopped them in the middle of the song & told them never to come back to his club. I tried to explain that it's an anti-American song, but she couldn't understand, all she knows is that the guys like it. But she didn't play it. . . .

Love,
Helen

LARRY BUETER served as a draftsman near Da Nang. His two letters below offer a view of how Americans celebrated holidays thousands of miles from home. (For a biographical sketch of Bueter, see chapter 1.)

November 23, [1967]

Dear Mom, Dad, and John,

My conscience is getting the best of me lately, and I feel a little guilty about not writing, to say the least. I know I haven't been writing much lately because of my state of depression but I think I'm snapping out of it. Plus the fact that I'm getting back to my old work schedule with all the free time. So, I promise I'll write more often in the future, like I used to. In fact, this makes two I've sent you in about a week or two.

Today was Thanksgiving Day, and I sure have a lot to be Thankful for. Our base staged a football game as a Thanksgiving Day event, with free beer and hot dogs. It was Supply Bn against Headquarters Bn and the final score was 6–6.

I was really surprised at the thoroughness of the planning of the whole affair. The sand playing field was leveled off, goal posts put up, sideline ropes, yardage markers, chairs on trailer truck beds, beer and soda in Jeep trailers, hot dogs under a huge tent on each sideline, 4 experienced referees, uniforms for players, a P-A system, and last but not least, cheerleaders. They were 2 Red Cross girls from the Freedom Hill U.S.O. and Red Cross Center. So I guess you could say it was just like being back home. I took a bunch of pictures at the game and as soon as I get them developed, I [will] send them to you.

Then we had a really decent layout for Thanksgiving Day Supper. I'd try to tell you what we had, but it would take up a whole page. So, I'll just send you a menu and you can read it yourself.

I'm up at work now and it's 10:30 and we are now listening to Johnny Carson on the radio. . . .

Love,
Larry

Christmas on a riverboat in the Mekong Delta. Courtesy Tom Hounsell.

January 5, [1969]

Dear Mom, Dad, and John,

. . . We had our Christmas party in the hootch. About 9 o'clock the impromptu fireworks began, and lasted for about 30 minutes. On every holiday or special occasion, a bulletin is sent out saying that no one will shoot flares and if caught, the wrongdoers will lose one rank. But, like clockwork, on Christmas Eve, the flares burst into the air from all over, and it was bright as high noon. Not just our base either, as all surrounding units pulled the same thing. Some were even original: one unit up on a neighboring hill sent up approx. 30 red flares, followed into the air by 30 green flares; and the intermixed flares floated lazily to the ground, providing a very appropriate colorful show. Others were more helter-skelter and haphazard as they just shot up their flares in no particular order, but it was very colorful also. So for about 30 minutes, we sat up on top of our bunker by the hootch, and watched the fireworks, bathed in the light of the flares, and hollering "Merry Christmas" to everyone who could hear us.

At about 10:45 all 8 of us from our hootch went to church for the Christmas Eve candlelight service. It filled all of us to overflowing with the holiday spirit, as we belted out favorite Christmas hymns between

excerpts of the Christmas story read by the chaplain. The small chapel
was bulging with Marines (the chaplain called it the best present we
could have given him as the midnight candlelight service was his idea,
and he wasn't sure it would draw a crowd because of all the parties in
the hootches) in contrast to the sparse attendance every Sunday. They
all came in groups of 2 or 3 with occasional singles, but they all had
one thing in common: faith in God and a faint home-sick twinge to be
with others on this occasion to join in singing in the hope that those
back home would sense our feeling and join us singing praises to
the Lord.

We were in a group of 12 (8 from our hootch & 4 from next door)
and were quite a sight to the chaplain as we filed in 5 minutes before
it began and filled up the 2 front rows. By the time the service started,
the last guys had to stand in the back. We sang with the lights on and
I'll bet they could hear us on the other side of the mountains. Then after
each song, it was startlingly and peacefully quiet as the chaplain read
the Christmas story accompanied by the lonely crickets outside. At about
2 minutes to midnight the lights were turned out, and everyone was given
a candle. Then the ushers transferred the flame from the 2 altar candles
to the 2 they were holding, and in turn to each person on the aisle, who
then passed his light to light the candle of the person next to him until
everyone's candle was flickering in the darkness. We then observed a
5 minute silent prayer to usher in Christmas Day after which we all took
communion then returned to our seats and sang "Silent Night," to finish
the service. It was really an experience, and one I won't ever forget. . . .

Love to All
Larry

3

Combat

Although American combat soldiers spent most of their time in the field humping the boonies, they had been sent to Vietnam to fight. But combat in Vietnam differed from that of previous wars. Instead of clearly defined opposing forces facing each other in a set battle, the fighting usually consisted of guerrilla warfare in which small units encountered each other at close quarters for relatively brief periods of time.

The basic American battle strategy was to send groups of men out to attempt to find the enemy. When contact with Viet Cong (VC) or North Vietnamese army (NVA) troops occurred, a firefight ensued. U.S. forces would then radio their location to artillery and air support units, which would pound the enemy troops. Thus, combat usually began when one side surprised an enemy patrol. In 1966, for example, 58 percent of all combat encounters involved such ambushes.

This approach had several drawbacks. U.S. forces had little control over the location or timing of a battle: nearly 80 percent of all combat in 1966 was initiated by VC/NVA forces. Furthermore, because the two sides were frequently close together, supporting fire could hit American troops. Although estimates vary, "friendly fire" may have accounted for as much as 15 to 20 percent of all combat casualties in Vietnam.

During the peak years of the war, 1967–1969, an average of nearly half a million Americans served in Vietnam. But although military analysts calculated that the United States would need to commit enough soldiers to overwhelmingly outnumber the communist forces, American intelligence consistently underestimated enemy troop strength. Furthermore, the U.S. military had a high ratio of support troops to combat troops, meaning that the actual number of fighting men was considerably less than the total number of troops in country.

The American policy of sending men to Vietnam for a fixed period of time, usually one year, often resulted in a shortage of experienced personnel. Newly arrived men were especially likely to be killed or wounded because they were not familiar with the types of warfare practiced in Vietnam: 43 percent of all Americans killed in combat died during their first three months in country.

Perhaps most important, however, American fighting men found the U.S. battle plan immensely frustrating. They seldom saw the enemy, and there were few clear objectives. The United States sought to defeat the

59

communist forces by inflicting heavy casualties that would destroy their will
and ability to fight. By contrast, in "conventional" wars both sides attempt
to conquer and hold territory. In this type of combat, progress can be fairly
easily measured, but in Vietnam, soldiers would fight to take a hill or a
valley, only to abandon it later. Success was measured by the number of
enemy killed (the body count), but accurate estimates were difficult to
make. The jungle terrain was daunting, and the enemy often carried off its
dead and wounded.

Because the VC included large numbers of fighters who did not wear
uniforms, including women and children, American soldiers often found it
impossible to distinguish the enemy from the general population. Friendly
villagers one day could become snipers the next. The VC also used other
means to hide their fighters from American troops, including disguising
themselves as allied South Vietnamese soldiers and constructing extensive
underground tunnel systems.

Finally, the communists used land mines against American troops.
Because mines could be detonated from far away or activated when an
unsuspecting soldier hit a hidden trip mechanism, they did not require close
proximity—either temporal or spatial—between opposing forces. The
devastating injuries inflicted by mines, including amputations, were
especially horrifying for soldiers to witness, and they took a toll on morale.

These factors affected most American soldiers to one degree or another,
but combat also varied greatly in different times and places within Vietnam.
As the following letters illustrate, this conflict was unlike any ever before
experienced.

Infantrymen and Marines

JEFFREY M. FIELDS (b. 1945) was born in Madison and was living there
when he enlisted in the Marine Corps in April, 1964. He served as a fire
team leader, automatic rifleman, and radio operator (M Co., 3/7th Mar., 3d
Mar. Div.) near Chu Lai and Da Nang from July, 1965, to May, 1966. Fields
was discharged in January, 1967, and now lives in Madison, where he is
president of a communication graphics firm. The following three letters take
Fields from his first week in Vietnam to the final months of his tour of duty.

Qui Nhon, July 9, 1965

Dear Family;

I received all your wonderful letters tonight and I'm really glad to
hear from you. This is my first full day aboard ship after about a week
in Vietnam. I'm glad I'm back on. On July 7th we were hit bad by the
VC, they are smart, so smart that they were using umbrellas that were
black in color that looked like the natural rock surrounding the hills.
We killed 47 of them, we didn't find any until recon went out and found
men & women stacked up and dead. I've never, never seen anything
like them before in my life. We were set in by the side of this hill and

waited for them; none of us moved, smoke, or set up. It started off at about 10:30 p.m. when one of them about 20 yards away, set off a trip grenade and blew himself up, we all opened up on the remaining three that were trying to drag him away. When they found out it was useless they tried burying him and he was still alive. The reason we could observe this is because we had night illumination that was fired by 81s and by ship, it makes night turn to day. So we shot all four of them. By the next time the illumination went off we seen about eight to ten Guerrillas forming a human chain to drag the wounded and killed off. We again hit them by grenades, A.R.s (Automatic Rifles) and M79s (gun which fires grenades). By the time the next flare went off about 5 or 6 of them which were trying to drag the other four off, were laying there dead, and the ones who moved we killed. We then tried to switch positions but were hit by Carbines and small automatic fire. We finally did and spotted three more down the road off their hill. By the next flare that went off in the skies I seen at least 40 of them all forming up in the road and by the time they shot the next one up (flare) we opened up and seen many fall to the ground. It was sickening to me. I was nervous and shaky by the time the whole thing was over. One VC came within 15 yards of my position and he set off this trip flare which brighten up the whole area around me. He went to run and Lablanck & I shot him. Lablanck is in my fire team. It got so bad that the flares that were shot started the trees & bushes afire about 500 yds to my direct front. When this happened we seen many more. The next morning (July 8th) we went out to see if we could find any, there was nothing. We did find blood on leaves, bushes, and ground. I don't think you believe this but look on the newspapers dated 7 or 8 July, maybe 9 July too. I'm still quite nervous on account of this. The first night up in the hills, I and two others were selected to be outposts. This is quite hairy because you are situated about two hundred yards from the main body on high level terrain. About 3 AM a boy named Parrish spotted three on our left flank, we threw grenades at them and called in and reported it. By throwing Grenades this gave our position away. They had informed us that about 20–25 VC were coming up our draw [baited ambush] to our direct front prior to having spotted those three I had mentioned. So Lablanck threw a hand illumination (like a grenade) but dropped it as he was about to throw it. I threw myself over this rock and hid until it went out. This is the thing though, the ships, 81s and 4 deuces threw flares in the sky from 3:15 AM until sunrise, if they hadn't of, I think I wouldn't be here trying my best way to tell you this. At one point in the game I had hallucinations (your mind changes things and distorts them) of a rock that was moving and it had hands & legs and a rifle, it was wearing [a] black silk garment with tennis shoes and some kind of a cover. This thing was about 10 yds from me, I took the .45 and emptied a magazine into it. A few minutes later I had realized it was a rock. I was so tired, I had about 2–3 [hours] sleep in two days alone. I am telling you the truth on everything I have written in this letter, may God strike me dead if I am lying. Please look in the papers and find an article about VCs found dead in a cove in Qui Nhon. It's the only way you will believe me I think. Our plt is up for some kind of citation. If I get [it] and when I do I'll send it home and then you will believe me. It was a nightmare and I'm glad it's over. It's the first time I've seen combat and it's the last time too. The kids over here beg you for food & cigarettes but we can't give it [to] them because 70% of Qui Nhon is VC. At any given time they can form a Regiment in one hour, their methods of fighting are ones that no one can believe. They used bird calls and signals of hitting sticks together, it's something that's hard, very hard to believe. I'm on way to the Philippines for some R & R (rest & relaxation) and to tell you the truth I need it. I'm hoping this will arrive home soon because I can imagine you are worried about me. I'm safe & sound and no gooks can get at me. A couple boys in my co. were hit by grenades they threw and another was killed by his own sq. leader because he didn't know the password when challenged.

Well family I've got to go, again I say, everything I have told you is the truth, not one bit is put on. It's nothing to brag about, I just want [you] to know how they fight and what kind of war we are fighting. Got to go.

Love all of you very much, God answered my prayers when he let me come aboard this ship alive.

love your son & Brother
Jeff

March 2, 1966

Dear Family,

 . . . I lost two damn good buddies yesterday and another good friend. We were coming back along Highway #1 and Williams tripped off a 155 Mine (gook). He took Zoboblish and Fears with him. Williams was in my squad. He said "I'm getting too short with this stuff." He had a "Cat of nine lives." Williams, Zoboblish Smith and I went out on liberty together. What a rotten way to go. . . .

I received Mom's letter last night along with one from Frye, Amato, and Di Salvo. Don't worry Mom about me I'll be okay when I get home,

Heat, fatigue, and danger all took their toll on weary American combat troops. Courtesy Jim Carlson.

I just don't want to hear anything all the time about this screwed up place. I won't be able to even stomach the rotten name of this place. I get a big kick out [of] hearing what everyone else says how this place is (service guys writing home), they say it's okay, sure it is because they're back in the rear setting on their big fat behinds typing, lifting boxes etc. They don't go on patrol all night, pull 50% sleep on the lines, take showers every three weeks, sleep on a stinken poncho on the rotten filthy deck eating "C" rations. They aren't losing weight, they're always dry and warm in their tents, they never have to worry about being cold, wet, and miserable—they get their three "squares" a day, they see a movie every night, they get their beer & soda—I say to hell with those phonys! I'm so sick I really am. I'm tired physically and mentally—I've got 60 rotten, filthy days left.

Chow's going and I'm going up to the lines at 1:00 pm—I just got back from that Co. operation (revenge) last night. I'll write later.

> Love you all very much
> Your Son & Brother
> Jeff

March 6, [1966]

Hi Family,

. . . I haven't too much longer, I'll be out of here in 60 more days!!
Lippian (one of my buddys who got it Christmas day) returned today
from Casual Co. in Okinawa. His face has but one little scar, he didn't
really want to come back but he said at least he's back with the best.
. . . So far 1st plt leads in WIAs & KIAs (wounded & killed) and the
rest are behind. I don't care what anyone says, I'm with a fine bunch
of guys who know their stuff and I'd go anywhere with them. I just hate
seeing stuff like the "mine affair" a couple days ago. So far I've had
to help carry four people I've known real well in ponchos to some helo
to take their last one way ride and I hope I never do it again. On that
day when those three got it we had 30 to 40 prisoners with us, I was
so mad, upset and all the rest of the crap which goes along with it, I
was seriously thinking of turning around zapping the old lady that was
crying before it happened and then going to the prisoners and doing the
same. I was really hurting, I hadn't had anything to eat for two days,
I was tired, and was walking the whole day—it was really hot out. I
wrote that letter the next morning and had to let myself go in it. There
have been times around here when I've been so depressed at things that
I could of almost cracked up then again it has changed so fast. The same
applies to every individual here, I know. I really can't explain it. Alls
I know is that I'm counting my day like everyone else in this country
today. I was told more troops are on the way, 20,000 more for a bigger
build up. . . .

Love your Son & Brother
Jeff

DENNIS R. WOLF (b. 1945) lived in Kenosha prior to November, 1965, when
he enlisted in the Marine Corps after receiving an army draft notice.
Corporal Wolf served as a rifleman grenadier (M Co., 3/7th Mar., 1st Mar.
Div.) in Chu Lai and Da Nang from May, 1966, to June, 1967. He remained
in the reserves until November, 1971. He still lives in Kenosha, where he is
a truck driver. Because of the extensive use of helicopters, soldiers could
move very quickly between the hardships and danger of life in the field and
the relatively safe existence at base camps, as Wolf reveals in this letter to
his friend Victoria Jeuck (Hekkers).

June 21, [1966]

Dear Vicky

. . . Yesterday we came in from an operation and I said my prayers
last night. I do every night but last night was special. For we got shot

at yesterday and that is the close I ever want to get shot. The bullets were right around my head. Within the area of a foot. I could hear the rounds going past. Our squad leader got shot in the knee. So then we got out of that and the helicopters came to pick us up and running over to the copters we got hit again no one hurt. They were seven of us and a machine-gun on the helicopter we put out 212 shots in 30 seconds. When we got off the ground we could see that we got three of them. So we came back and went to a U.S.O. show. The person there was the one and only John Wayne. He is sixty years old, sounds like, acts like, and looks like just in the movies. He is pretty big and he also use to be a "Green Saint" (MARINE). So I had quite a day. . . .

Breathing Light,
Dennis

S. Robert Peterson (1940–1994) was born on a farm near Soldiers Grove. He was working for the U.S. Agricultural Stabilization and Conservation Service in Crawford County when he volunteered for service in March, 1966. Peterson served in the army as an infantry staff sergeant and a squad leader (C Co., 1-14th Inf., 3d Bde., 25th Inf. Div.) near Pleiku, Bong Son, and Chu Lai between October, 1966, and August, 1967. He was discharged in January, 1968, as a result of injuries from friendly fire that left his legs paralyzed. After the war Peterson served as president of the Village of Soldiers Grove for ten years. He died on April 23, 1994. In these two letters to his family, including his younger brothers, Arch and Ole, he vividly describes the peculiar nature of combat in Vietnam.

November 16, 1966

Greetings Folks—

Well, it's been a hell of a week—last Thurs. we choppered out here in the boonies again—we're about 4 kilometers from the Cambodian border—we're not supposed to get closer than 2 Ks so ol' Charlie is pretty thick here. We've been treading pretty lightly here. I don't know if you read it in the papers or not, but we were involved in the biggest battle of this area on Sunday—13th. We were waiting at our LZ for ammo when we heard shooting—A company made contact—we saddled up and headed out to help them—it was a good fight—A Co. killed about 20 and got 7 of theirs wounded. They found an LZ, choppered out their wounded, and set down to eat—We were about 250 meters away, and in radio contact—we also set down to eat C-rations. In the middle of our meal—all hell broke loose—A Co. had finished, got ready to move— when the Cong ambushed them. They hit them with everything—machine guns, grenades, mortars, and snipers in the trees. We saddled up and practically were ready before we got the word. There were an estimated

Helicopters played a crucial role inserting and extracting troops in Vietnam. Courtesy Dale Reich.

500-700 Cong attacking A Co. They didn't know we were there. But still—700 against our 2 companies (200 total). A Co. had 15 dead and 40 some wounded and the Cong were putting on a human wave attack when we came at the SOBs from the side—screaming at the top of our lungs—we killed 50 right away and they were so surprised they turned and ran—all the way to the border. Artillery and air strikes followed them killing more. There were at least 200 Cong killed in this battle. It was like a movie—us arriving to save the day. Believe me, I was pretty scared moving into all that shooting and noise, but we all were. Several men in A co. are recommended for Medal of Honor & Silver Stars for their valiant stand. Our company is up for the valorous unit award for our gallant rescue. Boy—the guys in A co. love us for coming in there— they knew they were done for when all of a sudden they heard us charge and yell—it was great, but I hope it doesn't happen again. I saw too much GI Blood that day—we lost 2, A Co. 15, and about 45 wounded. We still kicked their butts—but they're after us—or somebody—they have orders to wipe out somebody—but I don't think they can. Actually, it was our second big rescue of the week. Last Thurs. nite we moved on a 6-hour night march to find and protect some Montagnard troops with Special forces advisers. It was scary as hell, too. I was wondering if we were ever gonna find them. Boy, I'll be glad to get out of this area.

Right now—we're in an LZ with the Battalion—A co. is patching up. I don't know where we'll go or when—I've given up on ever getting back to base camp—it sure hasn't been any picnic for me, but after Sun— I'm sure the good Lord is smiling on our Battalion—I've found it's a lot easier to believe in Him over here—no commercialized, hard sell religion—I just ask him for the strength & endurance and thank Him when I make it through each day. I believe this way I'll be ready for anything—I hope you people are, too. . . .

See ya
Robert

Chu Lai, May 30, 1967

Dear Arch & Ole—

. . . As you probably know, we're just a few miles south of the DMZ and our area of operations is a "hot" one—in more ways than one. We've been battling it out with some hard-core VC for a month now and we can't get them where we want them—they move quickly, silently, using the natural terrain to hide and maneuver in, and they have tunnels running everywhere to hide in. So, they open up with automatics, throw grenades, and disappear—we can't find 'em. So, we pulled back out of the big valley (Sniper valley we called it) and are trying to cut off their supply routes. We caught about 8 of them sneaking around the other day—I was on top of a small hill with my squad and a radio, calling another squad waiting in ambush along the trail. Well, I called them and said here they come—wait, wait—but the fools opened up too soon and got only the first one—oh, was I mad—they could have gotten all 8 if they would have waited—that's the way it goes over here. The one we got had a Chinese Communist "burp" gun, Chi-Com grenades & booby-trap mines, 1 U.S. grenade, some ammo, 3000 piasters ($30) and some important looking documents, so we might have gotten a wheel of some kind—but we should have gotten all of them.

So, we've been busy, dodging bullets and grenades, springing ambushes. I'm getting pretty good at hitting the dirt now—one crack and I'm eating dirt—there must be a better way to make a living—don't you think so? I don't want either one of you dudes ever to get in the army—although it would make a man out of you—there has to be an easier way. . . .

Well—we gotta move out—we're just pushing around this area trying to draw out some VC—they want us to come northwest to their stronghold—kind of a standoff—and believe me it's a dangerous spot to be in. If anything happens to me—take care of the folks for me—ok?

Take it easy and be good.

Your brother
Robert

GERALD L. PAUL (b. 1946) was born in Baraboo and was living in Sparta when he enlisted in the Marine Corps in June, 1968. Paul served as a helicopter crew chief and door gunner (Medium Helicopter Sqdn. 163, Mar. Aircraft Grp. 36, 1st Mar. Aircraft Wing) near Dong Ha, Hue, Phu Bai, and Quang Tri from September, 1966, until April, 1968. Discharged in September, 1969, he now lives in Cottage Grove and works as a systems programmer. In this letter Paul describes ground combat to his girlfriend, Patricia Schaller, who is now his wife.

Phu Bai, July 13, 1967

Pat:

Hope everything is okay back stateside. We've been getting hit every other night with rockets. The NVA are getting brave. I guess it isn't the VC. As of a few months this stopped being a "police action" in my definition. We are fighting trained units from North Vietnam. They are just as well equipped as we are. We carried some NVA KIA gear a couple of days ago. In their packs they have everything that you or I have.

They even have 2 bars of soap & 2 toothbrushes. They have Swedish MK-61 assault rifles which are second only to our own M-14s as far as quality and firepower go.

I will tell you this. The new M-16 isn't worth anything. You may have heard of "Hill 881." On the assault of this hill 50% of all KIAs were killed because of the new rifle jamming up on them. That's the same as murder in my book, sending guys out with rifles that don't work.

If we are ever issued the M-16 I will refuse to take one. I will keep my M-14. At least I can depend on that weapon. Even the M-1 is better than a M-16.

The bodies are piled up at Dong Ha. The smell of death is all over up there. It make you retch. . . .

Love
Jerry

ROGER E. KASCHNER (b. 1947) grew up in West Bend and was drafted into the army in August, 1966. Corporal Kaschner served as an infantryman and supplyman (C Co., 1-18th Inf., 2d Bde., 1st Inf. Div. [Big Red One]) near Di An from March, 1967, to March, 1968. He was discharged in August, 1968, and returned to West Bend to work as a tool-and-die journeyman. The letter below is addressed to Marilyn Knuth, whom he married in 1969.

[October 22, 1967]

Sweetheart,

I am really sorry I haven't written very often in the last 10 day[s]. We were on a bad operation and I just didn't have time.

Combat duty in Vietnam demanded great physical and mental sacrifice.
In this photograph, a group rests for a moment in the field. Courtesy
Doug Bradley.

The last 10 days were the worst I have had over here. We seemed to be in the middle of all the V.C. Every time we went on a patrol we had contact with the V.C. It was really bad because the V.C. even try twice to attack the perimeter.

Of all the patrols we only completed two with no contact. We would go out a few hundred meters and find Charlie. Pull back about 100 meters and call in artillery and air strikes. All together we had 5 guys killed and about 20 guys wounded. Our body count of VC was close to 100 of which 50 were found die outside the perimeter after the night attack. I never want to see anything like that again as long as I live. They flew us out today because everyone was about [to] fall apart.

I want to leave Viet Nam so bad it scares me. I want to come home and try and forget some of the things. It don't take a man to be over here because there is no way to leave till your time is up. For the first time in my life I was really scared I wasn't going to make it. But the scareder I got the closer I seemed to God. But it is all over with and maybe I can relax again. . . .

Please Love Me
Roger

MARVIN S. ACKER (b. 1948) lived in Middleton prior to enlisting in the army in March, 1967. He served as a reconnaissance sergeant (E Co., 1–501st Inf., 2d Bde., 101st Abn. Div. [Airmobile]) in Hue and Phu Bai from December, 1967, to December, 1968. Following his discharge in March, 1970, he attended college, and he later worked as a builder. He currently owns a spa and whirlpool bath business and lives in Madison. In the following two letters to his fiancée, Acker describes the dangers involved in the jungle, especially for the "point man," who led the team. The men who walked point had to be particularly aware of mines, booby traps, and enemy soldiers, and one misstep could mean death for several men.

December 31, 1967

Today and yesterday were two very hard days for me. We had to go on an operation to look for Charlie. Yesterday we left here early in the morning and went five miles into the "Ho Bo Woods." I saw a lot of VC tunnels and a couple of their wells. Besides that it was hot. We had to carry twenty-five full magazines, our pack and a rucksack full of clothes, food and other accessories. We were the recon platoon for the battalion. It was when we hit our overnight base camp that all the action started. One sniper round was shot. We don't know if it was aimed at us or where it landed. We finally got settled down with the battalion. We had to move our position three times because other companies came in. That means two foxholes I dug and got blisters for nothing. We finally moved the third time and said, "The hell with it," so we slept the night without foxholes. Every hour and fifteen minutes one of us has to be on the radio. I had it from 9:30–10:45. All I can say is that I thank God that we didn't stay in our first position. At 10:00 I saw a mortar round go off very close to it. One of our mortars fell short and killed one man and wounded five others. Today we moved out another six miles to another area. I was point man again. We had to go through the thickest part of the jungle. I had to take out my machete and start hacking away. I'm glad Charlie didn't get in the way because it is impossible to clear your way through a jungle, look on the ground for booby traps, watch for him in a spiderhole and at the same time look in the dense jungle for him. If you ask me it's just plain luck and God's will if you live or die. Each step I made I prayed like I never prayed before—I was scared, stiff scared! I was the lead man, 50 meters in front of the whole battalion. So scared I can't even describe it. When I get doubtful I just said to myself, "All right, Marv, keep it cool, you've got a special date with someone across the ocean when this mess is over." I don't want to die. For this I'll be back and walk through all dangers. Tonight is New Year's Eve and I'm not even drinking. All I feel like doing is being alone and just dreaming. That's one thing the Army can't keep me from doing. . . .

All my love,
[Marv]

February 22, 1968

I finally have the time to write you a letter. Usually I just don't have time or if I do there's no way to get them mailed. Right now we're resting at this house in a village after a week of pretty fierce fighting. Believe me, I need a long rest. I'm so tired and my mind is going in all different directions. A lot has happened since I last wrote. One thing I know for sure, I'll never stop thanking God for still being alive. It all happened four nights ago. I knew it would happen sooner or later because every night we go on an ambush further up north in an area where no American troops have been for a long time. That night we went on a squad ambush in a new village that was certain to have VC. . . .

We left the Friendly Village A and then moved up the path. About 200 m. from the VC village we stopped and waited for dark. At dark we moved into the VC Village C. The path in the VC village was only about ten feet wide and you couldn't go to the right because of the lake and you couldn't go to the left because of the dense bamboo trees. We also couldn't go back very fast because of the bamboo fences. When we hit the fence with the star over it I really got scared because I knew it meant VC headquarters. We called up our company commander and requested not to go in, but he ordered us to keep going. We were about 100 m. from the fence with the star on it when it happened. Someone spoke to us in Vietnamese—after 7:00 p.m. the only thing moving outside is VC. The voice came from right in front of our point man who was Naylor; behind Naylor was Sgt. Travel and behind him was me. Naylor immediately opened up with his M-16 on automatic and then we all opened up. In return the NVA opened up on us. The whole fire fight lasted about 30 seconds. The only man in our squad that was hit was Sgt. Travel. We wanted to move back immediately but we had to spend a whole five minutes at the ambush site because we couldn't get the equipment off Travel. When we finally did, we had trouble lifting him. Every 30 feet we had to set him down and a new guy would carry him. To make a long story short, when we got out of the village we called in a medevac chopper which took fifteen minutes because at first he didn't want to land. We had to keep throwing flares to light up the land zone for the chopper and the flares gave away our position. We were just lucky the NVA didn't decide to come after us because we would all have died. He must have thought we were a bigger force than just a squad. Sgt. Travel died in the chopper. They don't understand how he lived that long because he was shot twice in the heart. When he first got shot he kept choking up blood and when we were waiting for the medevac he came to for a couple of seconds and kept yelling he couldn't breathe. The next morning the whole recon platoon went in the village. We burned all the houses. It seemed like there was a sniper in every other house that would keep us pinned down until we killed him. I killed one of them by running up to the side of the house and throwing a grenade in it. We killed a lot of VC and a lot of our men were wounded. Finkle got shot in the leg and will be going back to the States. Hinote got shot in the chest and is going to Japan, but will be ok in a couple of months. Four other men got wounded by shrapnel from the Russian Rocket Launcher. Sgt. Kenny got a slight wound in the nose and Parker got wounded in the leg but they're back with us already. Poncho got wounded in the leg. At first I was real worried about him but he'll be ok and will be back with us in a couple of weeks. Even last night we went on another squad ambush, but luckily didn't see anything. What I need is a long R & R! I've got to have time to put myself together. We just keep moving day in and day out, night after night. I've been sleeping on the ground so long I forgot how it is to sleep in a bed. If that

A "tunnel rat" enters a well-concealed VC tunnel. Courtesy Dennis Bries.

farm deferment was still open I would take it. I've seen my share of dead and have killed more than one. A man is not easy to kill. I've seen men with their legs blown off and holes in their chest and they're still alive! Sgt. Travel was shot twice in the heart and lived for over twenty minutes. At the same time, I've also seen how easy it is to die. So very, very easy. One second you're alive and the next second you're dead. I can't wait until I'm home again where there's *peace* and not half as many worries as there are here. . . .

With all my love,
[Marv]

The area around Cu Chi (about thirty miles northwest of Saigon) contained approximately 125 miles of tunnels measuring about three feet high and 2.5 feet wide. These complexes often had multiple levels and contained barracks, weapons, classrooms, factories, and hospitals. VC fighters could engage American soldiers and then disappear underground almost immediately.

When U.S. forces found the entrance to a tunnel, they would commonly throw grenades and other explosives into it in the hopes of killing anyone or anything that might be hiding below. Then a U.S. soldier would go into the tunnel, armed only with hand grenades, a flashlight, and a pistol. In addition to the possibility of encountering enemy fighters and booby traps, these "tunnel rats" had to deal with bats, rats, snakes, and other creatures.

TODD R. JACKSON (1947-1968) was raised in Manitowoc and enlisted in the
army in November, 1965. He was sent to Vietnam in November, 1966, and
served as a LRRP member (D Troop [Air Cav.], 3-4th Cav. [Armored],
25th Inf. Div.) in Cu Chi. Corporal Jackson was killed in action on January
28, 1968, while on a reconnaissance mission in the Ho Bo Woods.

January 4, [1968]

Dear Mom & Dad,
. . . I went down a tunnel today and got the surprise of my life. I
had thrown a grenade down there, and figured if there were any VC
down there, they would be dead, I was wrong, I turned a corner in the
tunnel, and was looking at a North Vietnamese regular, a major, and
three of his body guards. It got very exciting, and loud for a few seconds!
I sure was glad I brought my .45 cal with me. At any rate it started a
political issue, this major was from Cambodia, Cambodia is suppose
to be a neutral country, what was he doing training VC in Cambodia,
and carrying a Cambodian passport. . . .

In the two letters below, MICHAEL KASTERN describes the difficulties caused
by an encounter with an enemy mine. (For a biographical sketch of Kastern,
see chapter 1.)

April 7, 1968

Dear Mom and Dad,
. . . Last week my squad walked into a minefield. 2 of the guys were
killed and 4 were seriously wounded. There were 10 men in my squad;
now there are 4 left! The 4 of us left all received minor shrapnel wounds.
I caught a few small pieces in my arm and hand but like I said it was
very minor and I didn't have to get evacuated or anything. The medic
just picked the pieces out with a needle and tweezers (ouch)! So I guess
Fatty got put in for a "purple heart" (big deal).
Dad, I guess I don't have to tell you what a mine or grenade will do
to a man. I imagine you've seen more of that than you care to talk about!
I gave first aid as best I could to some of the guys that were hit bad
(the medic was busy with the others) and it made me feel good when
I heard that the guys I treated were sent back to the states and are
recuperating well and won't have any permanent injuries or be crippled.
Most of the guys here don't write home about stuff like that because
they say it will make their parents worry and stuff, but I don't really
like the idea of pretending that nothing ever happens here, (or something
like that)! I don't know, maybe I shouldn't have written about it, also.
Oh well, it's written!

Also last week, my old squad (the one I was in before) was on an ambush patrol one night when suddenly a grenade came flying into their position. One of the guys in that squad, and a very good friend of mine, quickly grabbed it and threw it out. It blew in the air and he only got minor "frag" cuts on the arm. He saved at least 4 men's lives and he was put in for the "Silver Star." I'd say he deserves it! . . .

I listened to part of Johnson's speech about stopping the bombing of North Vietnam a few days ago. I sure hope something good comes from it. I also heard about Martin Luther King[1]. . . .

Love,
Michael

June 10, 1968

Dear Mom and Dad,

. . . I didn't realize that West Allis has 10 KIAs so far (Killed in Action), Wow! But when you figure it out, there is roughly one American GI killed for every 8,000 American people (25,000 KIA into 200 million people) and that works out just about right for West Allis! Really a shame! . . .

I see Dad, that your feelings toward landmines are the same as mine! The bad part about them is that they are so demoralizing because when one goes off there is no one to shoot back at—all you can do is try to control your anger and go on with your mission! But like when a sniper or two fires at you, at least you have a target on which to take out your "wrath!" Not that way with a mine, right? You're right about me being lucky not to have gotten injured worse because the guy who stepped on the mine walked exactly the same path as me about 15 feet behind me. I must have stepped right over the mine! Whew! . . .

Love
Michael

WILLIAM C. JUNG (b. 1948) was raised in Randolph and enlisted in the Marine Corps in February, 1966. He served as a rifle squad leader (K Co., 3/27th Mar., 1st Mar. Div.) and a land surveyor (7th Engr. Bn., 1st Mar. Div.) in Chu Lai and Da Nang from February, 1968, to March, 1969. Sergeant Jung returned to Vietnam for another tour of duty as a land surveyor (9th Engr. Bn., 1st Mar. Div.) from August, 1969, to August, 1970. Since his discharge in June, 1972, Jung has continued his surveying work. He is currently employed by La Crosse County and resides in Onalaska.

---

[1]Martin Luther King, Jr., was assassinated in Memphis, Tennessee, on April 4, 1968.

May 25, 1968

Dear folks,

Well, my good luck finally ran out on me. I was wounded for the second time in eight days yesterday. This time it was bad enough for me to be taken out of the field.

It's all a long story. The last time I wrote, I said we were going on an operation against the NVA. We prepared for two more days after that. "K" was all ready to go. My squad had enough fire power and explosives to level Friesland in one hour.

On the 17th, "Operation Allenbrook" began. "K," "L," and "H & S" Companies went in by choppers. Our company fought its way to "I" Company 3/27 and "G" Company 2/7 and linked up with them. Those two were almost wiped out by the time we got to them. I was wounded that night, but not bad enough to be taken out. The next day we assaulted the NVA positions north of us. The battle lasted all day in temperatures up to 130°. "K," "L," and "M" (who were dropped in to help us out) Companies all took very heavy casualties. The battlefield was covered with dead, wounded, weapons, and every type of gear imaginable. The place was really a mess. I lost a lot of good friends that day. The NVA withdrew that night. We spent the third day bringing in our dead and collecting the scattered gear that had to be flown out. The next four days our battalion traveled the area searching for the NVA. All we got was exercise and a few sniper rounds. Yesterday, the eighth day, we moved south again. "K" and "L" were the lead assault companies. Around noon we reached a long hedgerow with a plowed field separating us from a thick bombed out tree line. Our company assaulted this area. We immediately ran into NVA entrenched in spider holes and reinforced bunkers. They hit our 1st platoon hard. Our 3rd squad went to help them out. Then they got surrounded. I then took my squad up to help them. Heavy enemy fire made travel difficult. I was almost to them when they cut me down. An NVA shot me from behind. One bullet went through my left shoulder. The rest hit the wall in front of me. I crawled to the surrounded squad. I fought with them for another hour. We used everything we had. "M" Company came up to save us, but NVA machine guns cut them to pieces, so they never did come. We finally fought our way out, taking our dead and wounded with us. We had to leave one dead man behind. It was really a shoot out all the way. Bullets flying and grenades and mortar rounds exploding everywhere. I used up almost all the 300 rounds I was carrying. We lost so many men; it was almost pitiful. A chopper took us to the Da Nang Naval Aid Station. They treated me and kept me there for the night. I'm at the air base now with a lot of other wounded. I guess I'm going to Cam Ranh Bay tomorrow. I'm not sure. I've got a clean wound, no broken bones, just a flesh wound. I'll be back with "K" in no time.

There's not much left of good old "K" or 3/27 for that matter. This operation has almost wiped us out. Our company went out with around 170 men. There's around 30 left out there. War is no picnic. Hell can't be as bad as war. We fought hard and well. The NVA hurt us, but you can bet they paid heavily.

At any rate, I'm O.K., so don't worry. They give us good care. I'll write again in a couple of days.

Love,
Bill

P.S. I sprained my ankle too.

KRIS F. BLUMER (1949–1969) grew up in Albany and enlisted in the army in July, 1968. Private Blumer arrived in Vietnam in November, 1968, and served as a rifleman (D Co., 2–16th Inf., 2d Bde., 1st Inf. Div. [Big Red One]) near Di An. On May 15, 1969, Blumer was wounded by the detonation of a mine, and he died in Vietnam on June 25, 1969, from complications related to his injuries.

January 29, 1969

Dear Mom & All,

This letter has been a long time in coming, but it will eventually get there. Letters from now on will probably be kind of scarce from now on. You needn't feel obliged to write if you don't feel like it. I have little urge to write. Don't ask me why because I don't know. It's just one of those things that change with time over here. Please inform all concerned that letters will be scarce for a while. . . . I have been off ammo for about a week and a half at this writing.

I am in first squad and am doing well I think. We are supposed to go further north sometime in the middle of February. I have been walking point lately while we go out on ambush. I don't really like it because the VC have been booby trapping around here lately & they are hard to detect in the dark. We lost another track & its driver a couple of days ago. Hit a mine & blew the hell out of it. The driver was 19 and had only been in country two weeks. Oh well, easy come easy go. I will hate to move from here. We have been getting two hot meals a day and we have rigged up a barrel so we can fill it with water and take a shower. Things have gone pretty well for me here so I really don't want to leave. . . . The gooks over here have a new trick now. They dress up as ARVNs and hit you when least expect. They did that the other day and tore the

Armored personnel carriers (APCs) transported troops across much of Vietnam's varied terrain. Courtesy Jim Carlson.

1/18 cav unit all to hell. We have orders to kill anything that moves after 7:00 PM even if it looks like an ARVN. The ARVNs are supposed to stay out of our A.O. If they don't, that's their tough luck. Half of the ARVNs are VC anyway. They are worthless bastards anyway. When I get back in the world, I am going to start my own movement to help legalize peace. It would be nice if someone would start it. Just kidding! I'll just be glad to get out of here. . . . Well, that is all I have to say for now. Will close now.

Love
Kris

STEPHEN J. PIOTROWSKI (b. 1950) was born in Stevens Point and was living in Amherst when he enlisted in the army in June, 1968. He served as an infantry sergeant and radio operator (C Co., 3–503d Inf. [Abn.], 173d Abn. Bde.) near An Khe and Bong Son from February, 1969, until February, 1970. Piotrowski now lives in Madison and works as a staff assistant to Senator Herb Kohl.

June 1, 1969

Dear Folks,

Got your letter today, glad to hear from you. Congratulations to Tony for the placings in track. The 10.6 isn't a bad time. Sounds like there isn't much going on at home. I'd like a couple of pictures of the wedding if at all possible. We went on a patrol and captured a couple of VC women. It's a strange feeling to be shot at by women. We have a fairly good sized force of them working in this area, and almost all the action of the last couple of weeks has been against women. I really haven't got much to write but that I hope Al and Tina have the best of luck.

Love
Steve

TOM MCCABE, an infantryman, described some of his combat experiences in the following letter to his family. He was wounded just a few days later. (For a biographical sketch of McCabe, see chapter 1.)

June 5, 1969

Howdy—

. . . Well life in the jungle hasn't changed much for me. I'm still with the gun & Don & am humping as heavy [as] ever. The system of supply hasn't changed for this mission as we had hoped so we are still struggling on little food & water & irregular log times. This mission is going to be rougher than the others that we have been on, because the enemy is all over the area. We saw them come in from Cambodia on May 31st (Buddha's Birthday) during a cease fire & could do nothing about it. For me the action started before the Charlie Alpha even began. About 6:30 on the morning of June 2nd I started the day out right by killing a 5'-6' cobra that had penetrated the LZ. I'm beginning to be known as the "snake killer." After the area had been bombed by B-52s we moved in to our AO just north of Dolly. Supposedly there was supplies strewn all over the jungle by the arc-lite. But we didn't find any. The area was rough going because the bombs uproot so much vegetation & trees that it becomes almost impossible to move around. On the 4th day we made contact with an unknown size of Gooks. They hit us about 1 o'clock while we were resting. We had just taken five because we found what appeared to be an old bunker complex & the CO wanted to investigate. The patrol from 1-6 (the 1st platoon) got hit first. At the time Don and I were leaning up against a tree on the edge of a crater talking to 3-6 (our platoon leader Lt. Clemons) when all of a sudden the jungle erupted with fire. The ironic thing about the moment was that we were discussing how the complex was so old & was more than likely empty. Don, 3-6 & I jumped over the log and took cover, I landed smack-dab into a large pricker bush & picked up some dandy cuts & thorns. Since we were the leading platoon in our column we had to go up to help out. Don & I were first gun so we were needed immediately to lay down supporting fire for 1-6's patrol. We moved up slowly then found a good position & started firing up the area. We couldn't see anything but we sure put out a lot of lead and noise. At first Don's gun wouldn't fire correctly, but after a good dousing of gun oil he went crazy with the bloomin' thing. I was buckling belts on so fast that I didn't have any time to fire my own weapon. After about 500 rounds I shut down Don & his gun so that they could both cool off. It was almost comical to see Don lying there with a dazed smile as he held the trigger back & casings were spewing from the gun & the barrel smoking & getting red hot. If I hadn't stopped him I think he would have burned the gun up before he let go of the trigger. When Don's gun stopped I commenced to lay out fire power with my M-16 until after some 300 rounds I could no longer hold on to the hot barrel hand guards. At this point we slowed down our firing to reconnoiter the situation & wait for further instructions. Word came that all the dead & wounded were out & we were to move back. Again my gun stayed to lay out fire as the company moved back. After we withdrew some fifty meters all was quiet. It is now that the impact of the battle is felt. We spent the next two hours removing men and equipment from the fire fight area. I carried a double pack & several litters, until I was too exhausted to move. I took over a security position & rested; it was during this short period of rest that the weight of what war is fell on my shoulders. As I sat watching the men file by my gun I saw a friend brought out on a home-made litter with his head hanging loosely over the end with his blonde hair hanging in loose curls. Now I know why war is so meaningless & wasteful—my heart is heavy. Not one square inch of Vietnam was worth that young soldier's life—not to mention the 35,000 other boys that have so far died over here. It seems that firefights are the only time we get really good food in the field. It is undoubtedly to keep up the morale of the company, but it is a heck of way to earn a hot meal. After resupplying we moved back towards our old FOB & set up. Tomorrow we'll move back into the complex to drive the gooks out.

It will never cease to amaze me how unorthodox this war seems compared to how I imagined it. There are no set lines of battle & it is usually over as fast as it starts. We move a 100 meters from the battle & set up almost as nonchalantly as we would on LZ Dolly. This is truly a strange war both physically & mentally. . . .

Love to all
T Mc

In the following three letters, STEVE PLUE, another infantryman, echoes McCabe's sentiments about the ugliness and senselessness of the war. (For a biographical sketch of Plue, see chapter 1.)

April 28, 1970

Dear Mom & Dad:

. . . It's so stupid and ridiculous of how so many of our boys are killed by accidents due to some careless mistakes.

Like the guy I saw die, the helicopter crash killing 13 people. And for another example, 2 nights ago, B co. blew an ambush on their own people due to a simple communication mistake and these two squads started blasting away at each other. Two men were killed instantly by Claymore mines, another lost his legs and 5 more injured. All due to GI mistakes. They say as high as 50% of deaths and casualties are caused by our own men and so many parents never know how their son was killed because all the Army tells them is that they are combat casualties.

That's why I was afraid of this mission. Because our commanding officer is insane. Gungho lifer looking for nothing but a body count of enemy so he can make a stupid promotion.

Like on this last 9 day mission, one night he made us fire mortars from our night position ambush saying we needed practice. All the VC had to do was zero in on the noise with their mortars and we'd be hurting. The Lieutenants tried to explain the hazards of doing this but he pulled rank on them and that's all that could be said.

I know for one fact. With the hatred his men have for him, that if we ever got in a firefight someone will knock him off. It happens quite a bit and I'm for certain It'll happen here. I've never seen such hatred.

With all the war atrocities, people act like animals. That's why they happen. It seems these lifers go nuts. Army means battle, death and victory to them.

Enough about him. . . .

Love
Steve

May 2, 1970

Dear Mom & Dad:

Am I beat, and I do mean beat. For the last 3 days, I think I can say have been the roughest 3 days in the field or at least the most frightening. On the 30th I was taken out with the re-supply to the field. The company was to come in on the 30th but were extended because of the sightings and contact they had made during that mission.

So the minute I touched down by chopper we had to move out and spent the day humping through muck and bamboo. And right away they gave me the 292 to hump, a super long antenna about the size of a bale of hay when wrapped up.

And I could really tell some stories about bamboo. It's nothin like cane poles that's for sure. It's thick like a wall of thorns that wrap around you and jab ya in the eyes and arms and knocks you down and you're all tangled up in these vines. I've really got some beautiful cuts.

So we humped 4 klicks about 2½ miles that day and set up near a stream for an ambush. Everything went alright during the night. Nothing wandered into the ambush but at 7:00 the next morning I was awakened by a hell of an explosion and it sounded like the sky was falling in.

The position to our left about 50 yds away was in contact with Charlie. They had spotted 8 Gooks and they returned fire for about 15 min with AK small arms and RPGs something like a bazooka.

The Gooks didn't spot our position so we didn't receive any of the big fire but AK rounds were whizzing around our heads and we were tryin to find a hole to hide in.

Everyone was scrambling for ammo & helmets and my heart was pounding so hard I couldn't hardly pick up my rifle.

We called in Gunships and cobras and really brought hell on them.

It might seem like it's easy to shoot back and there's nothing to get upset about but I've never felt this kind of fear before. Just listening to the crack of rounds and actually hearing the rounds go over your head makes you clam up and wish the Lord would make some kind of miracle and take away all the nasty happening but it's just you and your own ability to keep a clear head and know what to do. As of yet I don't think I've ever been so scared.

After they drew back and ran all we found was some shed clothes where one had been shot and stripped to patch a hasty wound.

So we swept the area and set up another ambush that night. Beautiful place for Charlie to walk into.

What makes it so freaky is that he's as quiet as a mouse and it was so dark that he'd be upon us before we knew what happened. Luckily we had negative contact and we were radioed an urgent message that we were to be brought into base as a support element for a suspected ground attack tonight on our base camp. And about 10 min before we boarded choppers this morning we had to change plans again. They had spotted a helmet, rifle and pack with blood on the ground so our Co. was dropped in that area and the choppers sprayed the area for we were certain of enemy in the area. We call it a "Hot Landing Zone" marked

Operation in the Tay Ninh area. Courtesy Dennis Bries.

by red smoke. That's what scares me the most. I can just picture the VC shooting at the choppers as we make a landing and fighting to set up a perimeter of small arms fire. So we moved into the location of this spotted gear and it turned out to be GI's gear.

It was raining all this time and it was pretty miserable. After we picked up the gear they choppered us out to base here because they're sure of getting a ground attack and we're needed pretty badly.

So here I am, 2:00 in the afternoon waiting til dark and then I don't know what.

And another bit of good news. Troops were moved 20 miles into Cambodia yesterday and guess who goes to the border in 28 days. Damn this war is all I can say. We'll never get out [of] here.

10–1 Scott will be over here in a few years and if I could I'd buy his ticket to Canada before I'd let him come over here. . . .

Guess I'll go for now. Sorry if this is so messy and hard to read but my knee doesn't make a very good table.

Love
Steve

May 20, 1970

Dear Mom, Dad & Family

Well, I guess maybe I'll have a little rest time now. I'm in the hospital again at Long Binh, Vietnam, arrived about 2:00 last night. I've earned one medal last night that I had hoped to avoid during my tour, the "Purple Heart."

After I had written my last letter from Cambodia, we moved out on armored tracks again on a three day mission supposedly to secure a bridge, road and a water purification point on a nearby river about five miles from our fire support base.

We dismounted the tracks at about 4:00 on the 19th and for some off the wall reason our commanding officer led us off the side of the road about 300 meters. Told us to eat chow and be ready to move at 6:00 into a night ambush position.

We sent out a recon party about 5:00 to check the area and decide on the best place to set our ambush.

The recon came back and had picked out a clump of trees across an open field in which to set up.

Things have been awfully shaky as far as leadership is concerned. Like I had mentioned about our Captain and just that day we lost our only person with any sense, our platoon Lt. to another sgt who is too old to be out in the field and no experience in field operation.

So at 6:00 we started across the open field to our location. It was still daylight and way too early to do any moving unnoticed.

We proceeded into the woodline setting up 3 positions forming a triangle with my position, the machine gun as rear security.

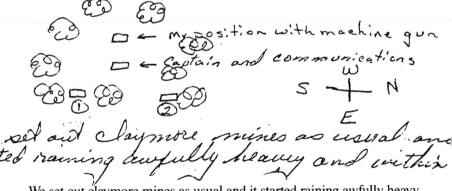

We set out claymore mines as usual and it started raining awfully heavy and within a half hour the ambush was set.

Things were getting pretty miserable, tired, wet and the lack of leadership was bothering everyone. My guard started at 10:00 and at 10:00 I called in a negative set-rep, meaning no movement, everything calm.

Five minutes later, small arms fire started coming in from the south onto position (1). I no sooner got my helmet on when I received an AK round through my helmet and luckily just creased my ear exiting out the front of my helmet. The sergeant in my position got hit in the shoulder and hand.

At the same time grenades and rocket grenades were thrown in on position (2). One of the rocket grenades hit between myself and Jim Alt, the machine gunner and all I saw and heard was one hell of a sharp blast and something striking me in the head behind the right ear and burned like all hell and blood was spurting pretty badly. Jim caught shrapnel in the head also. That sort of did our position in. Two boys were killed in position 2 from grenades and 3 more wounded, 1 man lost his fingers. 4 men in position 1 received shrapnel wounds and 1 man in the captain's position lost his hand.

Everything was over in five minutes and apparently the NVA snuck in the dark, hit us and ran.

It took almost a half hour to get gunships and artillery in on our position and I was so worried they hit us again and perhaps overrun us. But God was with us and they didn't return. It took an hour for the Medevac chopper to come in and dust us off. We had to leave the dead behind because of too much weight. They flew us to Tay Ninh for immediate application of wounds and then flown to here near the coast again.

They didn't take the metal out of my head til 5:00 this morning. Lost quite a bit of blood but that's all. So all day I slept and rested. Got a bandage the size of a turban on my head and my head hurts an awful lot. I don't know how long I'll be here or what. All I know is they dug five pieces of shrapnel out and the top part of my ear is cut off but hardly noticeable.

All I could do was cry for the 2 men killed. It's so hard trying to realize that your friends are dead and all messed up. The screaming and moaning was so horrifying it makes me shudder to bring back to mind of last night. . . .

Love
Steve

JOHN W. KRECKEL (1948–1970) was working in Milwaukee when he was drafted into the army in May, 1969. He served in the infantry (A Co., 2-506th Inf., 3d Bde., 101st Abn. Div. [Airmobile]) at Phong Dien between April and July, 1970. He died on July 22, 1970, when he pushed a fellow

soldier out of the line of enemy fire, an action for which he received the
~~Distinguished Service Cross.~~

June 4, [1970]

Hi Timmy,

I just got a letter from Steve so I guess I don't have to ask how things are going. There's times when it seems like everything just goes wrong, isn't there!! During these times we usually feel depressed, dejected, and as though the world was against us. It's then when we have the least optimism and then when we're most likely to go the wrong way—usually because it's the easiest out. But that easy out will destroy a man's pride in himself, destroy his sense of being, thus destroy the man. That's the time to stand up and fight back, so to regain our lost pride. Life doesn't seem fair at times but then who says it has to be—it's what we make of it—our attitude.

Yesterday we were on patrol and ran into an ambush. Our CO told us to move on but the point man (person leading the patrol) refused. Then one guy said that he'd lead us up the trail. Pretty thoughtful of him, wasn't it! He's dead now! It wasn't too bad a fight though—1 dead; 3 in critical condition. (One with a head injury, bullet in his left arm, & right leg. Another with a bullet in his stomach. And another with a bullet in his chest); 6 in fair condition with various injuries of the legs & arms. It was my second firefight. We advanced on line up the hill shooting everything we had in front of us. We then formed a perimeter and tried to sleep. . . .

Do you know what fear is? I do!! So things are going bad for you hey—want to trade places? But I'm a man and I'll live through this because I know I must. A year from now I'll look back at this and feel proud for I'll know I served my country well. I may not believe in this war but I believe in my country so I'll do my best. You're as much a man as I am Timmy, and when I get home I expect to meet one.

Sincerely,
John

Armored Combat

Armored vehicles played primarily a supporting role during most of the Vietnam War. The communist forces rarely used armor prior to the 1972 Easter Offensive, and the United States generally used tanks and armored personnel carriers (APCs) to escort convoys and to break jungle in support of infantry patrols.

Armored units were extremely vulnerable to mines, which could do tremendous damage. Not only could the explosions themselves have catastrophic results, but a disabled tank left its crew stranded with little protection and no means of movement. Tom Reneau, Darrel Lulling, and Lynn Columbia all served with armored units in Vietnam, and their letters offer vivid descriptions of tank warfare.

THOMAS A. RENEAU (b. 1944) grew up in Beloit and enlisted in the army in July, 1963. He served as a tank commander (B Trp., 3–4th Cav. [Armored], 25th Inf. Div.) around Cu Chi from July, 1967, to July, 1968. Reneau remained in the army until his retirement in October, 1985, and currently resides in Beloit. He wrote the two letters below to his parents.

September 14, 1967

Dear Mom,

. . . I've got something to tell you, I feel you should know.

The night of the 12th, about 8:15 P.M. my platoon, the 1st Platoon, was hit by a Viet Cong ambush. We had a tank in the lead, APCs and two tanks at the end, the tank I commanded was the very last tank.

The lead tank was fired at with an RPG-7, (an anti-tank weapon) but was missed. Then fire started coming from both sides of the road we were on.

Mom, I don't want you to get all upset and worry so I'm not going to tell you the rest of what happened.

I will tell you this, because of what I did, I was promoted to the rank of Staff Sergeant E-6, by the Commanding General of the division, personally. I also received the Silver Star, the nation's third highest military award and my crew received the Bronze Star, the nation's fourth highest award. So, I guess you may say, we were heroes, in a way.

The tank commander of the tank in front of me that night, wrote up an eyewitness report of what happened that night.

When I get a copy of the report, I will send one to you.

Don't worry Mom, my men and myself got off of the tank and to safety okay.

Mom, your prayers, my prayers and everybody else's prayers, timely were answered that night. I said a little prayer that night before I went out, as I usually do. (SMILE)

Well Mom, I may just as well tell you what happened. The tank was hit five times, caught fire but we stayed and fought until the last minute. But before we had to leave the tank, we were able to get out 9 to 12, 90 mm main gun rounds at the Viet Cong. In all, the platoon killed 10 Viet Cong, the crew of B-15, my tank, was given credit for killing 3 of the 10 Viet Cong.

Just as we got off of the tank, it started to blow up.

So, now you know what happened. . . .

Love always,
Tom

Tank commander Thomas Reneau at Cu Chi, 1967.
Courtesy Thomas Reneau.

October 28, 1967

Dear Dad,

I'm now going to answer your letter of the 17th of September.

Dad perhaps that was quite a feat my crew and I did the night of 12 September. By no means do I intend to make a habit of it. (SMILE)

Dad, that night I happened to be in the wrong place, at the right time. I was in a place that night where I had to fight for my life, so I did. With the commands to fire, I gave to my gunner, I did not know until the next day that three men had been killed, Viet Cong. The night we were hit by the ambush, the area was checked and four bodies were found.

Dad, I did stand tall on that tank. I saw the fire start across the rear of the tank, I saw the two rounds hit the left side, one of which went through the hull, into the left fuel tank. I saw the fire start down the left side of the tank.

Seeing all of this, I was scared, but I made up my mind I was going to stay and fight because I knew God was with [me] and I knew God would tell me when to go off the tank. So I stayed until that time fighting.

Dad, I'm still going to look up to you, you are my father, a father I am very proud of.

Always,
Tom

In this letter, DARREL LULLING, who served as a mechanized infantry squad leader, describes a tank battle to his girlfriend. (For a biographical sketch of Lulling, see chapter 1.)

August 19, 1968

My Dearest Darling Jane

Yesterday I went out on my third patrol. We were headed straight toward the DMZ. When the front portion of our company was hit by a manually detonated mine—I was supposed to be up there with them but they were going so fast and I was so tired that I was lagging behind. They had just gone down this hill when I saw the explosion. I hit the ground and then later ran to a safer position behind a large rock—and had a drink of water. I heard someone say that someone was wounded. It later turned out to be a sergeant from my platoon who had a piece of metal hit his arm tearing the flesh and breaking [the] bone. Several men where the explosion had been were knocked down. A Radio Man had a piece of metal go right through his steel helmet and was stopped by his helmet liner. So his helmet saved his life. Shortly after I heard over the radio that another section of our company also encountered a mine and one man had a slight flesh wound.

The medic gave the sergeant some morphine and then we moved out to a level area where we called in a "Dust Off" (a special helicopter that evacuates wounded). Then we came back to our base camp.

Today we had incoming rockets in our base camp. Pretty far away from me but someone was hurt because I saw the "Dust Off." . . .

All My Love
Darrel

LYNN F. COLUMBIA (b. 1949) grew up in Waupun and enlisted in the army in August, 1969. He served as a tank loader and in the arts and crafts shop (L Troop, 3/11th ACR; HHC, 26th Gen. Spt. Grp.) while stationed in Di An and Phu Bai from July, 1970, to July, 1971. Following his discharge in March, 1972, Columbia returned to Waupun, where he works as a guard at the Wisconsin Correctional Institution.

August 31, 1970

Hello everyone,

. . . Well, things have been pretty low down around here. Remember I wrote you about Twiggy (shot with a 45), well he died about a week and a half ago. What a way to die. Just a stupid stunt to get somebody killed. Anyway about a week after Twiggy's death, an armored personnel carrier hit a mine. A soul brother was killed and the 3 crewmen were badly injured. It happened at night when 3rd platoon was returning to the NDP. Some more bad news. 29 Aug. 3 men from my platoon were badly injured. Someone stepped on a mine. One of the men lost his right foot and they hope they can save both legs. The second man got shrapnel in his arms and badly in his left shoulder. The last man got shrapnel in his buttocks. 2 of the men will be sent back to the world. The buttocks case will be back in the field in another couple weeks.

Last night was my first firefight. (30 Aug.) We had just set up our SP (strong point) and in the distance a green flare had been popped. Immediately we cranked up the engines and headed for a village where we had an NDP set up a week earlier. I could hear a lot of shooting (AK47s) by the VC and south Vietnamese (RVNs). The village was lit up with flares. 4 VC were killed just as I arrived. After the shooting we moved through the village, knocking down some hooches. We reconned by fire after we went through the village. A cobra helicopter fired its mini gun & launched rockets in front of our position. We opened up with everything we had. I didn't see any VC, but they were out there. Later we returned to a new strong point.

That same evening a little while before the firefight someone else accidentally got shot in the stomach with a .45 pistol. I can say this. This is hell over here. You have to be on the lookout *all* the time. Believe me this isn't a picnic. I hate it and I sure don't like writing about it. I know you're probably going to get really worried now. Please try not to get too upset. If I can live with it you can. I have to not only be careful during a fight but also the elements and insects are bad. . . .

Now that I have really shaken you, relax. I will come home in one piece. I have a lot of living ahead of me. I just can't wait. I'll probably be a different person to you. I love you all so much.

Lynn

Helicopter Pilots and Crew

Vietnam was the first war in which helicopters played a crucial part in combat. In 1969, at the height of the war, U.S. helicopters flew nearly 8.5 million missions over Vietnam, transporting supplies and troops to the field, performing reconnaissance, evacuating casualties, and providing fire support. By the end of the war, 4,642 U.S. helicopters had been downed, 3,013 American helicopter pilots, crew, and passengers had been killed in combat, and another 2,276 had died in nonhostile incidents such as accidents. The following letters from Scott Alwin (who piloted troop transport helicopters known as slick ships), Jerry Paul (a helicopter door gunner and crew chief), and John Abrams (the pilot of a gunship) describe different aspects of the air war in Vietnam.

SCOTT R. ALWIN (1944–1976) was raised in Fort Atkinson and enlisted in the army in July, 1966. He served as a helicopter pilot in Bien Hoa from August, 1967, until the summer, 1970 (68th Avn. Co., 145th Combat Avn. Bn.), and from the spring, 1971, until January, 1972 (117th Avn. Co., 222d Avn. Bn. [Combat Support]), receiving a battlefield commission as a first lieutenant in February, 1970. A much-decorated pilot, Alwin died in an auto accident in the United States in 1976. This letter was sent to one of his younger brothers.

September 20, 1967

Dear Lance,

. . . I'm meeting a few new situations myself. We fly long hours usually and quite frankly under situations that money couldn't pay me to fly. You get into the air with a load and a weak ship and you're assaulting a landing zone in some rice paddies and so help me God I don't honestly know whether we can get the ship down in one piece.

We've lost three ships since I've gotten here but only one to enemy fire (this is just from my company and just the ones totaled). But the crews all came out pretty well. We took some hits in our ship the other day but I suspect they were the result of the gunships shooting too close to us and not enemy fire. When we were taking off from the LZ one of the ships dropped out of the formation about 300 feet in the air. At first I tried to follow him because someone had just been on the air talking about seeing some VC and they were going to go and throw out a smoke grenade and leave their gunners work the area over. But the aircraft commander (A/C) told me to close up the formation and I realized that the other ship was making a forced landing. They did a beautiful job and the ship was salvaged and is already flying again.

I don't tell mom and dad much about what I do so don't you mention it either.

There is a misconception that the gunship drivers are the real fearless

Army pilot Scott Alwin. Courtesy Walter Alwin.

bunch but the common way of looking at it here is that gun drivers are
"slick" pilots who have lost their nerve. I've been given the chance to
go into guns but don't think I'll take it. Those people whose delight is
in recounting their kills at little risk to themselves aren't my group and
quite frankly I'm not much of a killer myself . . . .

God Bless you,
Your loving brother,
Scott

In the following two letters to his girlfriend, JERRY PAUL describes life as a
helicopter crewman and some of the problems he faced. (For a biographical
sketch of Paul, see earlier in this chapter.)

Base X, November 9, 1967

Darling Pat:

Sorry I haven't wrote for a while but I warned you. Everything is okay here but wish I were with you. I've been flying just about day & night. Most of the birds in the sqdrn are down. We just can't get parts up here.

It's a pretty hot area up here. At least it doesn't get boring. You can get shot at flying admin runs. I wish I could take movies of some of the things that go on. It would be the best John Wayne flick ever made. Call it "Flying Leathernecks 1967." I'll have some good flicks if my pictures turn out okay. I wish I were a writer. The stuff we do doesn't seem the same when I put on paper.

I think I'll try though. I'll take today and won't add anything or delete anything.

It starts at 0430 when the Duty NCO comes into the tent & wakes me up. I get up, put on my flight suit & leather jacket. It's cold here in the morning. I walk out to the line and preflight the bird then sign off the "yellow sheet." I get my gunner up and we go out to the bird and make some "C rat" coffee and wait for the pilots. Time for a cigarette.

The pilots finally come out and preflight the bird and brief us on the first mission. We're going to Quang Tri and pick up some officers for a recon overfly.

We go pick up the officers and head for the mountains in the west. There was a group of gooks caught there last night by the "arty." They said they got a lot of secondary explosions which might have been rockets. The area is all torn up with shell craters overlapping each other but nobody in sight.

Suddenly our wingman spots a sampan on the river. It's in a free fire zone and we go down after it. It ducks in under the trees over hanging the river & gets away.

Next we sight about 150 gooks carrying bundles. We go down after them but they are out of the zone so we can't shoot.

It's almost noon so we go to Dong Ha and shut-down for chow. "Cs" again. We take off again and start resupplies to a bunch of isolated grunts along the DMZ. NVA arty is dropping in the same area. The whole area looks like the moon. Nothing but craters and blasted trees.

They're short on water so we haul mostly water. They have heat casualties, must be 18–20 of them. We get them loaded. Only able to take 4 at a time. The zone is real bad. One of them is in shock. We don't have a Corpsman so I take rags and soak them with water. I've got to keep his temp down. We're about halfway to Dong Ha and he seems to be coming out of it. His color is better. Suddenly he's conscious but he's like a maniac. It takes 3 of us to hold him down. He fights like a madman. We hold him down but he tries to bite. We finally land at "D" med. It takes six of us to get him on a stretcher. We finally get done with the resupplies thank god.

One more mission. Tomorrow is the Marine Corps birthday. They've got a special treat for the guys at Ca Lu and the Rockpile. 2 huge cakes, beer & soda. We're so loaded down we can barely get off the ground. We deliver the cake, beer & sodas. Boy now I know what it feels like to play Santa Claus.

Home we go. Haven't hardly enough fuel but we make it. We shut-down and watch the sunset. I grease the bird and go to the line shack. I find out I'll be launching early again tomorrow. Got time for a shower and to write a letter to Pat. Which brings me up to now. Every day is about the same with little variation. Where the action is.

I miss you. I think of you real often. The mail service is pretty bad here so I get a bunch of letters all at once. I do appreciate them. Must close now. Be good, study hard & say hello to everyone.

Thinking of You

Love
Jerry

Ai Tu, February 17, 1968

Hi Honey

. . . We're getting shot up pretty bad. We've had 7 planes shot up in the last 2 days with 5 people hurt pretty bad.

I'm short of people now so I'll be flying myself tomorrow on medevac. That's where the action is. You can't ask people to do something you wouldn't do yourself. The battle is still going strong up at Khe Sanh. They have even sighted MIG-17s north of Khe Sanh. Wouldn't even want to come up against one of those with only a M-60 MG. . . .

Not too much more news. Just trying to keep 8 birds in the air when the gooks try to shoot them down. Had a gunner "freeze" on a gun. Have to replace him, could get someone killed if he's too shook to fire. These new kids they are sending us are never going to hack the load unless they learn fast. If I keep getting crews shot up all I'll have are new "kids" who don't even know what's going on. A person needs a year over here just to get working good and then he goes home. It's too short a time as far as I'm concerned.

I'm losing what few experienced crews I have at the end of the month. They'll be going home then. I haven't got too much more time here but you sure wonder when you see these "kids." They don't even know the bird. Much less how to work on it and what to expect under combat conditions from the A/C. . . .

Love
Jerry

JOHN ABRAMS, a navy helicopter gunship pilot, described aerial combat in the following excerpt from a tape he sent to his wife, Jane. (For a biographical sketch of Abrams, see chapter 1.)

[May 6, 1968]

. . . You want to know what I'm doing and all that good stuff? Well, there's really not too much I can tell you, at least not much you really would want to hear. A lot of it's not too pretty. I wrote you about some of it a few weeks ago, and it hasn't changed. It's just the same thing day after day. It's like I wrote, sort of like playing God, with your finger on the trigger deciding whether to let him go or to finish him off there before he gets a chance to finish you. The hard part, the really hard part, is trying to decide which ones are the bad guys and which ones are the good guys. . . . Usually we always fly two gunships—we call the helicopters gunships here, it's sort of another one of these Vietnam-created military words. They're gunships, not helicopters. Anyway, we'll be flying over with two gunships, and flying over a loaded sampan with maybe one or two men in it and some miscellaneous cargo-looking things. They'll see us coming, and what'll they do? Hell, they'll jump over the side, or they'll paddle like hell for the bank to get under some brush. They're obviously trying to avoid being seen. Well, if they'd have just kept paddling along, we'd have figured they were just farmers or fishermen or some damn thing. But they're not that way. Every time we see one evade, we know it's Charlie trying to get away from being seen, and by that time we've already seen him. So, we shoot him up, sink the boat, and try the best of our ability to annihilate Charlie in the attack. The other day, we were flying some low surveillance over an area, just looking, not bothering anybody, not—hell, our guns weren't even armed. We were just flying along, and all of a sudden a guy runs out of one of these shacks—we call them hootches. This guy ran out of a hootch, running like hell, and starts throwing big branches over a sampan that he's got pulled up on a shore along the canal. We'd have flown right over him. We never would have even noticed him. Sure, we'd have seen the sampan, but bags of rice look like bags of rice whether they've got ammunition inside them or not. So we quick armed weapons and swung around and destroyed the sampan and got a secondary

*Lt. John L. Abrams, a navy
helicopter gunship pilot.
(Courtesy Ellen Abrams
Blankenship.) Helicopters
helped define the nature of
combat in Vietnam. This Huey
was photographed flying in the
northern sector of South
Vietnam. (Courtesy Ed
Beauchamp.)*

explosion out of it. Guy must have had some high explosives or some ammunition or something hidden in the bags of rice. And we never would have seen it if this guy hadn't run out of the house and started covering it up. So in the ensuing attack he got killed, and the sampan was destroyed.

Charlie just doesn't seem to have any common sense. He's determined, and he's mean, and he's got one thing on his side—that's time. He really has time on his side, it goes without a doubt. He can sit and wait, and wait, and wait, just wait for us to let down our guard then, bang, he's gonna zap us just when he gets a chance. That's the way this guerrilla warfare is. In their favor is time. Of course, in our favor is resources and resource management. He has a lot of logistics problems and supplies and supply routes and methods of supply that we don't have. But having time in his favor certainly is an asset. Of course he does probably 90 percent of his work at night. He kills—that's something that's very strange—flying along in the middle of a jungle, there'll be a rice paddy, neatly tilled rice field. We'll watch it for maybe a week or two weeks. We'll never see a water buffalo and a farmer out there tilling it. And it's in an area that you know is a Charlie area—it's a hot area. Never see anybody tilling it. So one night we'll go out there, on a real black night, no moon. We'll pop a few parachute flares out over the area, and there the silly bastard will be down there in the middle of the night in the dark with his water buffalo tilling his rice. One night he tills his rice and the next night he walks around with a rifle sniping at the ships or the airplanes. So he's got his problems. The nights belong to Charlie. And with the oncoming monsoon season, it's getting to where parts of the days belong to Charlie too. This weather is getting real bad for flying, for operating. And every time it's too bad for us to take off, it's that much more time that Charlie's got on the ground to operate. He's getting pretty bold. He's taken a few potshots at the LST, the ship that we're on. In fact, a short time ago, he tried to mine this ship, just before I got aboard. They had some swimmers swim out with some gasoline cans filled with some type of explosive and tied them to the anchor chain. Luckily, they had some pretty alert guards around the flight deck that spotted them. . . .

At any rate, what I'm doing isn't real pretty, and I guess it's probably something I'm gonna want to forget a lot about when I leave here. The flying is exciting. There's no two ways about that. It's a certain scarf and goggles and leather helmet-type flying. It's a window open and a scarf blowing in the breeze-type thing. It lends a little hero image-type thing. But it's not all glory, it's excitement, it's all excitement. And a

lot of it is being real, real scared. I guess I've probably been more scared
here already in the last month and a half, six weeks, than I've ever been
scared before. I won't go into it. Someday maybe we'll talk about it.
I don't think this is the time or place. But it's no picnic. It's really not
a picnic. I don't want to make it sound all glorious or anything. It certainly isn't a glorious thing either. It's just a job that has to be done.
It's a dirty job, and it's a job that has to be done. That's about all I can
say about it. . . .

At least here you go out on a mission and we fire our rockets and
our machine guns or what have you, and we can see ourselves hit the
target. We can see if we're missing the target. We can make corrections,
we can criticize ourselves, we can criticize each other, as we do. We
can really see an actual physical reaction to our actions. That's kind of
confusing sounding, but I think you know what I mean. We actually
can see what we're doing, what we're accomplishing—in any particular
instance. What we're accomplishing overall, I really couldn't say. But
we go out and put in a strike on a target. We can see how well we hit
the target or we don't hit the target. That's a big thing, it's a mark of
maybe a little professionalism. You can take a little pride in being able
to hit a target maybe a little better than the next guy. Of course, that's
how we all try to look at these things, as just targets. We try not to think
about, try not to really look at what is in the target or around the target.
Of course, we have to make a recon after each attack and get what they
call a body count and structures damaged, this type of thing. After the
attack is over and you go back to take a look at it, it's a lot different
than thinking about it while you're actually doing the attack.

I won't say that I regret coming here. It's been an experience, and
I guess all our experiences add up to something good. I think you and
I have had enough experiences together where I guess probably, maybe
all of our experiences might add up to something really great. I'd like
to think so. . . .

4

Why Am I Here?

The Vietnam War divided Americans in ways that were unthinkable to the generation that grew up during World War II. Bitter debates at home profoundly affected GIs in Vietnam, who were well aware of these divisions while fighting a war that lacked clear objectives and measurable victories. Although there had always been some opposition to American involvement in Vietnam, the antiwar movement grew substantially in 1965, when President Lyndon Baines Johnson drastically increased the number of Americans sent to Vietnam. Opposition was at first concentrated in religious groups and on college campuses, but as death tolls began to rise, opposition to the war increasingly began to come from the general public. The conflict and domestic divisions stemming from the war dominated American politics during the late '60s and '70s. Facing challenges from antiwar senators Robert Kennedy and Eugene McCarthy, President Johnson decided not to run for reelection in 1968, and Vice President Hubert Humphrey lost in the presidential election to Richard Nixon. During the campaign, Nixon stated that he had a secret plan to end the war, but deaths continued after his inauguration, and the antiwar movement gained momentum. On October 15, 1969, millions of Americans took the day off from work or school to protest the war in what was billed as Moratorium Day. Publication in November, 1969, of news about the March, 1968, massacre of unarmed civilians at My Lai and subsequent revelations about the clandestine bombing of Cambodia increased public skepticism about the war. Whereas a 1966 Gallup poll showed that only 35 percent of the American public viewed U.S. participation in Vietnam as a mistake, by 1969 this figure had reached 52 percent.

The invasions of Cambodia in April–May, 1970, and of Laos in February, 1971, and the publication of the Pentagon Papers, a secret Defense Department report that revealed government duplicity about Vietnam, further increased American antipathy toward the war. President Nixon's "Vietnamization" policy, announced in November, 1969, reduced American troop strength in Vietnam from more than a half million when he took office in 1969 to about 150,000 by the end of 1971, partially defusing the antiwar movement. By 1971, however, polls showed that 61 percent of all Americans believed that the United States should not have become involved in Vietnam, and 58 percent considered the war immoral.

Divisions at home, of course, affected the attitudes of American soldiers in Vietnam. Some resented antiwar protests, others encouraged them, and still others disagreed but believed that they were part of the democratic process. But even GIs who disagreed with antiwar protesters were frustrated by the lack of progress in the war. As troop levels fell during the Nixon years, disillusionment among American soldiers grew. Many of those who remained in Vietnam wondered if they would have to give their lives in a war that their government no longer found critical.

The letters in this chapter, arranged in roughly chronological order, reflect the divided feelings of American soldiers about the war and show their reactions to public attitudes and politics at home. Each writer sought in his own way to answer a vital question: *Why am I here?*

LANCE P. SIJAN (1942–1968) of Milwaukee entered the U.S. Air Force Academy in 1961. Sijan began a tour of duty in Vietnam in July, 1967, flying Phantom jets on combat missions out of Da Nang (366th TFW). On November 9, 1967, he was shot down over Laos. With a broken hand and leg, Sijan evaded capture for forty-six days before he was taken prisoner by the North Vietnamese. While in a POW camp, Sijan remained a model of defiance, refusing to answer his captors' questions and repeatedly attempting to escape. He died of pneumonia, untreated wounds, and malnutrition on January 22, 1968. He posthumously received the Congressional Medal of Honor, one of only twelve members of the air force to be so honored for their service in Vietnam. While at the Air Force Academy, he wrote the following letter to his father, commenting in part on criticism of American involvement in Vietnam by former Federal Reserve Board chairman Marriner S. Eccles.

[February 13, 1966]

. . . I'm just trying to look at this article and many others like it that the American public accept at face value. I have seen "propaganda" from the other side. I have seen movies of the hostility and insane dogma that the VC possess. I have talked to officers that have been over there and have told me of the need that the South Vietnamese have for our help. I am convinced that we are not over there for personal gain. I am convinced that we are needed over there. I am also proud of the fact that we are a country that is proud enough to stand fast to its commitments and promises. Maybe I'm a little bit too tied up in this thing to see the big, overall picture, but I am a firm believer in Eisenhower's "Domino Theory." I don't want my kids to grow up under Communist rule. The Communists have to be stopped somewhere. Someone has to do it. The one thing that is good about all of this is that the American public is no longer apathetic about the world situation. Since Roman times great nations have fallen because of an apathetic, disinterested public spirit. They were always content to sit back, big, dumb, fat and happy and watch the world go by . . . until it was too late. This almost happened to us

Lance Sijan at the U.S. Air Force Academy. Courtesy Jane Sijan.

just before WWI. The "Isolationist Policy" kept us out of world affairs. But not really. The U.S. realized after this that they had a role in world affairs. A role of leadership. It's a big responsibility and not one without its hard knocks, including anti-U.S. demonstrations, flag burnings, and Peace demonstrations.

I'm sure you too can find many arguments to refute the things I have said here. I don't have time to debate the issue. I just thought I'd let you know a few of my feelings on this subject. Everyone has a right to his own opinions. These are mine. And that's what makes this country great. The fact that Eccles can say what he wants and I can say what I want are precisely the things that I would probably have to fight for some day ... in Vietnam or elsewhere. If for no other reason, I *have* to believe this way, in order to believe that what I am fighting for is right.

Love,
Lance

ANTHONY SUMINSKI (b. 1943), a native of Kansas, was living in Milwaukee when he enlisted in the Marine Corps in September, 1963. His first encounter with the burgeoning conflict in Vietnam occurred in January, 1965, when the ship on which he served was deployed to the Gulf of Tonkin. Corporal Suminski returned to Vietnam and served from March to September, 1966, as a machine gun squad leader (E Co., 2/5th Mar., 1st Mar. Div.) in Chu Lai. Following his discharge in September, 1966, he returned to Wisconsin and attended the Layton School of Art. He currently resides in New Berlin. In these two letters, he illustrates that American soldiers knew early on that the war would be long and hard.

March 10, 1966

Dear Mom & Dad,

We have been training with choppers for about a week. It's pretty dangerous, working with them in Vietnam. They say the complete chopper must unload within 8 seconds or be "downed" by fire. The VC will first aim at the door and then the pilot. We lost 15 choppers two days ago. . . .

The war will last many years. The communists over the last decade have painted the minds of Vietnam. "The U.S. wants to get your crops. The Marines are barbarians. The Imperialist U.S. desires domination." But we are gradually winning friends. Without the support of the Vietnamese the United States had better give up. A guerrilla could live in those jungles undetected all his life—if he had support of the people. But the people are catching on. "How can these Marines be barbarians. Why they fixed my roof. The old woman no longer has sores since their doctor with his strange medicines took care of her." So it's a slow job. A slow war. . . .

Your Son,
Tony

May 22, 1966
Dear Family,
Sunday morning the firefights are heard and even our mortars and artillery return fire. In any event it wakes you up.
The U.S. knows it cannot win on the scale and type of fighting we are employing. Every inch of ground must *physically* be controlled in order to have hold over the Communists. Since the manpower is not available the U.S. must fight a "negotiable war," in other words hold out until North Vietnam initially requests some form of appeasement. So many times on our patrols, sweeps, ambushes, the VC have returned the next day and set up shop again. We control so very little of Vietnam now and would need millions of men to put a stand against the countless that China could pour in. It is not the fact that Communism is being fought but the lack of interest shown by the Vietnamese that makes this war so difficult for the Americans here to see.
An example: We received sniper fire from a village and returned a heavy volume of fire killing one civilian and injuring two others. Then 10 minutes later the women were out there selling us soda just like they always have. It's really funny.
A few days ago a grenade set by VC exploded and killed one of my close friends and the villagers just kept trying to get 50¢ per Coke from us. It's not only the fact that no interest is shown on their part, this is understood by the fact that they lived with war for 20 years. But they seem to lack desire for a democracy which we are trying so hard to win for them. . . .

Your Son,
Tony

ROGER S. BOEKER (b. 1942) was raised in Madison and enlisted in the Marine Corps in August, 1965. He served as an educational noncommissioned officer (Hq. Co., Hq. Bn., 3d Mar. Div.) in Da Nang, Phu Bai, and Dong Ha from July, 1966, until his discharge in August, 1967. After the war he worked for several meat-packing companies, and he still lives in Madison. The following three letters to his family reveal his changing reactions to the growing antiwar sentiment and offers of humanitarian assistance to the communists as well as his thoughts on the ambiguities of war.

May 5, 1966
Dear Family,
. . . In reading your letter, I notice that the Governor [Warren Knowles]

makes mention of the people who are protesting the war. It's hard for
me to defend those who oppose our effort, I've lost good friends, ac-
quaintances, and commanders for whom I had the greatest respect. But
if our mission is to defend freedom, (dubious motive), it's not to defend
the freedom to think as I do just because I'm fighting. That's not freedom
at all. That is just playing king-of-the-mountain. The strongest person
dictates policy. We must and are defending everyone's freedom including
that of the dissenter. I don't believe in obstructionism to the majority
decision, but to make known alternatives and faults of present policy
is never wrong. It's also too easy to blame the clothes a man wears,
or his beard, or hair—for his opinion. If we ever lose the Sen Wayne
Morses and R.F.K.s [Robert F. Kennedy], God help us. . . .

Love,
Roger

October 12, 1966

Dear Family,
     . . . Something really burned me up and keeps gnawing at me. They
don't censor the news in the Stars and Stripes, and the whole Marine
Corps must have seen the article about the Quaker group who is sending medical supplies through Canada. TO THE NORTH VIET-
NAMESE. There are quite a few Marines in RVN who are of Quaker
descent. I'm sure it wouldn't take a week to find one of them laid open
at charliemed (3dMedBn). Then there's RFK who wants to send blood
to the N. Viets. How can they ask us to come here, and then provide
medical care for our enemy to insure that we have an enemy to fight?
The Red who lives to kill another Marine because he got Blood from
America has shown us precisely the calibre of mentality which a free
people elects to office. I can't do anything about it here but you can
certainly bet there'll be hell to pay by someone when I get back. I hope
that someone has the courage to do something back there, our morale
is dependent on precisely such issues. We can go without food, or luxury, but not without the support of our country, in spirit. My God, do
we have to give them that also. I'm afraid you'll have to ignore the voting
issue in your letters if you choose to vote for my brother's killers, I.E.
the democrats. Ask me to fight Russian jets and missiles and I will, but
don't give the Russians a billion dollars worth of my tax money in wheat
so that he can release farmers to make more and better fighters and
missiles. Ask me to live in a stinking hole on the other side of the world
and die if need be, and I will gladly. But don't give the aid and comfort
to the enemy that you so bitterly debate giving me. Ask me to defend

free people everywhere and I will. But don't let the free people everywhere give my enemy the support he needs to more effectively destroy me. . . .

Love,
Roger

June 11, 1967

Dear Family,

. . . A couple days before I left, I witnessed one of the truly suspenseful moments of my life. I mentioned before that a sergeant had been given life imprisonment for murdering a Vietnamese. He had claimed that the Lt. had given him the order to do so. The Lt's trial took place in the courtroom only four hutches down from mine. I looked in on as much as possible. I saw the Father of the Lt testify, the summations and instructions to the court. The Lt's father had been an immigrant from Germany who served in the OSS during WWII. In very broken English he told of the atrocities that he had observed; he said that all of this had been told to his son and that he had agreed about such things. He said that he could not imagine his son doing such a thing. There were six witnesses for the prosecution and one for the defense. The six gave testimony saying that the Lt. had given the order but could not agree as to time, circumstance, and other specifics. I believe the Lt's radio-operator testified that he had given no such order. The case really looked bad for the Lt. despite the counsel of a retired admiral, one civilian New York lawyer, and the Lt Col the Marine Corps provided. When the Court went into balloting it was adjourned for about 2 hours or so. I reviewed in my mind the rationale of the situation and tried to relate it to the way I generally shoot off my mouth about this place. I have said mentally and verbally, "Kill them all, none of them deserve to live." And you'd be surprised how easy it is to believe when you've seen a few friends, dead. If I put a notch in my rifle for every friend who died here, there wouldn't be a stock on it. While mulling these realizations, it dawned on me, as if no one had ever thought these things before, that Germans and Jews, Christians and Islam, Russians and Poles, Romans and Gauls, Americans and Japanese, ad infinitum, had each a relationship of the same foundation. That each had rationalized the efficacy of their own cause and the necessity of genocide. The Germans had said, "What good are these people," and I had said, "Of what worth are these Vietnamese." And I was ashamed. Ashamed that I had the potential to put my Father on a stand to beg for my life. Ashamed that all the learning availed me had not taught me basic respect for human life. Then I prayed that the court made the right decision. The court found him Not Guilty. Short claps, a great gasp, a moment I'll never forget ... I saw a man given his life with a few words.

But now, with the perspective of five days or so, I wonder how I can have been so awed and excited by that event. The lesson has dimmed. I know that my thoughts run along the same lines, that these things will happen again and again. Futility corrodes conviction; morals will be relative to a situation and modified by temporary emotion; justice is only the security of the lawgiver; something is wrong.... The family is all that is constant.

LOVE,
Roger

HOWARD M. SHERPE (b. 1944) grew up in Westby and lived in Madison prior to being drafted into the army in December, 1965. Sergeant Sherpe served as a field medic (4th Engr. Bn., 4th Inf. Div.) near Pleiku from July, 1966, to July, 1967. Following his discharge in November, 1967, he returned to complete his education at the Madison campus of the University of Wisconsin. Sherpe currently works as a commercial artist and lives in Madison. In this journal entry, he reflects on his participation in the war.

August 19, 1966

I've been doing a lot of thinking lately about why it is we are here and what we're fighting for. So far I have yet to see even one Vietnamese soldier fighting or even in the field. The only Vietnamese I've seen fighting are on the other side and the rest of the Vietnamese around here seem to be on their side too or helping them in one way or another. So who the hell is it that we're supposed to be trying to help. No one seems to want our help. They all seem to be against us, unless they want our money or a free handout. . . .

I guess personally, after seeing how the people live here, I'm fighting not for these people, but for the people back in the states, so they never have to live like this, and so our kids never have to be like this. Even the worst slums in America are better than the way most people live here. I guess I'm fighting for the continued freedom and prosperity of America. But then when I think about it, that doesn't make much sense either. How the hell is my being here helping America keep its freedom? To stop the dominoes they say. Stop the Communists here or they'll eventually take over America. That's a bunch of . . . bullshit! As far as I'm concerned, unless we quit trying to kill each other there won't be anyone left to rule the world.

I don't think anyone wants us here. From the sound of the news we get in the Pacific Stars and Stripes, the majority of Americans couldn't care less that we are here either. Everyone's against us. Be that as it may, I'm stuck in this . . . place now and I'm going to get in a few licks for me and my family and we'll let the dominoes fall where they may. . . .

In this letter to his family, ROBERT PETERSON expresses his anger on hearing about race riots and protests in the summer of 1967. (For a biographical sketch of Peterson, see chapter 3.)

Chu Lai, August 1, 1967

Folks & Kids

Greetings from riot-free Vietnam. I'm beginning to feel relatively safe over here considering the outbursts in Newark, Detroit, etc. I guess my tour of duty will prepare me for stateside living. I wish they'd turn our platoon loose on those rioters—we'd clean them up in a hurry, using a few tactics we picked up over here, which I'm sure these rabble-rousers

Robert Peterson writes home. Courtesy Joni Peterson.

have never seen. It sure is hell to read about the killings and lootings back home—people taking undue advantage of the freedoms we are guaranteeing them. If they don't like our country, send them to another one and let them try to make it—but no, they can only riot and protest in a country like ours, in a time when we need support, we get nothing but violence and anti-everything riots. Damn 'em all!! . . .

2 months or less.
Miss you all
Son & brother
Robert

GEORGE S. KULAS (b. 1947) enlisted in the Marine Corps in July, 1966, following his graduation from high school in Sheboygan. Corporal Kulas served as a communications operator (Communications Co., Hq. Bn., 3d Mar. Div.) in Phu Bai, Dong Ha, and Quang Tri from March, 1967, to December, 1968. Following his discharge from the marines in June, 1969, he returned to Sheboygan, where he received training as an accountant. In 1972 he again enlisted in the military, this time in the army, for which he worked as an accountant from 1972 to 1990, retiring as a sergeant major. He now works for the Wisconsin Department of Corrections and is a freelance author in Fond du Lac. Kulas chose to serve in Vietnam for an extra six months after his first year there, and he explains his reasons for extending his tour in this letter to his family.

February 14, 1968

Dear Mom, Dad & Mike:

I received your letter yesterday. I know you want me to do what is best. Believe me I thought about everything that could happen to me. I didn't make a split decision, but I think I made it slowly. I started making it last April when I was here. When I walked to work & walked past the dead bodies lying on the ground. It scared me then to see anything like that. It still scares me, but I have to learn what life is all about. Life is different to everybody. But it has to be hard in times because if it gets bad you live better when it's over with. I guess I can't explain it. If life was easy there would be no happiness, because a person won't know what it is to be without certain things.

I don't know what I'll do after I get out, but whatever it is I'll be a better person because I was here. I could come home now & forget about this place, but that's the easy way, that's the way I really feel.

There's a lot of people who think the young Americans, my generation, are a bunch of hippies, draft card burners & bums. But who's dying over here every day!

I'm not intelligent enough to know everything about this war or the facts behind it. But we're here & too many lives have been lost in it that we can just leave & say forget them, they died for nothing. Sure our Government only asks 1 year of everybody. But they leave it up to you if you want to stay. This is where the government doesn't decide, you decide. It doesn't make you a hero if you stay or certainly not a coward if you want to go home to America. But I want to stay, not because I'm so patriotic or anything like that. But because I think it's the best thing to do for myself as an individual.

It's possible I could be killed here, think of all the families that have lost someone here though. I'm one person & families have to accept it, that's part of life. God only knows what will happen & I'm willing to trust in him that I'll be kept safe.

So I'm glad you understand the way I feel & why I'm going to extend here.

I'm scared, every time I hear a gun go off or am told we might get hit tonight. But there's guys that are a lot more than scared. The ones who face the enemy & see their buddies get hit & watch them die. While some hippy paints himself up.

I'll write soon again & I'll be home soon.

Love
Georgie.

JAMES G. PICK (b. 1943) was raised in Watertown and was studying at Whitewater State University when he enlisted in the Naval Reserve in July, 1966. Pick served as a hospital corpsman striker and as a medical assistant on the USS *Prichett* (OC Div.) off the coast of Vietnam. He was discharged in December, 1968, and now works as a computer programmer in Fort Atkinson. In this letter to his parents, Pick comments on President Johnson's March 31, 1968, speech, in which he announced a reduction in the American bombing of North Vietnam that had continued intermittently since early 1965. Johnson also declared that he would not seek reelection, leaving Democrat Robert F. Kennedy (who was assassinated in June, 1968) and Republican Richard M. Nixon as the frontrunners in the upcoming presidential election.

April 8, 1968

Dear Mom & Dad

. . . I know about the bomb stopping and feel we should go one way or the other, really hit them hard or get out. If they don't come to the conference table willingly we should make them beg for it. I think this should be their last chance for peace talks. If they don't come now— knock the shit out of them, we got more than necessary to do the job and that's not even thinking of our nuclear force.

I heard Johnson decline the next term and in all honesty wish I could hear Nixon and Kennedy debate. I like Bob Kennedy. I also feel Nixon would be a good president. If Kennedy makes it at the convention it will be a damn interesting race. Both are outstanding men. If other countries think we are weakening ourself by changing in the stream—I think they had better grow up and look at reality. It will not take any time at all for either to show the world we've got a good president. I know each could fit the ticket. I hope one does. . . .

As Always & Love
Jim.

In the following excerpt from a tape recording sent to his wife, Jane, JOHN ABRAMS, a Navy helicopter pilot, reflects on the nature of the war and his role in it. (For a biographical sketch of Abrams, see chapter 1.)

June 6, 1968

. . . Well this war is a lot different than any other war. You could ask somebody from World War II or Korea if they ever killed anybody, and they'd probably say, "Well, I don't know." And they're probably telling the truth. They were firing at long ranges, long distances, to emplacements, this type of thing. This isn't that kind of war. This is a people-to-people war. We're firing from 600 meters away. We fire, we hit, we see what we hit. We see the results of our hit. We see the wounded, and of course we oftentimes see the dead. Of course, Charlie gives it back to us too. We take a lot of hits in the aircraft. Occasionally one of us gets it too. We've had three door gunners wounded—one of which died—since I've been here. I've been shot at quite a few times, and I think I've got a purple heart coming for a minor thing that happened here a couple weeks ago. There's nobody here that's not getting shot at, although this part of the war isn't as highly publicized as the part that's going on in the north. The part we're doing down here nobody wants to talk about. It's a dirty job. It's women, twelve-, fifteen-year-old boys and grown men that we're killing because they're killing Vietnamese and trying to kill us. Some of atrocities that Charlie commits are unbelievable. . . . And Charlie's unscrupulous. Yesterday, for example, we were cleared into an area where Charlie supposedly had an arms cache. We went into the area—sure enough, there was all camouflaged arms cache. So we went in, circled the area one time at high altitude, rolled into our strike. All of a sudden, people started running out of the hootches—we call them hootches, they're grass houses—running out of the hootches that this material was all stacked around. And every one of them had a saffron robe on. A saffron robe is a bright orange robe—kind of the color of a flight suit, if you remember what that looked like—that the Buddhist monks wear, every one of them. Now, what were Buddhist monks doing where there was a large cache of Charlie equipment, and no Buddhist pagoda around the area? Charlie's not dumb, but he's not smart either, really. They ran out of the hootch, ran across the rice paddy, and they never got any further. Now maybe there were some Buddhist monks among them. Possibly there were. And Charlie was trying to escape along with them. But they all got it. . . .

Charlie's pretty smart in one way. He knows we don't put in air strikes on pagodas, and temples, and this type of thing. So he'll hide all his arms caches in and around a pagoda. Well, we'll get intelligence from the Vietnamese that Charlie's got a big cache in a certain area, in a pagoda, and they'll get all the Buddhist monks out, at least the ones that aren't VC sympathizers—and many of them are—haul the people out and we'll put in an air strike. We hit a pagoda the other night. Put two rockets in. We had a secondary explosion that leveled the whole building. Found out later that we exploded a whole cache of 82 mm mortar shells. They went along with the VC district commissioner, who was in the building. . . .

About the only other thing I can say about this is that I guess this war, this life, changes your outlook. It's not a permanent change, it's probably a protective change. You learn to accept things, things that you never probably ever dreamed existed. Yet, some of the things you can't accept. I'd be lying if I told you that a lot of things that we've done, we've had to do, we've been told to do, haven't bothered me. I'd be lying if I told you that I haven't gotten out of the airplane and thrown up. But still, you get kind of embittered, you get kind of hardened. And unless there's some evening factor, some direction that you can point yourself to, something to look forward to—a letter, a recorded tape, something of this order, a word from home, a magazine, just maybe a written thought or a spoken word from someone who means a lot, means something to you—can change this whole thing, it can help you keep things in the proper perspective. Here again, this isn't a plea for you to write letters and send tapes. I know you're doing your best, and I appreciate it. I know how busy you are and how busy you keep yourself, and how varied your interests are, and how quickly time passes for you.

But I want you to know how much I truly appreciate the letters, the tapes, the essays, the things that you send. They mean an awful lot. . . .

June 7, 1968

I just got done flying the evening patrol a little while ago, and I listened to what I had to say last night. I guess there wasn't too much pretty, too much good that I had to say last night, especially with all that sniper fire going on. . . . I guess I sounded pretty grim, didn't talk about too much good last night. Maybe I should say something about the good we're doing here instead of just the destruction and the destroying. For example, one of the villages near here that recently was taken over by Charlie. The people evacuated the village, they got out, we went in, put in air strikes and leveled it—the school, primitive school that it was; the hospital, primitive hospital that it was, and the town. Well, the people moved back in and they rebuilt their hootches, their stores, primitive as all of them that there are, and we all chipped together, those of us here in the detachment, along with the sailors of the river section that drive the river patrol boats, we chipped in $10, $15, $20 apiece and bought supplies from USAID—that's United States Agency for Interna[tiona]l Development—bought supplies and rebuilt their school, a lot better than it was. It has a concrete floor, cinder block walls, blackboard, school supplies, desks we built out of old rocket boxes. They're a lot better off in that particular case than others, than they were. So you see that along with the destruction that we do, we try to do as much rebuilding for the worthy Vietnamese that we can, and there are plenty of worthy Vietnamese. . . . The PF, the Popular Forces, which are a militia set up of the townspeople from the various towns, are tenacious little fighters. They're mean little bastards. They hate the VC with a passion. VC come in and they steal from these people, they rape their women, they destroy their homes. That's why these people leave, try to get out as soon as they find out that Charlie's coming in. They hate them with a passion. . . .

MICHAEL A. BURKE (b. 1942) was raised in Madison and joined the army ROTC in June, 1964, while attending the University of Wisconsin. He received his law degree in 1967 and subsequently served as an attorney with the Staff Judge Advocate (Hq., II Field Force) in the Long Binh and Bien Hoa areas from August, 1968, to August, 1969. Captain Burke retired from the service in November, 1988, and currently lives in Madison, where he is an assistant district attorney for Dane County. During the 1960s, protesters demanding equal rights called America's attention to its racial problems. Thousands of miles from home, Americans in Vietnam encountered similar racial divisions. In these two letters to his mother, Burke comments on one man's unsuccessful protest against racism.

July 15, 1969

Dear Ma,

. . . I have managed to become involved in another messy officer case. A young second lieutenant soul brother has decided to quit the Army, because the government is not doing enough to end discrimination. I agree; but he entered into a contract through ROTC; and he can't quit for another year. He talked to me before he submitted his letter of resignation to his battalion commander, but he ignored my telling him that he was destroying himself and accomplishing nothing. He wouldn't even try to resign legally. Instead he gave the letter to his battalion commander, and refused to do any work. Major Kulish is delaying the drafting of charges, and is trying to arrange a talk with a well educated Negro major who intends to leave the Army as soon as he can. We hope that someone will be able to talk him out of his rebellion. He can't possibly do anything constructive, and I can't do anything for him. . . .

Love,
Mike

July 22, 1969

Dear Ma,

. . . My officer case may turn out better than could be forecast. Yesterday, my client finally decided that he had proved his point, and went back to work. Of course, he is still guilty of a crime, but he may be offered punishment under Article 15 rather than a court-martial. A court-martial is not likely to give him much of a sentence now that he has gone back to his duties. . . .

Love,
Mike

THOMAS J. DOWNS (b. 1945) grew up in La Crosse and enlisted in the air force in September, 1967. He served as a life support technician (510th TFS; 8th Attack Sqdn.) in Bien Hoa from August, 1969, to August, 1970. Discharged in October, 1971, Downs has worked in several fields, including inside sales, industrial supplies, and the garment industry. He currently lives in La Crosse.

In response to growing antiwar sentiment, President Nixon announced in the summer of 1969 that the number of U.S. troops in Vietnam would drop by 25,000 by the end of the year. While this action meant that fewer Americans would be at risk in Vietnam, it increased the danger for those who remained, as Downs explains in this letter to his wife.

[September 20, 1969]

Dear Sandy,

. . . The next troop pullout Nixon just announced won't help me, it will hurt me, because the support troops are always the last to go, and the more ground troops he pulls out, the less secure this base will be. All he's doing is laying us non-fighting troops bare for an attack, and as North Vietnam has just spelled out, they don't consider Air Force prisoners to be under the Geneva Convention—in other words, they have declared before the world that they will treat us not as prisoners of war but as they feel like treating us, and Nixon, not being here and one of us, will take it and not beat [the] hell out of them. He's made his answer by announcing his troop pull-out. He'll leave us to rot over here, and then make his excuses when we're wiped out, and what's worse, it will all be in vain because this country is doomed to defeat anyway. Without us, this country will fall, and without the Army and Marines, the Air Force doesn't stand a chance. Yet here he is pulling more ground troops. All that does is intensify my desire to get back to you. I don't want to die, and not because I wouldn't if I were single but because now that I've found what real love can do, I don't want to lose everything by dying before that love even has a chance to develop. I want to come home to you so badly that it's tearing me apart inside, and the worst part of it is, I know there's nothing I can do about it. I'm stuck here to sink or swim, and you can bet that if we get attacked I'll try to kill as many as I can, because I want to come home and every gook I kill makes home more a reality. I just hope I make it, so I can spit my venom at the service system with a pen, and maybe be instrumental in keeping another guy in my shoes from being sold down the river the way I'll be. . . .

All my love,
Tom

RONALD J. DOERING (b. 1946) lived in Kaukauna and worked as a radar technician prior to being drafted into the army in January, 1969. Corporal Doering ran convoys and village checkpoints (218th MP Co., 18th MP Bde.) in Nha Trang from November, 1969, to November, 1970, when he was discharged. After leaving the army Doering worked as a service technician at an auto dealership and with a telephone company, and since 1985 he has been employed by the Defense Logistics Agency. He currently lives in Franklin. The letter below is addressed to his girlfriend, Nancy Brautigam, who is now his wife.

Nha Trang, March 8, 1970
A Soldier's Lament
—Dedicated to the One I Love—

As I look out at the sea, with waves breaking white on the sand beach, I think of you. Across these crystal blue waters, another continent lies. A continent of peace, a place where freedom is a meaning not just a word. . . .

As a soldier, I am obligated to fight for my country, right or wrong. Maybe my country makes errors and mistakes but it is the best country in the world. Other countries look up to it for leadership, for aid, for counsel yet they condemn it at the same time. This could be the very clue that indicates our country is the best. The others are constantly complaining and criticizing it. They want what we have but they fail to realize what the men and women of our country had to forfeit and had to die for. We were strong, willing to do the ultimate, so our offspring could enjoy the fruits we had.

For generations after generations, there were wars. The American Revolution, The War of 1812, the Civil War, the Spanish-American War, World War I, World War II, the Korean Conflict, World War II, and now the Vietnam War. Why is there war? Why does it continue? Will it ever end? These questions are very hard to answer. There never will be an honest answer, only myths.

These wars, they are understood by the mothers of sons, the sons, and the loved ones of these sons. Yes, they have a clear picture of the true meaning of war! It is an insane institution! People dying for the wants of greedy individuals. These pigs are not satisfied with their power or borders. They want more and for some reason these individuals believe the end justifies the means.

In the process many people suffer undue hardship, many people die. Mothers mourn, wives mourn, loved ones mourn, and fathers are outraged. War reaches all directly or indirectly.

Our country had to put up with aggression since its birth. This country does not believe in aggression but it had to go to war over and over because of other countries. The fact is, we want to be peaceful and left alone but others do not see it this way. That is why our country is the best! We are willing to fight for what we have and for what we are, the greatest nation in the world!

As a soldier in Vietnam, I see much suffering, killing, and despair. My way of life has been altered because of this. All that I have been taught, all that I have experienced, and all the goodness I have known is twisted and distorted here in a war zone. People are not the same, they do cruel things, their culture is much different, their viewpoints are much different. Only those who have experienced war can truly understand the predicament of war. It changes history as well as men's lives. . . .

Your GI in Nam,
Ron

JAMES A. CARLSON (b. 1945) was living in Oconomowoc and working as a journalist prior to being drafted into the army in November, 1968. He served as a reporter for the *Ivy Leaf,* the newspaper of the 4th Inf. Div. (2–8th Inf.), in the central highlands from June, 1969, to July, 1970, when he was discharged. He subsequently returned to his career in journalism and lives in Milwaukee. By late 1969, when Carlson wrote this letter to his brother, the lack of a clear American strategy for Vietnam had become glaringly apparent to the men in country.

November 5, [1969]

Dear Ralph—

I'm writing you my first confidential-type letter because there have been some things going on here that you might want to hear about and perhaps consider in relation to the current pull-out and Vietnamization talk.

For the most part my first 4 months in Vietnam were really soft and safe. My battalion had almost no combat casualties in all this time and our assignments were mostly road security on well-paved highways. However, a month ago there was a sudden change in the situation when one company was sent to Plei Mrong, an infamous village 15 miles northwest of Pleiku. The company first stumbled onto what apparently was a company-size enemy bunker complex. Two platoons were out on a patrol on foot in the afternoon and one walked right into the complex and spotted 5 dinks cooking chow around a fire. There was a firefight. We had a man killed and we got 6 NVA. Then there were small events—a few snipers and "enemy movement" reports—for the next week. Finally the same company hit another at least company-size enemy force, only this time the men were on APCs and the enemy was dug in for an ambush. The NVA have a weapon called the B40 rocket which they use to great advantage against our tracks. The rocket can go right through a track, and it explodes throwing shrapnel all over. They have all kinds of these rockets in the Plei Mrong area—I mean they have a lot of them. Well, I won't go into more details. We've had about 13 killed in the past 2 weeks and there have been many other casualties, with a lot of guys going home due to wounds—lost eyes, arms, legs—the whole gruesome lot. We apparently originally hit either a battalion or regimental NVA

Jim Carlson. Courtesy Jim Carlson.

headquarters, and each of our companies has been ambushed by company-size units. We've used artillery & air strikes and killed a lot of enemy troops—I think it's at least 200 and this is a fairly accurate count. Now I believe the enemy has split into squad & platoon size groups while the big leaders have most likely moved back into the mountains around the Cambodian border. But these small units with B40s can still cause us tremendous problems.

So that's the situation. As for me, I've played it pretty safe. Most of the time I am either at out battalion headquarters at Plei Mrong or at base camp. I've been out with 2 companies in the boonies for 2 days each, but I didn't see any real action. I hope it stays that way. So while most people back home think there is a lull in the war and think the war is slowly petering out, for the 2d of the 8th it has just started. We don't know how long we'll stay in this area. Activity has increased all around us lately, so we might be here a while. I am just lucky that I'm not out in the boonies with the other infantrymen—seven days a week,

come what may, seeing your buddies hit and just having to go on. I've
seen a lot lately. You see people change. You see guys jump at the sound
of a mortar firing—not just jump, but a guy's whole body makes a nervous twitch, a ducking motion. You see people really scared—leaders
who don't want to lead and soldiers who don't want to go—all becom-
ing harder and tougher and better, but no more willing. And then I watch
the commanders with their maps, designing attacks, patrols, and other
tactics, thinking they're doing well according to the kill ratios. It all em-
phasizes the big question of what we are fighting for. The answer—our
lives and our friends here. U.S. Policy means nothing because it was
simply a blunder on the part of the government. Most guys here would
agree that the biggest crime of the whole deal is this lack of definite
purpose—we didn't have it when we got drafted and we don't now.

Maybe I shouldn't burden you with this stuff, but I know you will
be able to accept it as information—a report on a sad state of affairs
that should never be repeated. . . .

Our recent action hasn't been all bad. Our reenlistment sergeant won
an award for having the highest number of re-ups in the brigade. Of
course, when a guy re-ups he can choose a new MOS or specialty, and
I think our guys have decided on non-combat MOSs. In other words,
taking 3 more years to get out of their present spot. Sorry to send you
such a gloomy-type letter. As I said before, I am learning a lot and this
is one bright spot in it. . . .

All for now
Jim

On November 3, 1969, President Nixon made a speech in which he
elaborated his plans for the Vietnamization of the war. American troops
would gradually be withdrawn from Vietnam, and the war would be turned
over to South Vietnamese fighters, who would then determine the fate of
their country. In the wake of this announcement, platoon leader BOB ROCK
wrote his reactions in the following journal entry. (For a biographical sketch
of Rock, see chapter 1.)

[November 5, 1969]

There were a lot of disappointed faces as we listened to Nixon's speech
on 3 Nov. We all knew he was right but still felt discouraged. I listened
to the whole thing with mixed emotions. There's no doubt in my mind
I want to be Home but at the same time I can't say, nor can any of my
platoon, whether we'd support Nixon or demonstrate against the [war]
but we're all convinced we'd do one or the other. Too many people are
apathetic to the situation over here. Take for instance Dodgeville or any

Bob Rock. Courtesy Bob Rock.

other hometown USA for the fighting troops over here. I'd be thrilled to death if once I could read in the Chronicle that Dodgeville took a stand on the war over here. It wouldn't make a difference which stand—but be heard.

To the majority over here maybe it doesn't make that much difference but to the "line doggies," the infantryman, it matters. These are the men dying here. If they're dying in vain then do your best to put an end to the war. If the cause is justified then let him know he's fighting for something worth dying for.

To the situation at hand—our (my platoon) main mission is to stay alive. We're fighting in place of a prideless ARVN Army. There's no doubt in my mind the ARVN fighting force cannot withstand the enemy for any length of time, let alone, defeat him. At present, we're in a backup (reinforcing) position waiting for ARVN forces to get overrun.

Another factor which adds to the anxiety of the fighting man's position is that the general populace, the rice farmers, the plantation owner, the cattle herder, will exist & continue to function regardless of the type of government set up in VN. I'm convinced that the U.S. is here, not because of a regard or consideration for the VN people and their way of life as some would like the public to believe. If it was, the program here would be different. We're here for personal reasons, the most important of which is the fact that WE don't want a communist government in this strategic location in the world.

Personally, I'm here because I want to live in my home, the U.S. &
not because of some idealistic goals our superiors apparently believe in.

PHILIP A. KALHAGEN (1947–1970) lived in Madison before enlisting in the
army in 1966. A career soldier, he married a Korean woman and lived in
that country prior to being sent to Vietnam. He served as a staff sergeant on
an armored personnel carrier (HHC, 1-61st Inf., 1st Bde., 5th Inf. Div.
[Mech.]) at Quang Tri from July, 1969, until June 19, 1970, when he was
killed in action. The following two letters to his parents offer his assessment
of the U.S. war strategy, its South Vietnamese allies, and the invasion of
Cambodia.

November 21, 1969

Dear Mom & Dad

Well I got back from the field today and just have to write to you.
I got the package that you sent me but Charlie got it too! That's right
while I was out in the field Charlie [h]it the base camp with Rockets
& mortars and the Mail that was coming to the field was lying outside
a bunker. They said there was black olives & ravioli lying all over. Thanks
so much for the package but I guess Charlie just didn't want me to enjoy it. A can of tomatoes & the Jalapenos & parts of Liz's date nut bread
was left & we ate that. Things up here are pretty hairy now, contact
every day. I suppose you read about it in the papers. Largest push in
the DMZ since the bombing halt. We were right in the middle of it.
Thank God we only had one man slightly wounded. The line companies
got hit real hard. One company has 39 men left in it. Lost 3 Company
Commanders in the battalion. What happen is that our battalion ran into
a NVA Regiment. It's really a messed up war. And I can't agree with
it at all. The way I see it we'd have to lose 300 GIs a week for the next
5 years and then it would all be under the pretense of helping these crum-
my bastards. They have no guts and they are corrupt as hell. Sometimes
they scare me more than the NVA. If we'd invade N. Vietnam and push
them back into the stone age I could see it but I can't [understand] what
we are doing now and that is nothing but killing more GIs.

3 battalions came to relieve us 2 days later. One from the 101st & 2
ARVN. Those choppers were the most beautiful sight in the whole world.
Well thanks to Chuck I also missed my R & R. They couldn't even get
choppers in for the dead & wounded let alone me. So I missed it. But
they got me a new one I leave for Korea today. I fly home the 24th.
Well that's all for now. I'll write while I'm home.

Love
Philip

P.S. Don't worry I'm fine, just very tired.

May 2, 1970

Dear Mom & Dad—

. . . Things over here are about the same as they have been for the past month, off again on again sometimes hairy, sometimes very dull & lonely. Everyone over here is wondering what will happen next. What a hell of a way to fight a war. But then for this unit, it's the only one we've got. Everybody is happier than a pig in garbage over Nixon's decision to go into Cambodia. It's about darn time we did it. It should have happened long ago.

. . . I'm sure that I'd never recognize Madison though and I'm sure that I wouldn't recognize the people. The city was much quieter when I was there. Speaking of quietness the newspaper we get over here had an article on how quiet Madison is not anymore so I ripped it out and am sending it to you. . . .

Your Son
Philip

JOHN R. GMACK (1951-1970) a native of Green Bay, worked in a department store before enlisting in the army in August, 1969. Gmack served as an infantryman, artillery observer, and radio operator near Quan Loi and in Cambodia from February through May, 1970 (A Co., 1-8th Cav., 3d Bde., 1st Cav. Div. [Airmobile]). On May 28, 1970, just a week after writing the second letter below, Gmack died of wounds sustained in a field accident.

March 18, 1970

Dear Mom & Dad:

This is going to be short but to the point because of lack of paper and daylight.

As of now I have made up my mind about re-upping and I think my decision will stand but I'll wait for [Senator William] Proxmire's reply. My answer is yes, I gonna re-up. For the following reasons.

1. In the last 11 days we have had 3 killed and 17 wounded. Call Kathy and she'll give you the details on them because I don't care to write it again.
2. I lost a friend today—killed—shot in the head (goes with #1).
3. Everybody including my squad leader says to re-up.
4. If I stay 11B I'll probably end up here for a second tour.
5. I WANT TO STAY ALIVE!!!

So that's my decision. You asked in your letter today how many guys in AIT were drafted. All but about 5. Storm is the same as me and he's going to re-up with me. . . .

John Gmack. Courtesy Bob and Gert Gmack.

Sorry this was so to the point but the conditions here are forcing me to and I have about 7 more letters to get out.

Write Soon
Love
John.

May 21, 1970

Dear Mom & Dad:

. . . You asked what I thought about the demonstrations. Well I think most of them are good. After all the people who are demonstrating are the ones who have Vietnam to look forward to! They also are letting the "brass" know what *many* people over here think too!, because once you're in the army your ideas and thoughts don't mean *anything!*

So more power to 'em.

Not much more
Love
John

STEVE PLUE, an infantryman recovering from wounds sustained in battle, disagreed with Gmack's assessment of the antiwar protesters, particularly in the aftermath of the events at Ohio's Kent State University on May 4, 1970, when National Guard troops fired upon demonstrators protesting the invasion of Cambodia, killing four students. (For a biographical sketch of Plue, see chapter 1.)

May 24, 1970

Dear Folks:

. . . They took my bandages off yesterday and the other side of my head looks like Frankenstein with all those stitches. . . .

Tomorrow I'll probably be presented my Purple Heart and all the ceremonial stuff.

Wish they'd bring my mail to me. Sure would like to hear from home. . . .

Been catching up on my news reading and it makes me sick and angry about the young people and their demonstrations.

When they protest this Cambodia issue they just don't realize.

I wish they could experience what some of these soldiers do and they'd realize you can't fight an enemy with boundaries.

I really feel Nixon's finally getting his head out of his ———— and doing some major steps in ending this thing even if we have to push beyond the 20 mile line or even as far as Laos. Can't these kids see that we just can't up and leave all of a sudden without losing what we've accomplished so far. I don't see how the police, citizens and schools can tolerate such actions on the campuses. Things worse than Kent U. killings will happen if they don't practice peaceful rallies or such actions.

Oh H—— with them just makes me madder to talk about them.

Well have to go again. Stay well everyone.

Love
Steve

In this letter to his parents, ED BEAUCHAMP, an infantryman, expresses his feelings that the war is wrong and that Americans don't care about those who were fighting it. (For a biographical sketch of Beauchamp, see chapter 2.)

June 8, 1970

Hi Everyone

. . . I had a weird dream last night that when I came home to friends & everyone I was greeted with a welcome home like as if I were on a vacation. And then I wanted to tell them about this place but I saw it was no use because they weren't directly affected so they didn't care. To them it was only news. I've learned how to appreciate what I had & to understand people a little more. After seeing these people & how they live I really feel more strongly that we shouldn't be here, that we haven't the right to decide what's right or wrong for other people. We can't even take care of our own country much less someone else's.

I thought I better stop. I was getting a little carried away. It's just that I feel the army is a dictatorship in a democracy. . . .

Lots of Love & I miss you all.

No 1 son

Ed

DENNIS L. BOYER (b. 1949) grew up in Pennsylvania and enlisted in the army in November, 1967. He performed tactical scale studies with the area analysis branch, terrain section, of the Combined Intelligence Center of the MACV. Based in Saigon, he worked on missions throughout Vietnam as well as in Cambodia and Laos from July, 1970, until he was discharged in July, 1971. In 1978 he moved to Milwaukee to work as a Milwaukee Road freight carman. He currently lives in Dodgeville and runs the government relations program for a labor union in Madison. In the following two letters to a Vietnam veteran friend, Boyer expresses frustration over the disparity between government pronouncements and what he observed about the American presence in Cambodia and Laos.

Somewhere near Svay Rieng, Cambodia, October 10, 1970

Dear Pete:

Just a quick note. As you can see from my dateline our President is not truthful about GIs being out of Cambodia. Surprise!

Actually, I'm not supposed to be over here. On kind of a private mission as I explained earlier. Hopped a ride with some Army 1st Aviation Brigade friends.

No fighting right here (or I'd be gone!). Artillery in the distance. Strange stories over here. The war seems more brutal here than Vietnam, if that's possible. Mutilations, hacked up corpses. In Vietnam it seems like it all comes down to bullshit politics. Over here the Khmer Rouge sound more like bandits and psychos. . . .

Well, I'll let you know if anything else happens over here in looney land.

Take care,

Dennis

Saigon/Tan Son Hoa, April 18, 1971

Pete:

. . . By the time you get this you'll probably be reading about what we called Lam Son 719 (the invasion of Laos). You'll also hear the usual crap about no Americans going over. I know some Marines went over, some Rangers, and quite a few helicopter assault units. I'd say maybe 2000 GIs in with the ARVNs.

The whole thing was a big mess. The ARVNs really got beat up. Their taking over here is a big joke.

By the way you should have seen all the bones and skulls that engineers plowed up on roads and landing strips up there. Some of them of the size of Americans, probably Marines from 3 years ago. Then they say they can't find the missing.

I think up to now I thought of all this as a dumb game run by shitheads. Now it's finally sank in for me that lots of people are getting hurt. I'm a little slow, right?

Going in up there the huey got shot at, tracers right by the door. Guys got wasted up there over really stupid stuff. I saw stuff that finally just made me blow up. What happened then still scares me. We'll talk when I get back.

Up to now you could call me "disgruntled." Now I'm 100% pissed off. Me and some of the others at CICV have started to send maps, documents, and pictures to Senator [George] McGovern's office. Don't worry you'll get everything he gets. By the way we are starting to put McGovern bumper stickers on hueys, jeeps, and trucks. It's driving the lifers crazy.

While I was up north my attitude changed. I'm not going to study forestry. I think it will be political science or law. Somebody's got to stop stuff like this. I slept in a hangar up north. At night I heard people come and go. When I woke up there were bodies laid out around me. Don't mean a fucking thing, right? . . .

> Hanging in there,
> Dutch

In this letter to his family, JOHN KOEPPEN, an infantryman, described the effect on American troops of the trial of Lieutenant William Calley for the massacre of unarmed civilians at My Lai. (For a biographical sketch of Koeppen, see chapter 2.)

February 1, [1971]

Blood—

. . . Our new area of operation is just within spitting distance of Long Binh. It's about 20 miles from Long Binh and it's right along Hy 1. We probably will be working alot of rubber and banana groves and working around the villages. There supposedly is two VC (Leaning) villages in our area. The area is pretty heavily populated and naturally the rules of war are different. From our viewpoint the new situation is going to be tough and there is no room for any error. It all boils down to using your head and we can't engage until the enemy is positively identified or we are shot at first. Naturally with the My Lai trials and stuff, everybody is a little leery of what to do. The only sure thing is that we are really going to bend over backwards to protect the innocent civilians in the area. So much for the tactical situation. . . .

Love
John

KENNETH M. ANDERSON (b. 1937) grew up in Florence and volunteered for the draft in 1956. He served as an army A-Intel sergeant and LRRP member (5th SFG) during his two tours of duty in Vietnam from December, 1968, to December, 1969, and December, 1970, to December, 1971. Since his discharge in 1976, Anderson has worked in oil field sales and service and as a letter carrier. He currently lives in Fort Worth, Texas.

May 2, 1971

Dear Mom Joe and boys,

. . . Anyone who says this war is over with is out of their ever loving mind. Flying over the A Shau valley and over Laos where we put in teams, Charlie has complete control and would you believe four lane roads and he really uses them. He has radar controlled anti-aircraft guns all over the place, tanks, armored personnel carriers and the whole works in these areas.

Our areas where we are working are getting so bad that we can't even get the teams on the ground. Every open area, Sir Charles has got covered by ground fire. He's been tearing up our people, & our choppers. We had a 7 man team get hit a week and a half ago by a company sized unit and the only thing that saved the three that got out was they stacked up the NVA Bodies in front of their positions so Charlie couldn't get them.

If you hear Charlie is a dumb stupid ignorant person that can't fight, or don't know how to fight, or doesn't have modern equipment, don't believe it, because most of them are highly motivated and dedicated to their cause. Every one of us have a high respect for charlie and we know how dangerous he can be. Once he knows we are on the ground in his area, he'll just keep hunting until he finds us and then he'll try and wipe us out or to take prisoners. He really likes to get after our people because we work in such small units. We only go out with 6 to 8 people. Usually two Americans and the rest Commandos who have worked with us since we've got into this war.

They have taken our berets away from us but you can better believe that we'll be here running this type of war long after the other people move out. We have probably got one of the most dangerous jobs in Nam, for the simple reason we are fighting with the little people. . . .

Your very loving Son
Ken

GREGORY E. "SANDY" CUSTER (b. 1945) was raised in Madison and enlisted in the air force in April, 1968, receiving his commission two months later. Captain Custer flew cargo planes between the United States and Vietnam prior to receiving permanent assignments at Cam Ranh Bay (458th Tactical Airlift Sqdn.) and Phu Cat air base (483d Tactical Airlift Wing [Forward Operating Location]) from September, 1971, to September, 1972. He flew airlifts to fire support bases and worked as a flight instructor with South Vietnamese pilots. Custer received his discharge in June, 1973, and attended dental school at Marquette University. He currently lives and practices dentistry in Mequon. Custer sent the following two letters to his family commenting on the final stages of the war.

December, 1971

Several of you have asked about the war. Here are some reflections ...

Though not very religious in a conventional sense, throughout my adult life I've always found myself reflecting on things of deep meaning to me at Christmastime. The feeling of good will, love and family togetherness found during the Christmas season forces one to reflect upon the motives of his own ways, his lack of effort in performing good deeds, in general, his failing to live up to his responsibilities as a human being.

The common expression here in Vietnam is that Christmas only exists in the "world." For myself, I find that can't be true, as this year especially I need the soul cleansing process of the Christmas season.

As a pilot and an officer my view of the war has been distorted. I return each night to my air-conditioned room, to eat well prepared food, almost embarrassed by the contrast of my circumstances to those circumstances I see during my daily flights.

No matter how much I disapprove of this war and no matter how much I hate everything it represents to me, it must be recognized that there are a lot of heroes here, in the conventional sense, that will spend the rest of their lives unrewarded, bewildered and frustrated by the war around them. These boys, remember many are about Bob's age, have lived in jungles, in filth, in fear and they have performed well for the most part. I've carried them into action and I've seen the looks on their faces. I feel our slow withdrawal has hurt many of them. We've pulled them out of combat to keep the casualties low (We see this in the lower body counts), however, we haven't sent them home as fast as we've pulled them out of combat. This leaves a lot of free time on their hands which has resulted in increased drug addiction, VD varieties for which no cures have been found and disgusted, disillusioned young men. This waste of personnel is not just an Army problem. . . .

The poverty of Vietnam doesn't shock me. I've seen similar poverty in other underdeveloped nations I've visited as well as our own United States. However, the way we've helped perpetuate that poverty is astonishing. Mile after mile of natural resources that will be unusable for years. Whether the defoliation has actually helped in a military sense I can't answer. However, to fly over the defoliated jungle is to question again the sanity of the human race. The pock marked rice paddies, where the water buffalo can move only with great difficulty is also a depressing sight.

Part of the reason I have a hard time adjusting to this war is that I don't hate the Vietnamese. Most Americans refer to them as zips, gooks and Nguyens, friend and foe alike. There isn't much consideration for the feelings, thoughts or religious beliefs of the Vietnamese. The typical American is here for a year and wants to win the war in that year. He doesn't care what is left when he leaves. The Vietnamese have been living with this war for years and expect it to last for years more. The impatience of the Americans is a mystery to the Vietnamese.

Since I've been in Vietnam I've flown many missions that were purely for paper purposes. While I like to stay away from war stories let me just say that a person resents risking his life for the sake of logging another combat sortie for statistical purposes. We are so phased down right now that there are only a few missions left that warrant risking men and equipment. However, each day we fly a certain number of missions just to keep the planes in the air. It is my belief, after talking to pilots from other organizations that about half of the Air Force flying people could leave Vietnam tomorrow without depreciating the war capability. Every organization is overmanned for their mission. Why?

I've met some of the finest people I've known in my entire life here in Vietnam. Fine, intelligent, mature men who would make excellent career officers for the Air Force. This war is driving them from the service in droves. Believe me, the service needs them. We want military men with conscience and ability. The future of our military will certainly suffer for this war.

While entertaining these thoughts I've tried to stay away from the Communist threat and the international problems involved. I'm not schooled in these areas as I'm not schooled in the military "big picture." I've tried to explain some things as I've seen them and as I've interpreted them. Believe me, this Christmas, more than any in the past, I feel it from deep within me when I wish us PEACE ON EARTH.

Sandy

May 3, 1972

Hello Mom and Dad,

. . . Dad, you mentioned the extra Navy men on board ship and extra air force in Thailand that don't count as Americans in Vietnam. There are also thousands of people here on Temporary duty, here for 3–6 months at a time but not on the official rolls as they're on "temporary" duty and not "permanent" duty. What a bunch of lies they tell.

Speaking of lies—I don't know what they're telling you at home about this offensive but it is hell, and everyone is fighting for their lives and American air power does not make up for poorly disciplined armies. Every time I fly I see or hear someone on the radio in a lot of trouble who should be home in the U.S. with his wife and family. Oh well—vote peace.

Take care
Love,
Sandy

Under President Nixon's Vietnamization program, American troops steadily withdrew from Vietnam throughout 1970 and 1971. At the beginning of 1972, 156,800 U.S. soldiers remained in country, and that number dropped to 24,200 over the next twelve months. These reductions caused problems for those who remained behind, as HELEN WEIDNER, a Special Services worker, describes. (For a biographical sketch of Weidner, see chapter 2.)

February 19, 1972

Dear Mom and Dad,

. . . I got upset today. One of the companies that is standing down, pulling out, gave all their equipment to the Vietnamese trash men. There was office equipment & old mattresses, but also live rounds. I'm prejudiced against getting killed by an American made bullet. If Charlie wants me dead he can at least use his own AK-47 rounds instead of an M-16 round that the local VC trash man gives him. That stuff will all be in charlie's hands by tonight. You bet I was mad. I went & reported to my SSO [Special Services officer] who reported to the colonel who jumped on the Major. I suppose I shouldn't have gotten the major in trouble, but I think he should have a little consideration for those of us who have to stay here a few more months. He's leaving next week & just wanted to get rid of his company stuff the easiest way possible. I'm sure this is happening all over country. There's so much time & paperwork to turning stuff in to the army PDO [property disposal officer] dump that the companies standing down let anyone have it. They don't care; they're going home. Funny, a standdown used to be when a company came in from the field for a few days, like 3, after several months of combat. They would come back to base, get a hot shower, new fatigues & weapons, see a movie, get drunk for 3 days, then go back out for several more months of humping the boonies. . . . Now standing down is final. The colors are struck, the books closed, equipment & men are reassigned to new divisions. Some units Keystone—the whole unit, men & equipment, are reassigned to the states together.

. . . There's an across the board speedup to meet Nixon's quotas. No consideration is given to how critical a man's MOS is (Military Occupational Specialty). Some guys don't even want the drop, but they are no longer given the option of refusing it. Some want to stay for the money, or to date a local girl, but they're sent home.

. . . Phu Loi closes in less than 2 months. Already whole areas of buildings are vacant, the doors blocked by a white board with red lettering forbidding entry. Parts of the base look like a ghost town. Today's good friend who has promised to be at the picnic Saturday is gone tomorrow. It can be an emotional drain. . . .

Love,
Helen

On January 25, 1973, the Paris peace accords were signed, officially ending direct U.S. participation in Vietnam as well as military assistance to South Vietnam. Over the next sixty days, all American combat troops were withdrawn from the country. In the following letter, Weidner describes the final months of the war.

January 29, 1973

Dear Mom & Dad,

The war has never been so bad as since the peace was declared. You've heard already—TSN was rocketed Sunday AM. Also Bien Hoa, Pleiku, Da Nang. Heavy fighting in Tay Ninh. Sunday 4 helicopters were shot down. Two were birds coming to pick up peace teams, & striped white to indicate that. . . .

The VC have moved on post, as part of the 4-party military supervision team. They carry weapons & wear arm bands identifying them as VC. We are not allowed weapons, & not even allowed to have protective gear. All flak jackets & helmets had to be turned in Sat night. I'm tempted to write my congressman about that one.

. . . Deadlines are hitting fast. The pools, libraries, other non-essential services closed Sunday 28 Jan, which is X day. It is a statement of the army's attitude toward Service Clubs that they've asked us to stay open as long as possible. Our guys, 59th C[orps] A[viation] C[ompany], are the ones doing the flying. One friend was asked if he'd stay in Nam past 60 days to rescue POWs. He asked if they meant rescue men before or after they became POWs. They said before. That means they expect more aircraft to be shot down & pilots to be in danger of capture by still-hostile forces.

In closing, no matter how long we'd like to stay, we are dependent on other units for support. We need trucks from the motor pool, for instance, to haul out the furniture after we close. So we have to close before the motor pool does. With luck we'll stay open thru February. It's uncertain. We'll all be gone by early March. . . .

Wisconsin newspapers record the shocking events in Saigon that took place on the first day of the Tet Offensive.

5

1968: The Tet Offensive and the Siege of Khe Sanh

The Tet Offensive

Just as politics at home affected GI morale, perceptions of the progress of
the war in Vietnam helped mold public opinion in America. Two events in
1968—the Tet Offensive and the siege of Khe Sanh—attracted substantial
media coverage. Ironically, while Tet and Khe Sanh were major military
defeats for the Viet Cong (VC) and the North Vietnamese army (NVA), a
substantial portion of the American public perceived them as setbacks for
the United States and began to turn against the war.

On January 30–31, 1968, the VC, supported by the NVA, broke their own
holiday cease-fire agreement and launched an unprecedented number of
surprise attacks across South Vietnam. Nearly 84,000 enemy soldiers boldly
infiltrated and attacked the south's cities, including coastal Da Nang, Qui
Nhon, and Cam Ranh Bay, all supposedly beyond the reach of enemy
attack. They also assaulted numerous provincial capitals, district towns, and
hamlets in an attempt to severely undermine U.S. pacification programs.
The communists expected that the Army of the Republic of Vietnam
(ARVN) forces would defect and join the VC/NVA and that the South
Vietnamese people would rise up against both the United States and their
own government. With more than half of ARVN's troops furloughed for the
holiday and with substantial numbers of American forces moved to the
northern provinces, cities in the south were indeed vulnerable to attack.

Saigon, the seat of the South Vietnamese government, and Hue, the old
imperial capital, were hit especially hard by the Tet Offensive. With little
resistance, the communists invaded Hue on January 31 and then proceeded
with a horrible bloodbath, killing more than 3,000 civilians and foreigners
in their attempt to take the city. It took nearly a month of intense house-to-
house fighting for the U.S. Marines and ARVN forces to regain Hue.

Although shorter than the battle for Hue, the fighting in Saigon captured
the attention of the American public and changed the course of the war. In
addition to citywide confrontations, VC commandos blasted a hole in the
wall of the U.S. embassy at 3:00 A.M. on January 31 and moved quickly
into the building's courtyard. American forces resecured the embassy after
six and a half hours of fighting, but images of gunfire in the embassy
compound shook America. Then, on February 1, an Associated Press
photographer and a South Vietnamese cameraman captured one of the war's
most memorable images. As General Nguyen Ngoc Loan, the chief of South

Vietnam's national police, patrolled the city's chaotic streets, his men brought a VC officer to him. Loan immediately shot the man in the head at point-blank range. The next day, American newspapers published the still photograph, and NBC ran an edited film of the execution on the nightly news.

Despite the allied success at repulsing the offensive by February 10, the gruesome images from Saigon shocked the American public and increased antiwar sentiment. The VC had been decimated, and the South Vietnamese people did not join the insurrection, yet media images of the offensive left an unprecedented number of Americans wondering if the United States should be involved in Vietnam. After Tet, public support for the war effort began to erode. President Lyndon Johnson appointed Creighton Abrams as General William Westmoreland's replacement in Vietnam, and the president announced on March 31 that he would not run for reelection. While a complete military failure for the North Vietnamese, the Tet Offensive burst the belief of many Americans that U.S. forces were winning the war and that the troops would soon come home. The following letters contain the reactions of seven individuals who experienced the Tet Offensive as it burst upon Da Nang, Kontum, Pleiku, Quang Tri, Ai Tu, and Qui Nhon.

CHARLES ALGER (b. 1944) was born in Thorp and was attending Eau Claire State University when he enlisted in the Marine Corps in December, 1966. Alger served at a photo interpretation facility (Mar. Composite Recon. Sqdn. 1) in Da Nang from January, 1968, to February, 1969. He was discharged in December, 1970, and now lives in Solon Springs, where he works in sales.

January 30, 1968

Dear Mom & Dad.

I imagine you heard about the rocket attack on the base at Da Nang on the radio & TV. It sure was a rude way to be woken up. They started the attack at 3:30 in the morning. I heard the sirens blowing and a rocket whistling over head, I jumped out of bed grabbed my helmet and ran into the bunker right alongside the hut. It sure is a weird sensation to hear the rockets whistle over the top of you and explode. They hit a flare storage dump about ¾ to 1 mile from our huts. It was just like daylight when it caught fire. It burned for about an hour. I am sure glad I wasn't at work last night as they took quite a few hits at the hangars. Some of the guys that were working said they did quite a bit of damage to aircraft & hangars. They also hit a fuel storage tank. I sure am glad none of the rockets fell short of their targets as they hit the ammo dump about a ¼ mile from my hut. This morning a fire restarted there and a lot of small arms ammunition went off.

This morning we all stood outside and watched our planes make bombing runs on some trapped VC, the bombs exploding shook our hut so they weren't too far away.

All in all it wasn't too bad. I am fine, though I was a little scared last night, but everyone else was too. It's a strange feeling.

Well I better close for now as I start work tomorrow and I better get some sleep. I just wanted to let you know I was okay & it wasn't as bad as the newspapers most likely made out it was.

Love
Charles

Sergeant LARRY BUETER was serving as a draftsman in Da Nang when he wrote the following letter to his parents. (For a biographical sketch of Bueter, see chapter 1.)

February 1, 1968

Dear Mom and Dad,

Just a short note to let you know I'm alright. I suppose you've been hearing a lot about the Da Nang area, and probably all of Vietnam. The reason is because of the Vietnamese new year, and VC's efforts to end the old year on a good note. It's supposedly good luck for them to do something successful just before the new year.

So they co-ordinated their efforts all over the country, trying to capture or blow up all our major commands. So far they haven't succeeded, but they're still trying. Some of the hard-core NVA tried to get through our perimeter the last couple nights, but didn't make it. They captured control of the ville just outside our compound, so our planes and jets blew up the whole place yesterday. There's a real war going on over here now, as we have to wear our flak jacket and helmet everywhere we go. The last two nights we've spent in the bunkers and extra guards have been put on the perimeter. But, I guess for the most part it's all over now, as we're beating them pretty bad.

A lot of guys are saying that this was their last big effort to get a major victory. They didn't make it and supposedly the end of the war is close at hand. I sure hope so. . . .

Love,
Larry

Chief Warrant Officer DAVE OLSON was a helicopter pilot stationed near Pleiku when he wrote the following letter to his family. (For a biographical sketch of Olson, see chapter 1.)

January 31, 1968

Dear Everyone,

Please excuse the delay between letters. I know I sound like a broken record because it seems I start every letter like this. I don't know what to say except that for the last two weeks we have been going like gangbusters. You just get so that you don't think about writing or anything else but what you are doing. I know you like to hear what's going on but I haven't felt like doing anything but having a beer and going to bed lately. Lest you get the wrong impression, I wish to emphasize that I am not complaining. Quite the contrary. I would much rather be busy than sitting around.

In any case, I suppose I should get down to the local news. I've got better than half the amount of hours I got in 8 months of flight school, in the month of Jan. Seeing as how I had the third highest total of hours this month in the weapons platoon: Ronyak, Musick, and I were to have yesterday off. However the lift platoon had a man sick so I had to fill in for him. It was the first time I've been in a lift ship since I've been in Vietnam and it was rather interesting. Yesterday, as you know by now, was some kind of a day! The NVA started mortaring Camp Holloway about 12:15 in the morning. (In case you're not clear as to the locations of the camps I'm speaking of; Holloway, New Pleiku AFB, and Camp Schmidt are all right around the city of Pleiku. Camp Enari is just down the road a couple miles south.) They also had a ground attack but did not get through the perimeter. When we got up at 5:30 it was still dark but there were a lot of flares and we could see the gunships out of Holloway making their gun runs. (The anti–Dow Chemical people and the other assorted protesters ought to be real happy with their NVA buddies the past few days. While the nasty Americans have been using napalm, the NVA have been restricting themselves to such gentlemanly activities as destroying better than two-thirds of a helpless village a few miles from Dak To, shooting up the streets of Kontum city in addition to the attack on the air base, attacking the 71st Med Evac Hospital with rockets, etc, etc.)

Anyway yesterday when I was flying with the lift section, we were down at the airfield standing by when we got the word that Kontum was coming under attack. We cranked up 7 ships full of troops and headed for Kontum. We were to set them down about 50 yards off the north side of the runway. About 3 miles out the lead ship called the tower and said we were coming in. The tower replied:

"Rodger, be advised Kontum is under mortar attack at this time; land at your own risk. This is Kontum tower going off the air."

The mortar rounds were landing about 150 yards from where we were going to land and since the troops were badly needed we went on in. There were a bunch of people about 30 ft. away from where we set down crouching behind sandbags and revetments. They kind of looked at us as if we were crazy. I saw this one character shaking his head when I was looking out the window watching to see if the mortars were coming any closer. (That kind of amused me. I mean what the hell else was I supposed to do.) The troops unloaded in a hurry and by the time the NVA got the range it was too late. I was in the last ship and one round went off about 40 yards behind us just as we were leaving. The mortars had stopped when we got back with the second load and we kept carrying troops for 4½ hours, non-stop. We went out later that afternoon and finally finished up at 8:00 last night. Today (huzzah, huzzah!) I've got the day off. (It's amazing what ten hours of sleep can do for one's disposition.) Anyway, don't worry. I don't know how the papers are writing up the situation, but have got it under control. . . .

Hope all are well
Catch you later,
Dave

KENNETH L. ANDERSON (b. 1947) lived on a farm outside of Mount Horeb prior to his enlistment in the army in November, 1965. Sergeant Anderson, a heavy equipment mechanic (815th Engr. Bn., 937th Engr. Grp.), served in Pleiku from March, 1967, to April, 1968. After his discharge in August, 1968, he attended the University of Wisconsin-Platteville and Edgewood College in Madison. Anderson currently resides in Oregon, Wisconsin.

February 1, [1968]
Dear Mom, Dad and Carol,
    I guess I better write so you don't worry. You've probably heard a lot about Pleiku on the news. It was pretty exciting most of January. They wanted to make a good showing on their New Year's. We got hit 6 times in the past 3 weeks. We saw lots of action but it was all outside the perimeter except one night. That one night 9 VC got inside the wire but Dave and a couple other guys were on Rat Patrol (a ¾ ton truck with a machine gun mounted on it and grenades and stuff). They went over there and shot them. They killed 7 of them and another one died later. They were skinny and young. They found a can with opium in it on one of them so they were drugged. That group was a demolitions group of NVAs (North Vietnamese Army). They blew up 20 trucks in the 630th Engineers but none of our guys were hurt. Dave said it was like playing cowboys, they would poke their head around a corner and shoot.
    Other than that, all that ever happens is the guys on our perimeter start shooting if they see anybody. Then the helicopters are here firing

rockets and machine guns. Last night we watched three jets dive and drop bombs about a mile away.

I've got a pretty safe job in an attack. I take the radio to the secondary line. I have to call in and tell them what's going on and how many are out there. I've never seen any VC out there because we're a long way from the perimeter. Whenever we have an alert, we just sit and watch the shooting.

Anyway, Intelligence says over 5000 VC were killed in the past 4 days. They said it was the most intense fighting in the war. But it's about over now. The truce is over so I guess the fighting is too! They asked for a truce for their New Year's. It started at 6 P.M. the 29th. That next morning at about 1:30 we were called out on alert.

All this fighting going on, and I haven't fired my rifle yet! That's O.K. I'm like most guys, I don't care to be a hero, I want to be a civilian! . . .

Love
Ken

MARV ACKER was doing reconnaissance work in Quang Tri when he wrote this letter to his fiancée. (For a biographical sketch of Acker, see chapter 3.)

February 1, 1968

I'm sorry I haven't written in such a while, but a lot has happened since I last wrote. Two days ago we moved again. Now I'm at Quang Tri and about fourteen miles from the DMZ. Two nights ago we were attacked by around 20 NVA. They carried AK-47 Russian carbines, Russian rocket launchers and they all had demolition kits. Their main purpose was to harass the troops and blow up the artillery. A week ago when a "leg" unit was here they tried [the] same thing and killed a battalion commander and some of his staff and they also did some damage to valuable equipment. These NVA made a grave mistake—they tangled with the 101st Airborne Division. Believe me, they know it now! We killed fifteen of them and wounded three. The only damage they did was slightly wound one of our men. A friend of mine, Caputo, who I took AIT with killed two of them. I always wondered what my reaction would be to see a dead gook's body. Surprisingly I was glad, namely because it was him not me that died. It's strange—once there was life and now a riddled mess that was once a fully human body. . . .

All my love,
[Marv]

Jerry Paul (right) with a fellow helicopter crew member, December, 1967.
Courtesy Jerry Paul.

JERRY PAUL was serving as a marine helicopter crew chief and door gunner at Ai Tu Field when he wrote this letter to his girlfriend. (For a biographical sketch of Paul, see chapter 2.)

Ai Tu Field, February 1, 1968

Hi Hon

. . . I got hurt the other night. They started rocketing us when I was in the rack and I slowed down to get my rifle. I was just going out the door when one hit right next door. The concussion blew me out the door and when I got in the bunker I found that about ¼ inch was missing off one of my toes. Outside of that I'm okay. I don't get a "heart" for that. I don't think I rate it anyway. . . .

I'll be glad to get out of here. We don't have enough parts and you can't work on birds with one man watching the tree line for snipers. The NVA are all around us and right up next to the perimeter. So you're open to snipers all day long and then they try to come in at night with satchel charges to get the planes and the bunkers. My nerves are really frazzled. . . .

Love
Jerry

Judith Jenkins (Gaudino). Courtesy Judith Jenkins Gaudino.

JUDITH JENKINS (GAUDINO) (b. 1945) grew up in Appleton and completed her bachelor's degree at the University of Wisconsin in Madison prior to joining the Army Special Services in June, 1967. She served as director of several centers that offered social and recreational services for infantrymen on standdown in Di An, Lai Khe, and Qui Nhon from September, 1967, to December, 1968, and again in Long Binh, Lai Khe, and Phu Loi from January, 1969, to August, 1970. She currently lives in New Jersey, where she counsels veterans suffering from posttraumatic stress disorder.

March 27, 1968

Dear Sue,

Well, another birthday goes by, 23 yrs old, and it's hard to believe I'm in the middle of Vietnam. I never expected to be caught up in this. I'm a civilian, non-combatant—it says so on my ID card. If I'm captured I'm supposed to be treated under the rules of the Geneva Convention. Do you think the VC or NVA would read the fine print on the back of my I.D. card?

Last month there were the worst attacks ever all over Vietnam during Tet. That's what they call the Vietnamese New Year. In the city of Qui Nhon the VC were broadcasting from the radio station and flying their flag over the building. My military base is only a few miles outside of Qui Nhon. We were all scared. Military intelligence reported that our base might be in danger of being overrun from an NVA battalion in our area. We lived in underground bunkers for several days, but the major attack never came. We only had a few rockets and a small sniper attack on the perimeter. Afterwards one of the enemy they found dead was the Vietnamese barber on our base who had just cut my hair the week before. You really don't know who you can trust here.

At this transportation unit where I'm assigned, most of the soldiers face incredible danger every day when they drive supply trucks from Qui Nhon to the Central Highlands near Pleiku. Like ducks in a shooting gallery, they get attacked all the time along the road. Sometimes you get to know the guys and then they don't come back.

Last year we celebrated my birthday at UW two months before graduation. College life seems so far away right now. I know it sounds crazy, but I'm staying in Vietnam because I feel so needed here.

Take care of yourself,
Love,
Judy

The Siege of Khe Sanh

The siege of Khe Sanh began ten days before the Tet Offensive and ended nearly two months after Tet had made its mark on the American war effort. Located in northwestern South Vietnam, six miles from Laos and fourteen miles south of the demilitarized zone (DMZ), Khe Sanh overlooked Route 9, the main road from the Laotian market towns to the northern coastal region. In 1962 the U.S. Military Assistance Command, Vietnam (MACV) created a Special Forces camp near Khe Sanh for border surveillance and to train local Bru tribesmen. General Westmoreland ordered the marines to establish a base at Khe Sanh in 1966, and it was reinforced with additional troops the following year. In April-May, 1967, the marines fought NVA regulars for control of the surrounding hills, but by the end of the year, the North Vietnamese had blocked Route 9, forcing the United States to resupply its troops by air. Anticipating an attack on Khe Sanh, more than 6,000 marines and South Vietnamese rangers were prepared to defend the garrison.

On January 21, 1968, the siege of Khe Sanh began when the marine outpost on Hill 861 stopped an NVA infantry attack and the NVA used 152 mm howitzers to hit an ammunition supply area on the base itself, destroying nearly 1,500 tons of high explosives. From January through April, the marines at Khe Sanh endured hardship, deprivation, and the monotonous terror of artillery fire, mortar attacks, and rocket bombardment. The NVA mixed this continuous barrage with sporadic battalion-sized ground attacks on the more exposed U.S. positions. Between January 22 and March 31, B-52s and other aircraft dropped more than 75,000 tons of explosives on NVA positions, while air force and marine transport planes

brought food and ammunition to the besieged troops. Because heavy NVA
antiaircraft fire made it nearly impossible for American aircraft to land on
Khe Sanh's airstrip, the air force also used parachute drops to keep the base
and the hill outposts supplied.

As the siege of Khe Sanh extended from days into weeks, President
Johnson became particularly concerned that the United States not lose Khe
Sanh, fearing that it would be compared to the French disaster at Dien Bien
Phu in 1954. Operation Pegasus, a joint army, marine, and ARVN effort,
began the relief of Khe Sanh in early April, and the siege was lifted by
April 6. Ironically, after all the bloodshed, the marines closed the base on
July 5, 1968. The following letters describe the siege of Khe Sanh through
the eyes of the men who fought there.

RAY W. STUBBE (b. 1938) was born and raised in Milwaukee. After
spending two years in the navy (1956–1958), he received degrees from St.
Olaf College and Northwestern Lutheran Theological Seminary, was
ordained as a Lutheran minister in June, 1965, and then began work on a
Ph.D. in ethics at the University of Chicago. A member of the Navy
Reserve, Stubbe was reactivated in 1967 as a chaplain. During his two tours
of duty in Vietnam, Lieutenant Stubbe served at Khe Sanh (1/26th Mar., 3d
Mar. Div.) from July, 1967, to February, 1968, at Quang Tri (3d Shore
Party) from March, 1968, to June, 1968, and at Da Nang (Naval Support
Activity) from July, 1968, to January, 1969. He remained on active duty
until his retirement in 1985. In 1991 he published *Valley of Decision,* an
account of his experiences during the siege of Khe Sanh. The three letters
that follow describe the days just prior to the siege.

January 18, 1968

Dear folks:

Hi. I'm writing this letter on my new typewriter—yes, my own
typewriter. There is a church group in California that is giving a free
typewriter, small tape recorder, and an AM-FM radio to all the Navy
chaplains here. Isn't that nice? I just came back from Phu Bai yesterday
where I picked it all up at the division chaplain's office. I had a real
nice time down there. I sort of celebrated the fact that on the 14th of
this month, I celebrated my 6th month in country; less than 6 more to
go. It's always good to go down to Phu Bai and rest up a bit. . . . We
had quite a time getting back to Khe Sanh. Some of the people down
there had been waiting 9 days in the terminal, from 7 in the morning
to 5 at afternoon, on hard benches, day after day. The weather gets so
foggy here, that even with instruments the planes do not come in for
fear of crashing into the nearby hills. Then, on Tuesday, they brought
up another whole battalion up here, another 1200 men! So now we have
three battalions here—1/26, 2/26, and 3/26. I think we are the only regiment in the Marines in Vietnam that has all the three battalions together.
(We are the 26th Marines regiment). It is the first time the regiment

*Ray Stubbe conducts a worship service at Khe Sanh on January 28, 1968.
Shortly after this photo was taken, incoming mortar fire scattered Stubbe's
marine congregation. Courtesy Ray Stubbe.*

has been together since World War II. The reason they brought up 2/26
was that they think this place is going to be attacked by the 4,000 North
Vietnamese or so that are always surrounding us. Well, they've said that
for the 6 months I've been here now. One month it was the national
elections; they always attack then, and in fact did attack most of the
Marine installations, but not us. Then it was the monsoons. Now it is
something else. They really get all excited. We now have to wear helmets
and body armor (flak vests), and the Marines have to carry rifles—this
is on the base itself, during the day. They expect human wave attacks.
We also have to keep our gas mask with us all the time. I think it is
utterly ridiculous to see the whole base become paranoiac. Everyone
is digging holes and building bunkers out of sandbags. I rest secure in
my hooch-bunker that I built back last September. I have my office in
it, and I sleep in it at night, and they tell me it would take a 120 mm.
rocket. So I'm safe. . . .

I guess I have to close now. Please greet everyone. O yes, concerning the clothing for the people here—anything of a discarded nature will be able to be used. They are so poor that they can use anything.

Love
Ray

January 20, 1968

Dear folks:

. . . Well, the last two days have been quite terrible as far as casualties to our own men in this area. Yesterday they brought in one killed and about a dozen or so wounded; they also brought in two children about 3 or 4 years old that had gotten some shrapnel. These are all from the outposts, not the base, of course. Today by noon, they had brought in 22 men with various shrapnel wounds in their arms and legs, ankle, lip, etc., and one killed. They were going to Hill 881 North, the site of the bad battle last April and May. Last night, and at about 2 in the afternoon, just as I am writing this letter, there were B52 strikes against two suspected North Vietnamese regiments (about 3,000 or so men) to our south, about 5 miles or so. These strikes are called "arc lights" and consist of 5,000 and 10,000 pound bombs. They drop so many of them that it sounds like a real bad thunder even at this distance. So things are getting a little warmer around here. . . .

Maybe sometime this will all end. If the people back there could see all the suffering that the men go through, the "hawks" would be less "hawkish" and the doves would be more realistic (and focus their attention on the predicament of the fighting man, not on the immorality of war). War is obviously immoral. What so many fail to see is that man is not naturally good, and will not naturally do the right thing, and that the choices before men today are not black and white but of differing shades of gray.

I saw my first childbirth last night. Although miraculous, seeing life suddenly appear; it was simply awful—seeing all that come out, all the torn tissue and blood and horrible suffering of the woman. Then they asked for the placenta or afterbirth; they eat it. I think if every young man and young woman saw that they'd never have any children. But, of course, that isn't true. For the only way there is life is through suffering, and the only things that are held of great value in life are the things one struggles for, how much more one's life, if one struggles to keep that.

Well, perhaps that's the way this war is. It's ugly; it's painful, excruciatingly so; but maybe that's the only way new life can come to these people who have lived under terror for 40 years.

Well, I guess I have to go now.

Love,
Ray

January 21, [1968]

Dear folks:

. . . We are, as you probably hear on the news, under attack. It's the scariest thing I've ever had to face. I awoke at 5 o'clock to the sound of incoming rockets and mortars exploding just outside my hooch! They hit our ammunition dump, and rounds of ammunition were flying all day long. Practically half the base is in ruins, but the casualties were very few because everyone got in bunkers. The only casualties were from the lines on the perimeter of the base and from Hill 861. I am writing this as the sun is setting today. I don't know if you will ever receive this, but I must write it anyway. . . .

I feel I'm needed here. I give my every waking moment for these men. They are basically good men, but not particularly religious as such, although I'm quite sure many prayed today! Yet I love them all, and give my daily life for them, and I do it not for personal satisfaction or companionship or a sense of personal accomplishment, but because I feel it's God's will. . . .

Love,
Ray

JERRY PAUL, a helicopter crew chief and door gunner, was near Khe Sanh when he wrote this letter to his girlfriend. (For a biographical sketch of Paul, see chapter 2.)

Base X, January 22, 1968

Honey

. . . Everything is going to hell up here. Don't know how long we'll be here. The NVA are massing on the other side of the DMZ and Khe Sanh is already under attack. They're just barely holding out. They say the NVA want both of the northern provinces. We are building up up here. The 1st Air Cavalry is up here now but are getting wiped but good.

We've lost 6 planes in the last 4 days.

I'm flying again, don't have enough planes or crew chiefs. I took over a dead man's bird. . . .

Love
Jerry

HARVE W. SAAL (b. 1941) was born in Rhinelander and was working as a technical artist in Milwaukee when he was drafted by the army in May, 1964. Saal subsequently reenlisted and served from September, 1967, to August, 1970, with the Special Forces (5th SFG [Airborne], 1st Special Forces) and with a reconnaissance force (MACV Studies and Observation

Group) that operated near Kontum, Dak To, Khe Sanh, Phu Bai, and Da Nang, as well as in Laos and Cambodia. He retired from the military in August, 1984, and now lives in Olympia, Washington, where he is writing a multivolume history of the Studies and Observation Group Special Forces. He wrote the following letter, which he never mailed, to his family over a seven-day period near the start of the siege.

January 22, 1968, 9:00 A.M.

Hi peoples,

Well I guess the word must be out by now about Khe Sanh. The North Vietnamese have us surrounded at this time, they have been estimated at, up to 20,000 troops.

They started the attack at 5:30 A.M. 21 Jan, and we fought hard for 8 hours. The NVA have destroyed the landing strip of the marines—we in FOB 3 are the outer perimeter for the Marines.

We haven't as yet had anyone even hurt bad. The marines are taking some losses.

The B-52s are bombing steadily around us, I think they have killed quite a few NVA.

I saw one jet shot out of the air not more than ½ mile from here and also a chopper who was bringing in reinforcements. Right now the water is low, the NVA have mortared and rocketed our watering station.

Charlie didn't try a ground attack last night, but rocketed us several times during the night.

10:30

A C-123 just resupplied us with ammo by air and while I was writing *C-123* the NVA threw a rocket at us.

You will never read this if I am (another rocket) hurt seriously, but only if I'm all right!

I didn't do this in Dak To cause I didn't have paper, or my camera along, but I'm taking pictures starting today. I think the battle for Khe Sanh has just begun!

January 23, 10:00 A.M.

No incidents during the night not even an incoming mortar round. A patrol was sent into Khe Sanh yesterday late and found many, many dead NVA. It was a little foggy last nite and Charlie likes to move when there's fog or rain, it looks today as if it might rain. I hope not!

3:30 P.M.

Another jet shot down over us by NVA. Jets have been bombing all day now. Water is still rationed. It stopped raining now, thank God. Charlie has been real brave shooting at our flares with small arms fire!

January 24, 1:00 P.M.

Sort of foggy last nite, I can't understand why the NVA didn't attack. They just lobbed a shell (mortar 82 mm) in on us near a chopper, wounded one Bru.

January 25

Well last nite at 6:00 P.M. Charlie started rocketing us and the marines heavily—we had a few persons wounded but I guess nothing seriously, we waited for their ground attack but none came. There was a few fire fights here and there one Bru got killed. Charlie has two regiments out there waiting to hit us tonite. He's only got 5 more days to get us before Tet. I think he just may do it!

Every day we re-adjust our positions and wait. We expect a heavy artillery barrage tonite along (again) with a large force ground attack.

January 27

Well yesterday was the same regular day, no attack the night of the 25th, no attack last night. But naturally the NVA pumped some mortars into our area and pumped a few more at the marines.

On Thurs the Marines dug in on a hill to our North, today Charlie mortared and got fourteen people—marines. Also yesterday I got myself put on a 57 mm recoilless weapon, the kind Charlie just loves to capture, he's going to have to "whip" me to get it.

The air force continues to bomb around us—taking heavy casualties on the NVA. It seems as though Charlie has three Divisions moving to Khe Sanh to wipe us out. I couldn't count that high to guess the number of men in a Division so we'll just wait and count them periodically as they come along.

I took my first shave in 7 days today, and was able to wash my hands, it felt great!

Susie sent me a bottle of booze, bless her soul, and a letter asking me to answer as soon as possible—I hope she doesn't mind waiting.

A battalion of Vietnamese rangers went over to the marine camp today and have begun digging in.

We're all wondering how long the NVA will continue this siege for Tet, after Tet is over. But of course he's still got five *long* nights to try us.

It's 6:15 PM now and the clouds are beginning to engulf us. Another good nite for Charlie to fool with us.

I just don't really understand these crazy guys in S[pecial] F[orces], we should be scared to death, but they drink every day and guard every nite, and naturally make a complete joke of death.

It's getting so when the NVA begin to mortar us the guys just walk casually to their trenches and get in. The marines took five hits today at 4:30 PM., we finished our drinks and went to our perimeter. I'm now in my position with a "Coke" and the booze Susie sent me.

The sea bees here got us some steel helmets and bulletproof vests (flak jackets), they felt sorry for us wearing our soft hats and Berets. I love my Beret, but it won't stop a bullet—especially an artillery round! We're not used to these "stand and fight" deals, but we'd better learn here in Khe Sanh all about it. I'm used to hiding in the bushes and ambushing—not front line defense like this—well I don't really mind, I'm not that scared yet!

January 28, 3:30 P.M.

Well another night spent in these lousy trenches and charlie didn't come. Everyone seems to feel he may come tonight, who knows now after all the bad weather and he hasn't hit yet with a ground attack?

I really do believe he's hurting from our air strikes. Ten Charlie were found outside our wire last night and we called mortars in on them (for a present for Tet). And so now the North Vietnamese Army has two days until Tet begins and it only lasts three day until the 2nd of Feb.

The sea bees and Marines are repairing the air strip every day now, it seems the strip takes at least 20 to 25 mortars and rockets a day.

DENNIS L. GOETZ (b. 1945) was raised in Portage and enlisted in the Marine Corps in August, 1966. Corporal Goetz served as an engineer (C Co., 3d Engr. Bn., 3d Mar. Div.) in Da Nang, Dong Ha, and Khe Sahn from December, 1967, until he was discharged in August, 1968. Since that time, he has lived in Irma, where he works for a telephone company. Goetz wrote the following two letters to his parents during the siege.

January 26, 1968

Dear Folks,

I thought, that I'd drop you a quick note, to let you know I am all right. I had to bring a message from Khe Sahn back here to Dong Ha, and that is why I am getting a chance to write now. I left Khe Sahn yesterday noon. I had to get a plane all the way down to Da Nang, and then back up here to Dong Ha. Those are the only planes leaving Khe Sahn. I was on the plane with 3 CBS news reporters. One of them had a piece of shrapnel in his head. Just the 4 of us on the plane, and they took my

Marines at Khe Sanh running for cover, January 25, 1968. USMC photo.

picture loading the stretcher on the plane. May[be] you saw me on Walter Cronkite. Well, I'll tell you about Khe Sahn. To start with, I have seen more war in the last week, than I thought I'd see in my whole time over here. They are hitting us with everything up there. Rockets, artillery, mortars, and gas, besides sniper fire. Me and the good Lord have had many talks in the past week. I have never been so scared in my life as I was last Sunday morning. We started getting Rockets and artillery fire at about 4:30 AM and it lasted till about 7:30 AM. It was our first nite there, so all we had was small foxholes. The tent right next to mine got a direct hit, and was leveled. Ours looks like a screen door. All our gear has holes in it. I had a close one, when a piece of shrapnel went through one of my magazines on my belt. Tues. all the civilian refugees came in and left for Da Nang. The army special forces camp over the hill got ran over, and we had all kinds of people with us Tues. nite. I saw 2 jets shot down right over our camp. . . . Both pilots parachuted into our camp. The whole place is surrounded up there, but I don't think they'll be able to take it from us. We are getting all kinds of people and big guns in all the time. Without our planes, we wouldn't have a chance. Anyone that says quit bombing should be over here with us, and then see what they think. Those jets are beautiful, I love them. When they're around us, they won't shoot artillery or rockets in on us, because the jets will get them. In case I have confused you, I am in Dong Ha right now. I had to bring a message to the captain, and pick up the mail for the guys. I also have to get a case of beers and a saw someplace. Being engineers does have some advantages. We got the SeaBees to dig us a big hole with their dozer. We build a real nice bunker, and I think we can take a direct hit with anything the NVA has. So that lets us sleep a little bit better at night. Like I said, they have used everything. We get gas in quite often. We have the right gear for all this stuff, so it isn't too bad. A guy just has to be careful. They have brought the 101st Airborne up here to Dong Ha, in case we need them at Khe Sahn. They say that this Operation Scotland is going to last about 50 days, so I suppose I'll be up there till it is over. I sure was lucky to come back here. I got to clean up and get some hot chow. You wouldn't have believed how dirty I was. I never had my boots off for 6 days. Well, all I can say is don't worry. Just keep faith in the Lord. I'll be going back up there tomorrow morning. They are expecting a big one in the next week. I really don't think they can get much bigger than the last week. I'll write what little I can, when I can. Think of you always. Just 204 more days and I'll be out for good. Bye for now.

Love
Dennis

February 14, 1968

Dear Folks:

Well folks, how is everything going, back in Portage? Things are going pretty smooth here. I received a couple of your letters a few days ago, and I am finally getting a chance to write. I sure did enjoy your valentine card. At least it lets you know, that you're not forgotten. Well, they have been keeping me so busy, that I hardly have a chance to think of home. I have more responsibility right now, than I ever wanted. Like I told you before, we have a platoon up here at Khe Sahn. That is about 30 engs. We are supporting a whole regiment of Marines. That means, that just our platoon, has to support ⅓ of the 3rd Marine Div. I have six engs. out here with 2/26 (second battalion 26 Marines). I not only have charge of them, but also any and all demolition work in this battalion (1000 men). I have been fixing up some dandy things for Charlie, if he tries to get in our lines here on 558. I have set in some 55 gal. drums of ½ gas and ½ diesel fuel. I put 10 lbs of C4 (like TNT) behind it, and fix up a circuit, so any of those guys on the lines can put a battery to the wires, and blow all kinds of fire out. Also, I have been taking rolls of barbed wire, about the size of a basketball and stuff it full of C4 and set a circuit to that also. Also, I am trying to get some mines to put in. . . . We are like on an island. We are dug in pretty good, so I think they would need alot of men to get inside our lines. They don't mess with us too much here, but the hill next to ours, which is 861, about as far as from you to the high school, gets in a fire fight every nite. I sit up here on the hill and watch them hit Khe Sahn with Rockets every nite and day, 24 hrs. Then I just hope none of my buddies down there are getting it. I suppose that I'll have to go back there in a week or so. I sure hate to think of that. That has got to be as close to hell as any place on earth. I would rather have someone I can see shooting at me, than just those big guns and rockets. You feel so helpless down there. They make air strikes all arounds us 24 hrs. a day. That makes you feel a little safer. We don't get much of anything up here. They have enough trouble getting us food and ammunition. I finally got some electric blasting caps in today. My red bag and all my gear are at Dong Ha, I think I'll probably be up here till I rotate in July. It has been bad up here, but they say the big battle is yet to come. We live in holes, and eat C rations, which aren't as bad as you think, except the same old thing for a month now, is getting sickening. I got a shot of Scotch from the Chaplain the other day, so now I am all set for another 2 months. Like I said, we don't get anything up here. I even had to steal a tablet to write letters with. At least we (engs) have our C4 to cook over. It makes wonderful heat, if you know how to use it so it don't explode. Well, here I am again. I got interrupted yesterday, and it is the next day now. I think Thur. nite. I went to church services this afternoon. It was hid in the elephant grass and had a box of C rations for an altar. Took communion. It was a Lutheran Chaplain. A little different than ours. No more light so have to stop. Please send me a few candles and some canned foods. Anything is OK. Don't worry, everything is alright. Think of you alot. Say Hi to Fritz.

Love
Dennis

WILLIAM W. MAVES (b. 1949) was born in Edgerton and was living there when he enlisted in the Marine Corps in October, 1966. He served as a radioman with a line company (E Co., 2/26th Mar., 3d Mar. Div.) stationed near Phu Bai from September, 1967, until November, 1968. He was discharged in August, 1969. Maves now lives in Edgerton and works as a repairman for an automobile manufacturing firm. He wrote the following letter while serving as an air-ground liaison with the marines at Khe Sanh.

February 15, [1968]

Mom & Dad,

Hi, I received two more letters from you today, one containing this writing gear. It seems as if lately I've been making out like a fat dog on mail. I just hope it comes in like it has been. It sure does help alot.

Boy, you talk about a crud, I'm as dirty and scummy as anyone could ever get. The last time I took a bath and put on clean clothes was the 9th of January. Do you realize that was 38 days ago, and it'll be another five before I get the chance. I don't want to ever be this cruddy again. I can't even pull the poncho over my head at night cause it drives me out!

I'm really gonna enjoy myself on R & R. A bath will seem out of this world. . . .

Take care now and love always,
Bill

DENNIS GOETZ served as an engineer at Khe Sanh when he wrote his parents the following letter. (For a biographical sketch of Goetz, see earlier in this chapter).

February 26, [1968]

Dear Folks;

Well, how is everything going with you folks. As you can see I am still kicking. I don't know if they sent the word home or not, but I got another medal the other day. I was hoping, that I would never get that one, but it is over now. I got a small piece of shrapnel in the right forearm. About all I can tell you is, I was sitting on my little bed of grass, and a 82 mm. mortar hit about 2½ or 3 feet from me. I shouldn't have to tell you, that there aren't many people alive, that have had one of those hit that close. I was in shock for about 30 secs. I couldn't even get in my hole. There was a couple of sandbags around my bed, and they are what saved my life. It hit right on top of 2 cases of C Rations. I even had a bean in my ear. It couldn't of been more than 3 min. before that I was sitting on those boxes. It even took a chunk of metal out of my helmet, and throw it off my head. There is so many little ifs, like I just put my helmet on. I guess the only answer is, that the good lord was looking over me. I don't know how to begin to thank him. One of my Men . . . who was about 10 feet away, got it pretty bad, both shoulders, neck, and the whole left side. I forgot about him, and when I finally got enough sense to get in my hole, I heard him moaning. I went over to help him, and I almost fainted. He was hit in the head also, and there was blood all over the place, and even his brains were visible. We took

*Marines firing a 105mm howitzer during the siege of Khe Sanh,
January, 1968. USMC photo.*

him over to the Doc, and they got a chopper for him. He is on a hospital
ship now. It seems so unusual, that I get a purple heart on Washington's
birthday, when it is his picture on the Purple Heart. All I can say is,
thank God. Things are about the same as last time I wrote. We got our
mine fields in, and 3 of our own stupid people have stepped on some
of them. There is even signs up. Yesterday, Khe Sahn was hit with 1370
rounds. That is way too many. I don't really look forward to going back
there. I think I am going to blow up a spring hole, and make a little
dam. For a water hole. If they make up their mind. Well, I have to go,
for it is dark. I am OK, the shrapnel was no bigger than ¼". Think
of you folks always. Say Hi to Fritz.

Love
Dennis

DAVID T. KRAMARCZYK (b. 1946) enlisted in the Marine Corps in May,
1966, from his hometown of Menasha. He served as foot soldier and truck
driver (26th Mar. [FWD], Subunit 1, 3d Mar. Div.) in Phu Bai, Hue, Dong
Ha, and Khe Sanh from November, 1967, to May, 1968. Corporal
Kramarczyk was discharged in July, 1968, and returned to his prewar career
as a pressman in Menasha. Kramarczyk wrote the following four letters to
his mother during the siege of Khe Sanh.

March 13, 1968

Hi Mom

. . . Things are still the same over here, Charlie keeps shooting and we keep ducking. Pretty soon it should be over. He won't get this base. He might break through the lines, but he won't take Khe Sanh from us.

So what's new back home? We haven't gotten mail in almost a week now. We still get supplies from air drops. Nothing lands at our airfield except helicopters. There hasn't been a plane on it since the last one got hit last week. I think it was last week. I don't even know what day it is. I think it's Friday or Saturday. What's everyone doing back home? Is Clair still deer hunting? That wine we made got all fruit flies in it and it turned to Vinegar. I hope my bottle back home is alright yet.

Well I'll close for now. You better take care of that blood pressure of yours.

Say hi to everyone for me.
Your Son
Dave

March 20, 1968

Hi Mom

I got your letter today. The first one in a long time. Almost three weeks. I got all the letters from Phu Bai even the one from JoAnne. This was the first one I got with my new address. I wrote you about eight or more letters since I was here and quite a few to Al and Clair also. Mail is so slow up here and mail planes get blown up. I don't know if you will get them all or I'll get all of everyone else's. It's so lonely up here, I haven't seen a girl in over a month. I had a total of one beer in that month and not a cup of milk or fresh food since I was here. I'd be happy to just get a bath. We got some fresh fruit the other day. One apple and orange apiece. That was the first fresh fruit anybody had up here. . . . Right now I got 500 dollars in my wallet. I'm afraid to send it out of here because it might get blown away. I'll buy my tape recorder when I get to Okinawa and send it home from there. I wrote Clair and Al tonight and I'm going to write one more tonight yet.

Well I'll close for now.

Love
Dave

March 28, 1968

Hi Mom

Well things slacked off the last few days. Either the gooks are pulling out or are getting resupplied. He's still out there, this we know for sure. Every time a chopper comes in he throws rockets and mortars in on it. No big troop attacks lately either. Maybe he's planning something big?

It's getting real hot now and there are thousands of flies and a greater number of rats now. I can't even count the flies I accidently eaten while eating chow. They even fly into your mouth before you get the food in. When you make coffee you have to pick the dead flies out before you can drink it and you hardly know how many sunk and are at the bottom. I never seen so many flies, not even in the barn at Clair's. The mosquitoes are pretty bad too. We have to take malaria pills to be safe. I hardly ever took them before. You may find this hard to believe, but I still haven't had a shower yet. I got a haircut last week with a scissors and what a job. It'll be alright by the time I get home. (I hope.) My orders are in for El Toro Marine Airfield. I don't know if I'll get discharged or not when I get back. I sure hope so.

Well I'll close for now, write soon if you can. The papers are North Vietnamese propaganda papers. They exploded a shell over the base and they flew all over. Save them.

Love
Dave

March 30, 1968

Hi Mom

I'm back here at Phu Bai and am glad to be here. For awhile I thought I would never leave Khe Sanh except in a plastic bag. I don't know if anyone told you or not that I was wounded. The first time I got a piece of shrapnel in my arm. The 29th I got medevaced to Dong Ha with a piece in my leg. I'm back here with my old outfit. I'll be laying in the rack for a couple of weeks till my leg heals and I won't be going back to Khe Sanh. Now don't go thinking I'm crippled or anything, I just got a hole about the size of a quarter in my leg about six inches above the knee so it won't even show. I just have to take it easy for awhile. When that chopper lifted off and I seen Khe Sanh way below I was as happy as any person could ever be. You might say I was the happiest person just to be alive. Well I know for sure I'll make it home now, so *don't worry.* I won't be going to Hue anymore either.

Write Soon
Love
Dave

BILL MAVES was an air-ground liaison with the marines at Khe Sanh when he wrote the following letter to his parents. (For a biographical sketch of Maves, see earlier in this chapter.)

April 15, 1968

Mom & Dad,

Hi, I thought I'd write a short note again tonight. I may have some good news but as of yet I'm not sure. It's rumored we'll be going back to Quang Tri around the 18th. We're going to blow this hill off the map the 17th and rejoin battalion. They're going to do the same to theirs the eighteenth. Then I heard we're suppose to go to Quang Tri and operate just like we were at Phu Bai. I sure hope it happens, it'll be a pleasure. It doesn't matter where we go, when I leave this hill, it'll be a proud moment for the few of us who survived. Out of a full company of about 260 men who originally come up here, 34 were killed, and 173 were medevaced, most of which never returned. You can pretty much tell there's not much left of the originals. . . .

Your Son

DENNIS GOETZ was serving as an engineer at Khe Sanh when he wrote the following letter to his parents. (For a biographical sketch of Goetz, see earlier in this chapter.)

Dong Ha, April 19, [1968]

Dear Folks:

Well, as you can see, I have left Khe Sanh. I left there yesterday and it was like taking a ton off from my back. I had a artillery round hit right by me, when I was getting on the chopper. I almost cried when I left, I was so thankful to be in one piece. As you can see I am in Dong Ha right now, and I have to be in Da Nang the 24th to leave for R & R in Tokyo. I guess I am what you might call a physical wreck. I lost 18 lbs. while I was at Khe Sanh. We have it nice here. We have cots to sleep on and hot meals and beer and even movies at night. I had a little meatloaf and potatoes last night and two beers, and I was sick all nite. All I did was throw up. So you can see I am not used to it. All I can say is I am really going to enjoy this R & R especially after the news about Tim. I don't think I could have taken much more up at Khe Sanh. . . .

Love
Dennis

6

Prisoners of War

During Operation Homecoming in February–March, 1973, Americans celebrated the return of nearly 600 prisoners of war (POWs) detained in camps by the North Vietnamese. While the war in Vietnam bitterly divided America, the return of the POWs provided a rare occasion on which all could display a heartfelt spirit of unity and healing. The initial group of POWs said little about conditions in the camps in North Vietnam lest they jeopardize their colleagues awaiting release, but as the months passed, their stories unfolded, disclosing years of sustained physical and mental torture.

POWs held captive in the north survived their ordeal by adhering to the tenets of the "Code of Conduct for Armed Forces of the United States." Adopted in 1955, the code provided fighting men in Vietnam with a doctrine for a unified system of resistance. Captive servicemen tried to replicate a military community in the camps, including a hierarchy based on rank, a tap-code communication system, and a moral duty to resist collaboration with the enemy. Torture sessions occurred regularly before the improvement of POW camp conditions in October, 1969, a change made by the North Vietnamese under pressure from the U.S. government, the public, activist groups, and the media. Evading the Geneva Convention Agreements of 1949 by labeling POWs "war criminals," camp guards attempted to elicit antiwar statements and sought to demoralize prisoners through torture.

Menasha native FREDRIC FLOM (b. 1941) was one of the POWs who returned home from Vietnam in early 1973. Flom graduated from Lawrence University in Appleton in 1963, and he subsequently enlisted in the U.S. Air Force, which sent him to Vietnam in January, 1966. Lieutenant Flom (354th TFS, 355th TFW) flew ninety combat missions over Vietnam and Laos before his plane was shot down over North Vietnam on August 8. For the next six and a half years he endured isolation, deprivation, and torture.

Flom kept a diary during his final sixteen days in Hoa Lo prison, known to POWs as the Hanoi Hilton. Meticulously written on twenty-seven 7½-x-4-inch Vietnamese cigarette wrappers and hidden from prison guards, Flom's diary begins on February 19, 1973, three weeks after he and his fellow POWs became aware that they would be freed as a result of the signing of the Paris peace accords on January 27. He summarized his years in captivity and on February 21 began to record his feelings and vent his

157

frustrations as the date of his release was further postponed. The diary concludes dramatically on March 6, when Flom boarded the plane that would take him to Clark Air Force Base in the Philippines.

Shortly after his return to the United States, Flom transcribed and edited his diary and distributed typewritten copies to family and friends to explain his ordeal. The text printed here is taken from the handwritten manuscript copy, with the exception of the entries written between noon on Tuesday, February 27, and Saturday, March 4, which exist only in the transcribed version of the diary.

Flom currently works as a commercial airline pilot and lives in Dallas, Texas. He retired from the Air Force Reserve in 1990 with the rank of colonel.

I am presently on the threshold of a kaleidoscope of emotional & physical excitement as I prepare to enter the real world after 6½ yrs. of physical & mental deprivation. I eagerly anticipate every aspect of life that awaits me. I hope that all of my senses can continuously react with max efficiency so as not to deprive me of any of the excitement that awaits me. I fear, however, that my senses may be somewhat numbed by over-stimulation & some weeks or months from now, I'll glance back over my shoulder asking myself "what happened."

I intend to maintain a continuing diary for at least one year beginning with the day of release. This will be an attempt not so much to put down my activities of the day but more to capture my thoughts & feelings so as to follow my adjustment to freedom & society. I feel that I am presently capable of a smooth & rapid psychological & physical adaptation to my new life. I have given much thought over the past years to my personal psychology, my goals & philosophy of life, & my association with my wife & family. I feel I am ready and will have few problems, however there still exists that unknown element of 6½ years of captivity with much physical torture as well as mental anxiety & almost complete mental or intellectual deprivation. The readjustment will be real. I am well aware that my family & friends as well as society has changed greatly but I await the challenge with great anticipation.

Because this experience has placed such a large unknown on my personal psyche it will be interesting & worthwhile to follow the readjustment. The forthcoming experience is almost unique & certainly unusual. In years to come I shall want to review this experience. The mind is so forgetful; particularly in regards to thoughts & feelings. Thus a diary.

Furthermore, as an introduction to this diary, I would like to put down an autobiographical sketch of the past 6½ years before my memory of these experiences fades too much. 6½ years of captivity alone is enough to have a large impact on a man's life & thoughts. However the details

Fredric Flom. Courtesy Fredric Flom.

a POW in North Vietnam will reveal a situation from which almost any consequences may be considered excusable. I do not seek sympathy nor excuses, but merely relate the facts for personal future reflection.

I was shot down on 8 August, 1966. I apparently had amnesia & remember absolutely nothing about the event. The last thing I remember was being on an R & R in Bangkok. The first thing I remember was waking up one morning in Heartbreak Hotel, cell No. 1. The details of my shootdown was related to me by Jim Kasler when I had an opportunity to talk to him for the first time on Jan. 21, 1973 6½ yrs. after the event: We had a pre-dawn takeoff with Baron (Jim Kasler) as lead, me on his wing, Norm Wells flying 3 with Roger Ayres on his wing. Our ordnance was CBUs & the gun. The target was a storage area north of Yen Bai for primary & a similar secondary target. We arrived in the target area just about daybreak under a 1500 foot overcast. As we came up a road heading for the target we split to a 2-ship a[nd] the Baron found 2 trucks which we set on fire with 20 mm. We went to the primary target & dropped 1 pod of CBUs then headed to the secondary target. After I dropped my CBUs & was pulling off this target Kas saw me take 37 mm in the belly tank. The aircraft immediately started burning & smoking. Baron said I'd better get out & I turned my aircraft to 240° to start heading out. He told me to get out again & then a third time as my aircraft did a violent roll to the right & started coming apart. He saw the canopy come out through the fire & smoke & then the seat. Then the aircraft blew up with a yellow-orange fire ball like he'd never seen. He said my chute opened immediately as my 0 lanyard was hooked. He saw metal debris rip thru the chute & I was hanging limp. He saw me on the ground & I was in the middle of a road on top of my chute just outside a little village & I was not moving. He could get no radio contact & headed out, picking up Wells & Ayres on the way. By the time they got to the tanker Saigon called & told him to go back & try to get radio contact. Kas said I was way north of the Red & even if they got contact there was no chance for a pick up. Saigon told him to go anyway & confirm I was alive. So they came back, found the spot where I had been & I was gone apparently captured & no radio contact.

With no chance of contact they headed out & just as they started climbing out Baron took a hit with 37 mm & had to bail out. Norm & Rog got contact with Kas on the ground but he was captured within an hour. He had a badly broken leg. (Norm Wells was shot down & captured some weeks later 28 Aug.)

Kas & I eventually were taken to New Guy Village that night. He was in the room next to mine & could hear me in much pain. He remem-

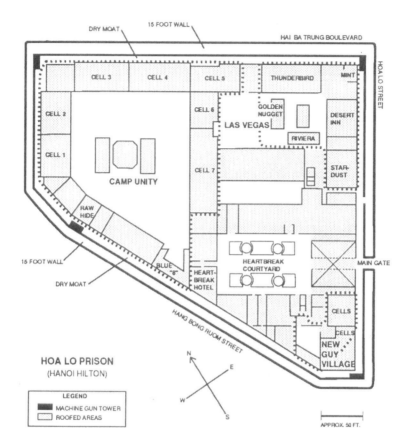

This schematic drawing of Hoa Lo Prison in Hanoi is loosely based on a sketch plan in Jim and Sybil Stockdale's In Love and War *(rev. ed., Annapolis, Md.: Naval Institute Press, 1990) and is used courtesy of the U.S. Naval Institute. American POWs called Hoa Lo the Hanoi Hilton. The perimeters of major sections of the camp, with the names given them by POWs, are marked with dotted lines. Drawing by Roberta Couillard.*

bers my saying "can't I even lie down." We were both taken to a hospital that night for x-rays—Kas with a broken leg & me with a broken arm. From there we went to the main hospital where Baron stayed for a couple weeks & he thinks I was there for 3–4 days after which time I was apparently taken to HBH [Heartbreak Hotel]. Here is where my living memory of my existence in NVN begins: Hell on earth—I feel my debts are paid.

I woke up one morning in HBH-1, no date, in a body cast from my waist up with a broken left arm set out parallel to my shoulder & bent at the elbow. My right arm was in a splint with torn ligaments & tendons. There were small cuts & scratches all over my body & blood everywhere. The heat was unbearable & I was starving as I gazed with horror at the iron fetters or leg irons at the foot of the concrete slab upon which I lay. The cement walls & high ceiling of the small 7 x 8 foot room. The barred windows which were boarded up to prevent prisoners from looking out & the heavy locked door with a small sliding peep in the middle which the guards used to look in. It is difficult for me to recapture the feelings & thoughts I had as the realization of what had happened came over me. I prayed immediately: "Oh God if I ever see my wife & family again ..." I did a lot of that in the next weeks, months, & years, but especially those first six horrible months.

The experiences to follow are beyond my capabilities of description. The feeling of loneliness & fear as you face a completely adverse situation, totally alone with no means of defense or recourse as your enemy uses every deceptive trick at his disposal, mental & physical, (trying not to leave permanent marks on your body & often failing at that) to totally destroy your spirit & resistance. This enemy of gooks are not wise & clever, however but bungling fools, something to your advantage, although painful.

I would not see nor have contact with a fellow American POW for the next month, nor the opportunity to talk to one for the next six months (All told, I was solo or in solitary confinement for slightly over 1 year in NVN) only the unfriendly faces of gook officers & guards. All I had was a mat, mosquito net, blanket, set of pajama-like clothes, shorts & T-shirt, cup & water jug, & a bucket for a toilet. Washing was very infrequent & shaving even more so (sometimes more than a month at first). Two meals a day: a plate of rice, bowl of water & grass soup— very thin, & a small side dish of pumpkin.

I began quizzes immediately & learned quickly to hate & fear the sound of keys. There were many questions & name, rank, serial no. did not work. Several beatings convinced me it would be best to answer some: where born, home town, what father do, sqdn, base? I lied about most of them but found they accepted lies & were happy whereas silence only got more beatings. Tactics? Details about my shootdown. Believe me I took a lot for that—they did not believe my amnesia story. I learned from an interrogator that I was shot down 8 Aug. north of Yen Bai & that Kas was also shot down & captured & for the next 6½ years that's about all I knew.

I recall that I was truly afraid for my life that first month. I was often threatened with my life & I almost believed it. I didn't put much value on the life of a POW before I was shot down. The word around the base & sqdn. had led me to believe that. Then there was the scare of War Crimes Trials in June & July & I wasn't really sure of the results. I had about decided I'd never let them capture me alive & now here I am. "Good God!" I really wasn't aware of my value to the V & indeed was scared they might kill me but it would take more than threats. (The V did kill many POWs in torture sessions not by shooting them but by going too far).

What the V wanted now was a war crimes confession. I could not give them that. I was beaten, put in stress positions, & shown confessions they had tortured from Kasler, Risner, & Denton. Finally I was beaten till my cast was completely broken & they worked over my broken arm which they had now rebroken. I couldn't go on.

I wrote a paper in which I said I was sorry I bombed N.VN and I would never do it again (half of which was true). They wanted more, but perhaps they felt they shouldn't take the chance of going further with me, but more likely they didn't need more confessions. They had been on a big push, as I found out later, & had more than they needed. At any rate they seemed satisfied & that night or the next I was taken back to the hospital & my arm was reset & put in another cast of the same type. That was on 9 Sept. the first time I learned a date (The gooks would never tell me what day it was or the time. This is typical, as I was to find out: they lie about every thing, even if it is easier or advantageous for them to tell the truth. Lying is a way of life for them).

That night I was moved to the Zoo or Camp America & put in cell 3 of the Barn. This cell was much bigger with 2 wooden pallets on concrete for beds & no windows. The heat coupled with the huge heavy cast covering my entire upper body & not being able to wash added considerably to my misery at HBH which continued at the Zoo; although for the first couple weeks I was allowed to wash more.

Here, I made my first contact with another American via the tap code. (A means by which we could tap thru the wall to other POWs. The gooks were fanatical about preventing us from seeing or communicating with other POWs.) Howie Rutledge was in cell 4 & was invaluable in giving me info about the system & picking up my morale. John Borling & Darrel Pyle were in cell 2 & also helped my morale. They said I'd probably get a roommate within a few weeks. Something I desperately needed was another American with whom I could talk.

The quizzes began again & the pressure would mount slowly. At first they just wanted me to write answers to biography questions. I was determined, however, to bounce back & never write another thing for those bastards. I was disappointed in myself for the first one & felt perhaps I had given in too easily. The quizzes were low pressure at first with the pressure building over a 5 week period. First threats then no cigarettes (if the heat was not on we got 3 cigs per day) no baths, no shave, & finally threats of serious torture. By now they wanted another confession.

I had moved to cell 7 of the barn after a couple of weeks next to Bunny Talley. It was the end cell, very small with one bed & no windows. We would comm via tap & were both optimistic. Bunny bet we'd be home by Xmas (he owes me a night's drinking at first bar we get to). I thought by April. On 19 Oct they moved me down to the Carriage House, a big old building that looked like a 2 car garage where they had been keeping some cows. They moved the cows out & me in. A 2 month torture session began & I knew I was in hell. I had been saving a banana I got a few days before & a piece of candy from Sept 2 (Gook's Independence Day) to celebrate Julie's birthday but I never saw them again.

I had been told to write a confession of crimes, a biography, & other information. I continually refused & now the real pressure was coming. Up to now all they had done at this camp was make me stand against the wall with my arms up for most of the day, after each quiz. When I got to the Carriage House, they beat me around then put my ankles in leg irons (I was still in the cast & the Qz man told me that because my arm was in a cast they could not tie me up tight (the ropes) but they could do things to my legs). I was sitting on a stool in front of a table with some paper & a pen on it. They tied the bar of the leg irons to the legs of the table holding my feet well off the floor & set the stool such that most of my weight was forcing my ankle into the irons. I was left in that position for 15 hours & harassed by the guards all night. My ankles bled & swelled such that the next day they had to pound the irons off. They then got a larger pair & had to pound them on. I was then tied to a stool with leg irons on & my free arm behind my back & beaten for long periods, with rest intervals, by the guards all day. I bled from my nose, mouth, eyes, & ears. That night they brought in a pallet, tied me to the pallet with leg irons & left me alone. I was so tired I could hardly see, yet I couldn't sleep. That night I had diarrhea & shit my pants. The next day I was beaten for that. For the next 3 weeks They left me tied to this pallet in leg irons in the middle of the floor of this big old bldg. Sometimes the guard would set the food out of my reach. A lizard fell from a rafter, landing 2 feet from my head & I watched it decay & rot. One night a rat or mole ran up my pants leg & was in my crotch before I woke up (I think it was a mole because it was so slow).

One day in Nov. they came in untied me & announced they were going to take off the cast. I had been begging for this for 6 weeks as it was driving me crazy. They left it on so long just to increase my discomfort. They drew a line around my bed with chalk & said I could not go outside that line (good luck) & left. For the next few days I could get around & looked out of cracks & saw other POW's: Jerry Denton, Jim Lamar, Sam Johnson, & Dave Hatcher (found out later). They often flashed a thumbs up signal toward my bldg which really helped my morale. I was not alone.

Another Qz found me still unwilling to cooperate & I was forced to stand against the wall with hands up for 18 hours a day. After about a week I was caught on my bed, was beaten then tied to the pallet with leg irons & cuffs. I stayed that way until 2 days before Xmas when I was let loose & given a bath, shave, & haircut. The day before Xmas I became very nostalgic thinking of Ginny, & the kids, & families & shed some tears. I was afraid I'd really let loose Xmas day but I kept control.

At the more recent Qzs the gooks had been asking me to write *anything* but I was determined. I was sure the reprieve was only for Xmas & dreaded the next day. Sure enough, they moved me the day after Xmas to the Outhouse, a solo bldg used for torture. Half of it was a pit. But I was left alone only to freeze in the bitter Jan. cold. On 24 Jan. I went to Qz & for the first time talked to another American. Hugh Buchanan was now my roommate & we went back to the Outhouse—I laughed for the first time.

2 days later, 26 Jan, we both moved from the Zoo to Vegas & I was put solo in the Mint. I thought: oh boy here it comes again, but a week later on 2 Feb, 67 I moved into Stardust cell-6 with Hugh Buchanan, Dave Burroughs, & Leroy Stutz. Rutledge was in 5 & Rehmann & Hatch[er] in 7. None of us knew very much about comm but I had done the most & took care of it. Most guys in Vegas were very optimistic at this time. 1 day I was caught in the window com[municat]ing with Howie & all of us were put in irons for 14 days. The cells were about 9' x 9' with heavy teak bunk beds & built in leg irons at the foot. The first night, Feb. 2, Root fell off a top bunk taking a bad blow on the head. I moved to the Golden Nugget (2) with him so the medics could take better care of him. We stayed only a few days & got contact with 2 new guys: Kramer & Bridger. The gooks wanted us to write answers to a few stupid, harmless questions for which I spent a night in the Riviera cuz I was still against writing anything.

On May 21, '67, Hugh, Root, & I moved to SD-3 & were joined by George Coker. We got the good deal of being dish washers & until the comm purge in August we were able to maintain good comm with the entire camp via the dishwashers. In early Aug Root was put in irons for whistling (accused of comm). A few days later I was also put in irons for getting into a pissing contest with Greasy over why Root was in irons. God it was hot. They made us wear long clothes for added discomfort & we both could reach into our crotch & pull out a handful of what looked like whipping cream. The first time we got out for anything (including a shit) was 10 days later & we could hardly walk.

About the 25th of August we were all moved. 2 at a time in a jeep to the Dirty Bird. We were each solo & were only there for a few hours & then brought back to Vegas 2 at a time driving all over hell & finally we all ended up together in the Desert Inn cell-7 with Root & I back in irons. We'll never figure that one out (all moves are with cuffs & blindfolds—the gooks are fanatics about blindfolds). We finally got out of irons for their Independence Day & were never put back in. George went to a Qz on 13 Sept & never came back. The gooks picked up his gear.

On 26 Oct, 1967, Ron Mastin moved in with Root, Hugh, & I & we stayed there in D1-7 until May of '68. On May 24 Ron & I moved to Camp Hope at Son Tay; Hugh & Root stayed at Vegas & moved out later (Hugh on 18 July & Root on Thanksgiving eve). I was put solo at Son Tay because Greasy didn't like me or my attitude. My room was 6' x 7' with no windows & 1 small vent that led out to a closed in porch. It was so God damned hot that summer I felt like I was living in a furnace. (There were 3 other Senior officers also solo in that camp). My cell was in the Opium Den cell-1. (Jeffrey & Moore in 2).

A few days before Xmas of '68 I was moved down to Beer Hall cell-2 & joined Hugh Buchanan, Bill Butler, Wayne Goodermote, & Dave Ford (the gooks apparently needed my cell for someone they were putting the heat on). A few months later Dick Brenneman moved in.

We got our first package in Feb of '69 & I learned for the first time that I had a son (Erik was 3½ then). I got 2 pictures in that first package, both of Julie & Erik, although I did not yet know Erik's name—we just called him Junior. I was very disappointed not to get a picture of Ginny, but loved those of the kids & was proud as a peacock. We sure enjoyed the Dots & nut rolls.

In May of '69 I had my first indications of intestinal problems. It began with diarrhea & was followed by 4 weeks of constipation. Up to this time I was exercising a lot & in as good a shape as could be expected under the existing conditions. I had trouble eating, much pain in my lower abdomen (left side) & began losing weight.

On Dec. 10, 1969, Hugh Buchanan, Dave Ford, & all the catholics in camp moved out. Before Xmas others moved in from Vegas. Butler, Goodermote, Brenneman & I were in BH-2 & were joined by Bob Jeffrey, Denny Moore, Ray Alcorn, & Jon Reynolds. It was an exciting night with 8 people in the room. The gooks had expanded the camp that fall by tearing down the back wall, making it bigger, & put up 2 new buildings for ping pong etc which were little used. Also that fall they took the pressure off everybody for writing things & making tapes. We speculated Hegdahl had blown the whistle on them.

That winter & spring my intestinal problem continued to get worse. It felt like a growth of some kind or an intestinal block. I could feel something hard in my lower left abdomen. I could not eat anything without getting very sick. Getting medical attention from the gooks was next to impossible. I was very weak, dizzy every time I got up & weighed about 105 pounds. Finally in May '70, the gooks took action. They moved me & Jeff to a special room out back that had big windows with plenty of fresh air. They gave me special food & medical care as well as letting us out in the fresh air & sunshine.

The day they moved us out there, they gave me my first letter & picture of Ginny. What a boost to morale. Also, I finally learned Erik's name (He was 4 yrs. 8 mos.). This, in total, I feel was the beginning of a long recovery.

At the end of June or early July 1970, Jeff & I moved back to BH-2. I felt better, was able to eat somewhat better (although it still gave me a sick feeling) & I began putting on some weight, about 125 pounds by then. On July 14 the entire camp of Son Tay moved to Camp Faith. This was truly a "good deal" camp by our standards. It appeared to have been recently built for the POW's. Cells with open windows & spacious cells. Half the camp was outside at the same time (3 hrs. per day) & eventually even permitted to talk to those who were still locked in. This kind of living was unknown to us. There were 57 men in our compound (A). I was in the large room (5) with 18 other men: Jeffrey, Moore, Reynolds, Alcorn, Glenn, Mastin, Fowler, Butler, Goodermote, Brenneman, Curtis, Forby, Collins, Temperley, McKamey, Bridger, Fer, & Hivner. A great bunch of guys who did much to bring me back to health. They gave me extra meat & milk & health foods from the packages & helped my spirits. Although the damn thing still gave me pain I was eating better, putting on weight & continually improving. As far as POW life goes this is the best we had it until the very last month.

This POW life, however, was short lived, as the night of 24 Nov, 1970 Everyone from Camp Faith was very unexpectedly moved to the big prison at Hoa Lo. The move was completely spontaneous & came as a result of the Son Tay raid[1] on the night of the 21st & early morning of 22 Nov. (If only we had still been at Son Tay—what a glorious way to leave No. VN.) When we learned about that raid later we almost cried.

On Nov 24, 70 all 57 of us from compound A of Camp Faith moved into cell block-3 at Hoa Lo, with Curly (Doug Clower) as S[enior] R[anking] O[fficer]. It was one big room about 25' x 70' but with 57 men we were very crowded—only 21" of bed space per man. The cell included the 19 of us from cell 5 of Faith plus Clower, Dutton, Stirm, Madison, Harris, Gene Smith, Terrell, Baker, Brunstrom, Jayroe, Swindle, Schierman, Frederick, Carrigan, Boyd, Gray, Thornton, Gaither, Seeber, Stutz, Ray, Chesley, Tschudy, Peel, Heilig, Brudno, Greene, Donald, Moe, Writer, Storey, Warner, Fisher, Ellis, Key, Galanti, Hatcher, & Clark.

The most significant aspect of the big room was the capability of exchanging ideas & intellectual information, particularly a conglomeration of what people could remember of foreign languages. I became conversational in French, Spanish, & German over the next year, & got an introduction to Russian. We had been living in a complete academic void & were thirsting for anything to occupy our minds. The gooks refused to give us anything of an intellectual or academic nature, including paper & pencils. This type of mental deprivation grinds on me as much as anything the gooks did. We also established chit passes with other cells so we could exchange info with them. We wrote on shit paper with cigarette ashes.

We were all very excited about moving in with so many men & were also quite optimistic that the war might end soon. A few days before Xmas we had a big inspection during which the gooks tore everything apart & took all we had except bare essentials. This inspection was triggered by the gooks finding a "grapevine" [contraband from the United States] in the possession of F. Crow when he was moved from Vegas. He had received it in a package from home. From this time forth the gooks cut up everything we got in packages before giving them to us, right down to the vitamins. Furthermore, they would not let us save items. Everyone was really ticked off about this and the inspection & we had

---

[1]On the evening of November 21, 1970, a team of seventy Special Forces troops raided the Son Tay prison camp, where Flom and other Americans had been held; however, the operation failed because the POWs had been moved to Camp Faith the previous July.

the Big Sing, which the gooks took for the start of a riot. They really clamped down on us after that for a long time & POW life was back to normal.

The first packages came for most of us in the winter of '69. The second in the fall of '69. The third was in Jan. of '70 & then they began coming every 3 months or so. We could take the entire package to our cell & consume them at our leisure including soap, toothpaste, toothbrushes, & gum. It was great, especially the parties we had in the big cell at Camp Faith. All this came to an end, however, with the big inspection at Xmas of '70. From then on—to the very last few days, getting a package was almost more frustration than it was worth. The gooks cut, chopped, ripped & smashed everything & withheld or stole much of it (which we never saw).

At Son Tay we wrote our first letter home in Nov. or Dec. of '69. From that time on we wrote nearly every month. This too, was frustrating, as the gooks censored to a ridiculous extent. In the winter of '71 at Hoa Lo, in order to try to gain some leverage to effect better conditions on our behalf, we had a letter moratorium. It lasted from Feb. thru Nov. 1971, during which time hardly anyone in the camp (about 350 men) wrote letters home. It was difficult to do as we knew it would be hard on our families, but our situation was grim & we thought we could eventually improve our living conditions & incoming mail. Toward the end, some were divided as to its effect as we had no real indications. We were happy to hear from new shootdowns in '72 that it had had a tremendous impact on the people back home. There is no way we could ever fully convey our extreme appreciation to the American people for all their attempts at putting pressure on the gooks to improve our living conditions & treatment. Our hearts swelled with pride when we heard of the letter siege on Paris.

On 13 May, 1972, 209 men left Hoa Lo & headed for a camp in the mountains near the Chinese border. Our hands were tied & we were blindfolded at first. There were about 12 POWs per truck in the convoy. This trip was about as miserable as you could possibly imagine. The road was unbelievably rough & we bounced around in the back of the truck like a sack of potatoes. To make it worse we got hardly any food & water & we spent half of one day parked with the sun beating down on the covered trucks. We arrived at the new camp (Dog Patch) on 15 May & you can't imagine how we dreaded the thought of another trip like that & how happy we were to have finally arrived. However, we felt that when we finally went back to Hanoi, we would be on our way home & we could go thru anything for that.

There were 12 bldgs with from 8 to 20 POWs in each. I moved into Curly with Clower (SRO), Jeffrey, Key, Glenn, Heilig, Curtis, Forby, Jayroe, Chesley, Frederick, Brunstrom, Butler, Gray, Fisher, Galanti, & Donald. There were 2 6-man cells, 1 4-man cell, & 2 solos. We used one solo to serve chow. We were allowed out of our cells during the day being locked in the bldg from 8–4. There was a very small court-yard for bathing, which the gooks covered with camouflage, thus no sun. The cells were very dark with 2 foot rock walls—much like a dungeon. There were only 2 good aspects—1. it was much cooler than Hanoi, & 2. the food was better—more protein with canned fish, although only rice, no bread. (John Frederick got very sick & left camp on 10 July, apparently with malaria. He has not been seen since).

In Sept. I was pulled from the room & put solo for 5 days in Casey (in a tiny dark cell). I had given a guard the finger behind the back, but, unfortunately, was seen by another guard. I think the gooks were looking for someone.

In late July, soon after J.F. had left, I got a very bad fever & the gooks took me down to Casey to give better medical care. Wally Newcomb was already there with a similar problem, but much worse. Larry Lengyel was taking care of him. A few days later Mike McCuistion came with the same type of fever. I was better in just a few days, but they kept me there over a week giving special chow & medicine. I think the gooks were a little jumpy after J.F. Mic & I moved back & Wally & Larry stayed a few more weeks.

My intestinal problem by now was well under control. I weighed about 160 pounds. It only gave me minor irritation in the lower abdomen & bowel movements were still irregular, but never went more than 4 or 5 days. I felt real good & was exercising. I was finally able to get off the CI list that Sept (Combat Ineffective). Also in Sept. Knutson & Ringsdorf, who had gone with Chesley to Hanoi for medical reasons, moved into our bldg.

On 18 Oct they had a small camp shuffle & Jeffrey, Key, Glenn, Clower, Ringsdorf, & Brunstrom moved out. Stavast (Lancer—camp CO), Pyle, Luna, Torkelson, Vogel, Hiteshew, Doughty, & Sawhill moved in. On Oct 25, 1972 they had a big campwide shuffle, as if they big boys had said—that's not what we had in mind. They arranged everyone by date of shootdown. I moved to Quicksilver, with Smitty Harris as SRO, Curtis, Forby, Pyle, Heilig, Galanti, Chesley, Knutson, Boyd, Alcorn, McKamey, Brazelton, Borling, Hatcher, Doughty, & ———. I felt pretty good about being in a group with some very early shootdowns & even then was getting ideas I might able to hang on their shirt tails & go out in the first group.

We were damned optimistic & then on Oct 31 when we heard the peace proposal we thought: "that's it, man, we're going home" till they read the last few sentences. I felt it was only a matter of time, though. If they are that close, surely it won't get away this time. I was still hanging on for Xmas—perfect.

On 2 Dec we saw some movies & half the camp was together at the same time. I met & talked to a lot of people & didn't see any of the movie. 9 Dec, magazines showed up for the first time. These were the first American magazines I had laid eyes on in almost 6½ years. Sport, Pro Football, Sports Illustrated, & some car mags. Great, even though they were 2 years old. On Xmas day half the camp was allowed outside together. This was another real thrill. By this time we were being allowed outside our courtyard on a designated area with another room—Aladdin (Al Runyan). We also had access to some textbooks (3—German, French, Russian) for the first time. Something had to be happening.

On 18 Jan, 1973 the camp filled up with trucks & I knew it was over. We'd go back to Hanoi & be home within 60 to 90 days. (Oh Ginny here I come). The next day almost everyone in the bldg was packed & ready to go by mid morning & definitely by mid afternoon. We sat around & waited till about 2 am on the 20th when we loaded up and moved out. We arrived at Hoa Lo that same evening (about a 16 hour trip). As we came in we waved & yelled at the guys we had left last May. All the fences & blinds were down. It was just one big courtyard now.

I moved into cell block 4 with 40 men. The 17 of us from Quicksilver at Dog Patch plus Al Runyan (Aladdin—SRO), George Hall, Keirn, Berg, Purcell, Spencer, Wells, Phil Butler, Schierman, Neuens, Neil Black, Means, Darrel Pyle, Brodak, Ratzlaff, Singleton, Perkins, Sima, Baldock, Byrne, Lockhart, Tom Barrett, & Halyburton. This was *IT* & we all knew it. The end was finally here.

The cell blocks at Hoa Lo were also arranged by shootdown date. The left side of camp, cell blocks 4, 6, & 7 were all early shootdowns— from Alvarez thru 9 Sept of '66. The other side blocks 1, 2, & 3 were from Sept '66 thru July '67. All shootdowns after that date had been moved to other camps (Group 3 at the Plantation, & group 4 at the Zoo). It appeared as though the left side of camp would be the first group (with the exception of CIs who would go first) & I was with them.

On 22 Jan the whole left side got outside together (either 4 hrs in am or 3 in pm—the other side was opposite) for half the day. Man it was great. The sad part of it is that that's the way we should have been living for the past 6 or 7 years. I finally got to see & talk to Jim Kasler & get our story. Jeff & I found we are still hot for the big trip & firmed up some plans. "Let's get going."

On 29 Jan, '73, the gooks read us the peace treaty & we learned it had been signed the 27th of Jan. A couple days later we got copies of the agreements.

31 Jan Knutson & Schierman left camp with all the other CIs. They went to New Guy Village. We were hoping the sick & wounded would go immediately, but it soon became evident they would be part of the first group.

On 3 Feb the ax almost hit my foot. They chopped the group at 7 Aug. I was 6 hours too late. I didn't make the cut & was somewhat disappointed at first but not for long. What's 2 weeks after 338 of them. (It turns out to be an agonizingly long 2 weeks). The early heavies moved out of Blue & Rawhide into the main camp—Risner, Stockdale, Denton, Rutledge, Jenkins, Franke. I moved into Rawhide with Norm Gaddis (SRO), Brady, Bliss, Nasmyth, Crow, Lawrence, Mehl, Moore, Blevins, Will Abbott, Stockman, Hughes, Wells, Fellowes, Brodak, Larson, & McNish. It turned out to be a real good deal from the standpoint of getting to know some of the big boys. We immediately started getting out with the other side of camp. On 7 Feb. Brazelton & North moved in as another cut was made which also included Burroughs, McSwain, Wendell, Pyle, Sandvick, & Gideon. I felt for them. Lawrence went to the Plantation.

The next day the entire camp got out together both morning & afternoon. This is the way we should have been living all along. I finally was able to talk to Risner, Denton, Stockdale & Rutledge under whose inspiration & policies I had been working for years. It was great being together & talking to everyone, but at the same time, we were anxious for them to leave so we could start our countdown. The gooks, typically, would tell us nothing as to the date the first group would leave or how big it would be. Each day there were many rumors & much speculation. Finally, Sunday night they shaved & bathed, got their traveling clothes & Monday morning 12 Feb. '73 before we got out the first group had left—116 strong.

The camp seemed almost lonely with half the men gone when we got out Monday morning, but now we could finally begin our countdown—15 days as we had it figured. These last days were really going slowly. There were many people with whom I could talk, but it was difficult to put aside the anticipation & expectations of the imminent release. I kept going over my expected relationship with Ginny, future plans, & philosophies of life & living that would be new to her. For the most part my mind was just caged on the all-important point that soon I was going home & would be with Ginny again & would be free.

On 14 Feb, at night, Norm went to Qz with the other SROs & came back with a list of 20 men that would be released within a few days. Immediately Nasmyth moved out & with the other 19 selected men— Purrington, Ringsdorf, Crecca, Flesher, Berger, Lane, Jensen, Fowler, Joe Abbott, Shively, Heiliger, Plumb, Milligan, McManus, Pirie, Mechenbier, Davies, Clark, & Bailey—& went to N[ew] G[uy] V[il-lage]. That night they shaved, got their traveling clothes, & were told they would leave the next day. They were not the next 20 men in shoot-down order & although the gooks had told Norm that it was a special release & they had been requested by the U.S. gov't, there was some question. 2 days later there was an exchange of notes between Pirie & Gaddis (via food) & it was decided they should not go as it was not according to the agreements—they were not in order. The whole thing smelled, surely the U.S. gov't would not ask for any other than the next 20 or a dire emergency family problem. We felt they were picked by the gooks for some unknown reason. (Maybe the gooks just wanted to show they could do something outside the agreements.)

By the way, in the morning of 14 Feb, all of us in Rawhide (cell-9) moved over to cell block-4 in the main camp. Pirie had told the gooks that he wanted to personally to talk to Col. Gaddis. That turned out to be unnecessary, however, as the evening of 16 Feb, the 20 "go homes" moved back into camp to cell block-1 from NGV. 4 men from cell block-1 moved to 3 & 13 moved in with us: Stark, Storey, Glenn, Monlux, Mecleary, Bliss, Hiteshew, Van Loan, Baugh, Cordier, T. Hall, Nix, & Wideman. (Wideman had been on the first list of 20, but was later replaced by Bailey from the Plantation). For 31 men in cell block-4.

On 17 Feb, we had a special "go home" meal. It was a last minute deal & appeared as though the gooks would be releasing 20 men the next morning. We felt the gooks were really squirming over what they had tried to pull. The gooks had announced to the world that they would have a "goodwill" release of 20 men & now they would have to come thru with it. We felt they would be forced to change their list to the next 20 men in order. Those on the present list wanted no part of an out of order release & would follow Col. Gaddis' orders to refuse to go.

It was very frustrating to me, as I was 11th & would be on the top 20. We kept waiting for something to happen. There were many Qz with Pirie & some with Norm G. We felt we were doing right & the gooks seemed to be knocking their heads against a stone wall. We hung on all night & the next morning expecting the gooks to change & "do it according to the agreements." The whole thing smelled so bad by now that even many of us in the top 20 were not so sure we wanted any part of it.

Col. Gaddis & Pirie kept telling the gooks that if this release was truly on the up & up all they had to do was let a representative of the Joint Military Commission verify it to Col. Gaddis. The gooks seemed so reluctant to permit this that we were sure something was amiss. Also, the gooks had said the release was to be 3 days ago. Why hadn't the U.S. aircraft come. Finally, at the very last minute, the gooks let Pirie see a U.S. L/C who verified the release & within 30 minutes (about noon 18 Feb—Sunday) The 20 were gone to the airport.

Man what frustration, wondering if you might be picked with the top 20 to go home within hours. Speculating on what kind of release it was, how those 20 men had been picked, & what the gooks were trying to pull. The excitement had made the past few days pass more quickly, but I was glad it was over. Now I could get back to our countdown. I expect the release to be the morning of 27 Feb, 15 days after the first group. Of course the gooks won't tell us anything.

Today is Wednesday, 21 Feb, 1973. I have been writing this for the past 2 days during the siesta period. A final countdown to something you have eagerly anticipated for 6½ long cruel years is slower than you might think. It is worse than the long hours of a Xmas eve for a small 6 year old boy who is awaiting the joys of opening presents on Xmas morning. Only 5 more days & I will be on the threshold of a new life. The expectations of new relationships with a wonderful wife & family in a manner few people have so vividly lived. My excitement & anticipation are real. The thoughts of dreams & plans finally being fulfilled are fantastic & satisfying. It's beautiful! I'll try to savor & absorb every moment. Ginny, I love you so very very much.

It is now Monday, 26 Feb. Saturday we all got our traveling clothes. Yesterday, 7 men from the plantation joined our group. Fuller, Waddell, McGrath, & Pollack moved into our cell block & Lawrence, Martin, & Hughey into 3. We now have a total of 106 men here in this group. Also 2 of the Thais, Pen & Dale are in Rawhide. It looks as though we will move out early tomorrow morning. The gooks are now preparing our special go home meal for this afternoon.

My feelings vacillate from being relatively calm to fantastic feelings of great expectations which bring butterflies to my stomach. The latter is usually aroused when I think of the initial reunion with Ginny. I'm ready to go, excited & anxious. I have no feelings of reservation or fear, but want to come out of here at mach 2 & live life to the fullest.

It is now the morning of 27 Feb. Yesterday afternoon we had our "go home" special meal & some men got back their rings & special effects. I slept better last night than I thought I would. I guess because I was

The cigarette wrappers on which Fredric Flom wrote his journal entries. (The pen has been added for scale.) Courtesy Fredric Flom.

emotionally exhausted. Right now everyone is putting their stuff in order & throwing out all kinds of crap. We expect to leave sometime this morning. The first group left very early, but I guess the gooks discovered they didn't need so much time.

This is going to be an exciting day & I'm super-anxious for things to get going. Ginny darling, our new life is about to begin. "My head is bloody, but unbowed."

If I could ever forgive these gooks for the inhumane living conditions, & physical torture for confessions, military information, good treatment statements, & propaganda; it will be even more difficult to find forgiveness for the mental deprivation they forced on us. Except for our last few months, we had a complete lack of contact with the outside world & educational materials. I can understand why they might not want us to have any contact with the outside world, but why couldn't they give us something to occupy our minds. The resentment & bitter-

ness I feel toward the gooks for this aspect of our treatment is deep &
undoubtedly enduring. They completely starved our minds & for apparently no other reason than an attempt to keep our morale as low as
possible.

When living conditions improved to the point that several men were
in contact with each other (direct or by notes—in '70) men began to
make up educational material, gathering information from memories.
Pens & ink were made from bamboo & ashes & the information written on shit paper. Whenever the gooks found such material—accidentally
or in inspections—they took it away & destroyed it. Things like poems,
vocabulary for foreign languages, history—all detrimental to the security
of the prison system, bastards. When they found we wrote on cigarette
wrappers they took the cigarettes out of packs & would not let us have
the packs, right up to 2 weeks before our departure. They also carefully
controlled the shit paper. It was not until Dec, 1972, that we saw any
U.S. magazines or got any educational material.

The mental anxieties caused by 6½ years with nothing to occupy the
mind controls my deepest hatred for these people. Time has healed the
physical pains & somehow eased their memory.

Equally as bad was their interference with letters & packages. In 6½
years I have received 14 letters, 3 this past week. The first letter I received
was on April 29, '70. It was written in Nov. of '69 by Ginny. Letters,
both in & out, could only be 7 lines long with only news of weather,
health, & family. Aggravating as it was with such a short supply of letters, the gooks made it even worse by not letting us to keep the letter.
They would allow us to see it only once for about 15 minutes, while
a gook officer was present & watching. It was great to get a letter, but
there was so little news & such a token effort by the gooks that it was
almost more frustrating than it was worth.

If the letter department was frustrating, the packages were exasperating.
The gooks found a "grapevine" in a '70 package & from then on they
reached us in shambles. No soap, toothbrushes, toothpaste, clothes—
except t-shirts & shorts, gum, & whatever the gooks wanted to steal.
Everything was opened & cut up in tiny pieces before we could have
it. We were allowed no containers or wrappers & would bring the food
in on plates from where the gooks decimated it. This occurred even during
our last week. Thank God they couldn't take the taste out of the food.

The food that we have gotten up here has ranged from bad to worse
by American standards. In the early years it was just enough to keep
us alive. 2 meals per day with, rice, very weak soup, & a small side
dish. It was not until 1972 that we got a reasonable amount of protein.
(Nothing compared to what we get in the states).

We had what was called "gastro-politics" up here. When the food would get better, we felt it was because something happened on the outside which indicated the war might be ending soon. It never really worked out however. At any rate, when the food would improve, our morale went up. When it went back to normal we decided that whatever it was, fell through.

In late '67 we started getting bread, which was a good deal. It was invariably very stale, however. In the fall of '68 the[y] started giving us a small piece of bread for breakfast early in the morning so we had 3 meals so to speak. In the summer of '71 they started giving us something with the bread—sugar, banana, milk, candy—which was the best deal they came up with. When we moved to Dogpatch it was back to rice, but we got more protein than usual; first with fish & later in buffalo meat. The food these past few weeks prior to release has been nothing special. No more shitty good food for me though. Tomorrow it's back to the land of good food & my own "World's greatest Cook."

The living conditions were miserable. Tiny dark rooms with no windows. Ungodly hot during the summer & bitter cold during the winter. There only 2 reasonably comfortable nights, weatherwise, October & April. The rats had free reign during the night & mosquitos made it impossible without a net. When the heat was not on, the daily routine called for: 1) dump shit bucket, 2) 1st cig, 3) wash, 4) chow, 5) 2nd cig, 6) chow, 7) last cig & that was the day. The rattle of keys at your door at an unusual time always caused the heart to sink & the excitement that fear brought. Unusual door openings were not good.

We have 2 very appropriate sayings up here that have raised our morale at various times throughout the past years: "Fuck em, we'll be going home someday & they have to stay" & "FAG"—fuck all gooks. These messages have been sent back & forth between fellow prisoners in all manner of covert methods. They were great for morale, especially when you were under the gun.

Great Scot, what happened? I was programmed to leave, and now it is Tuesday noon. Colonel Gates had a quiz with Frenchy this morning and two officers from downtown. They told him that Saigon made some violations of the agreements and our government endorsed them. Thus we were on "hold" and would not be released today, something for which I have waited and dreamed for six and a half years, and at the very last moment something goes wrong. I guess it's a fitting finale to this continued frustrating existence. But is it a finale? How long will it take them to settle their differences? When will we finally go—tonight, tomorrow, in a week, a month? Just another indication of what a POW's life is like.

Nothing is ever certain, and you never know what is coming, or what will happen next.

It is deathly quiet in the cell now. No one is saying anything. Last night there was a continuous roar of conversation. Everyone was expectant. Now we are all disappointed, and wondering—wondering how long it will be when we will go, what will happen. There is nothing left to do but wait, once again as we have had to do for over six years we must wait and wonder.

What will my total days in North Vietnam be? As of today, February 27, 1973, it is 2,395 days—it is only a matter of time—our standard cliche. How I hate it.

It is now Tuesday night. The realization of the magnitude of this disappointment has been sinking deeper all afternoon. I was planning for the past two weeks on being at Clark this very moment and having a telephone conversation with Ginny tonight. It is a difficult pill to swallow to be so close and then experience complications. I should have expected it, however, and, indeed, I had been suppressing those fears.

There is no reason for me to have expected my release to go smoothly as nothing else has for six and a half years. I will not breathe a sigh of relief until the wheels are in the well of the C-141 with me on board. These gooks are liars and cheaters and cannot be trusted. I have experienced that ever since I have been in their prisons, and I have no reason to believe that their leaders are any different, especially after having heard so much of their propaganda.

If I sound bitter, it is because I am—but at the same time, I speak the hard truth. I have been existing and waiting for one thing for six and a half years—my release. Then I learn it is imminent, and finally am able to start a count down to the final day. Then at the very last moment complications arise, and we are held. It is difficult for me to fully express my total disappointment and frustrations. Maybe it is a fitting climax to a horrible situation.

After so many years, what's another few days? The answer is threefold; one, not knowing how much longer it will be; two, time—when you are so close—seems so sadistically long; and three, even our release could not go smoothly. There is even that terrifying thought that it all could fall through, and that everything will start all over again. I am somewhat of an undying optimist, however. I feel we will go tomorrow, and if not, the next day, and so on. I feel these complications are only temporary, and that they will be settled quickly. I cannot fathom that things could be this close and then go to hell. Uncle Sam would not permit it. It may be only a matter of a day or two, but nevertheless it is very frustrating and damned disappointing. Great Scot, how I hate these gooks. I am almost glad they won't let me forget it right up to the end.

Friday night, and we are still here! I thought last Friday was the last beer call that I would miss. Wednesday, some of the men got back some of the money they had had on their persons when they were shot down. Wednesday night we saw some flicks—dancing, circus, the signing of the agreements in Paris, B-52 shoot downs and damage, and the capturing of the crew. Yesterday I got sick and had a fever last night, but feel okay today except being weak and tired. Many men have had the flu recently. If that's what I had, it was a very mild case, thank goodness.

Today a guard told Colonel Gates that if nothing changes we will be able to go tomorrow. My hopes are high again. Every time I think about where I should be, and what I should be doing right now, I get a horrible sick feeling in the pit of my stomach. I am very bitter toward the gooks for holding us these extra few days, but that's nothing new. I am somewhat bitter toward the gooks for damned near everything they have done. It is ironic my departure should be as frustrating as my entire stay, but it's a fitting finale, keeping the total experience in the proper perspective. Let's hope that tomorrow is the day—2,399 days now.

Guess what, it's Saturday night, and I am still in North Vietnam. This whole affair smells of a giant RF by the devil himself. Maybe a week or so ago if you heard some men declare they would do drastic things if they were here a day after February 27, and he wanted to see if he could witness some interesting reactions, if the devil could see inside minds, he would be successful.

Enough of this bullshit! Tomorrow is the day. Two turnkeys and a cooker said we will go tomorrow. They have some special chow in the kitchen for our morning meal. We shaved this afternoon—which is unusual. Finally Colonel Gates went to quiz a little while ago with the other SROs, and Frenchy told them we would leave tomorrow after the morning meal. This is it—it's got to be true. Tonight is my last—"last night!" I couldn't sanely take any more complications in this release operation. Tomorrow I will be free and talking to Ginny on the phone, and my new life will finally begin. I will be born again Sunday, March 4, 1973, 2,400 days of interrupted life.

It is now Tuesday, 6 March, about 5 PM. This is a new phase— "Freedom Phase." I am still standing in the threshold of my new life looking with awe, anticipation, & excitement at everything that is before me. It's wonderful. There is no way possible for me to express in words

the emotions I have felt the past 3 days. It has been continuous excitement, things happening, & no time to take a breath. This is the first
opportunity I have had to get at this, so we will have to go back to Sunday.

Sunday morning we were let out a little earlier than usual (6–6:30)
& given breakfast. Everyone was anticipating the release & very eager
for things to start happening (we remembered that the first group had
left camp by 6:30). Also we were very gun shy of complications & would
not breath a sigh of relief until the gear was in the well on our way out
of NVN. About 7:30 they gave us a semi-special meal with pork fat
& soup. Nobody ate very much, expecting to leave shortly. A guard
told us to be bathed & ready by 8:00. We were & nothing happened.

It was a dreary morning, rain & mist with low ceiling & viz. There
was some talk an aircraft could not get in. We sat around & the minutes
dragged, everyone anxious & wondering. By 9:00 the weather was looking better & we were sure they could get in. The minutes were agonizingly slow, creeping to 10 & then 11. What a battle time can be. Nothing
was happening—we were sure, but yet,—complications??

We had been put back in our rooms about 9:30 or 10:00. About 11:00
something finally happened—people, people,—photographers, newsmen,
military, poured into our compound. They came right to our door &
we saw it was the ICC. After a long hassle the gooks finally got rid
of the newsmen & photographers & the ICC came in. (We would not
permit the gooks a big propaganda show, & they were upset but had
to comply). The ICC made a brief pass around the cell shaking hands
with us & saying a few brief words. It was worth a few tears. "We're
here to take you home." "You're heroes." "The whole world is waiting
for you." This was our first real indication of what was coming, although
the new shootdowns had said we were heroes and wouldn't believe it.
Of course we thought they were probably just trying to make us feel better.

The ICC left the compound by about 11:30 & almost immediately the
gooks told us to get ready to go. It was almost a rush now. We lined
up in the compound, 106 of us, & they called off our names in order
of capture: Barbay, Hubbard, McSwain, Burroughs, North, Wendell,
Gideon, Sandvick, Pyle, Brazelton, Kasler, Flom... We went over into
the heartbreak courtyard in groups of 20, put our traveling clothes on
there, & then loaded on buses (in groups of 20 (always)).

While we were putting on the "traveling" clothes the excitement continually rose (& it hasn't dropped off yet). The bus trip to the airport
was very interesting from the standpoint that it was the first time we
have ever been able to look around outside prison walls. We had always
been blindfolded. We saw some bomb damage, but more than that we

saw what were once beautiful bldgs. Completely run down & dirty filth
& squalor those people live in. "Fuck 'em they gotta stay & we're going home."

When we came out of the prison there were thousands of gooks lin-
ing the street. They were not antagonistic, but not friendly either. The
bus trip was fairly quick, but not as fast as my heart. We got to the airport about 12:45. They gave us some beer & cookies, but that only took
about five minutes. We came around the corner in the bus & saw that
C-141 it was beautiful!! We got off the bus lined up—marched 50 ft forward & before I knew it we were going thru the change-over 1 at a time,
but quickly: FREDRIC R. FLOM 1/LT USAF a handshake & salute
with Gen Ogan & a few steps the same with Col Lowry & an escort
officer was taking me to the aircraft. I almost wanted to run. Americans
beautiful Americans!! I was greeted by a flight stewardess with a kiss
& into the aircraft. Shaking hands with everyone—& before I knew it
the rest were aboard & the engines starting—taxi—takeoff—wheels in
well & a sigh of relief & a big beautiful yell for freedom. It was all
so fast so smooth, so beautiful, so great, & so much before me.

7

Friends and Loved Ones

GIs coped with the danger and madness around them through the support of family and friends, and correspondence with those back in the States served as a major vehicle for maintaining those relationships. Young men compared their experiences with those of their fathers in World War II. Letters to younger brothers often contained unsanitized accounts of the war as well as hopes that siblings would be spared service in Vietnam. Some letter writers confided in their girlfriends or spouses, and a few of the older men tried to explain things to their children. GIs also developed friendships in Vietnam that helped them through their year of service. Some built relationships with the Vietnamese people who worked and lived around them; children especially captured their hearts. Others met future spouses while serving in Vietnam. Perhaps most vital for surviving the year were the friendships forged with one's buddies, for survival itself often depended on them.

Parents and Brothers

JOHN R. MILLER, JR., (b. 1949) of Madison enlisted in the army in March, 1967. He served as an airborne electronic countermeasures operator (1st Radio Research Co. [Avn.], 224th Avn. Bn., 50th Radio Research Grp.) near Cam Ranh Bay and Phu Bai from March, 1968, to March, 1969. Discharged in August, 1969, he now lives in Olympia, Washington, where he is a social worker. In the following letter, Miller shares his flight experiences with his father, John R. Miller, Sr., who had flown a B-17 bomber in World War II. (For the elder Miller's wartime experience, see Michael E. Stevens, Sean P. Adams, and Ellen D. Goldlust, eds., *Letters from the Front, 1898–1945,* Voices of the Wisconsin Past [Madison, Wisconsin, 1992], pp. 91–92.)

April 11, 1968

Dear Dad,

. . . I'm fine as usual, and enjoying flying in the old P-2. All the jerking around used to bump me around a bit at first, but I don't even notice it now.

Flying is really something in this type of a situation. Now I think

I know a bit more of how you used to feel. You get up early in the morning, too early to crawl out of the rack little more an airplane. You scarf down a quick greasy breakfast. Head for the briefing and get ready to fly. You've got your flight suit, with maps & your survival kit and 45, and helmet. Maybe you have to pull wheel pins, we do. You watch the props go round slowly then with burst of smoke the old recip kicks in. You run under the wheel bombay to check the fans, the prop wash pushing air at you, you give thumbs up to the crew chief who in turn gives it to the pilot. You then haul the fire extinguisher over to the other man who's to pull pins. You wait till he's done then comes the flap test. He pulls down 10° then 20°, you give him the up sign. The crew chief gives you the signal to pull pins, you run up and pull them then move up into the aft section and you're ready to fly. Water-wings, harness and all.

You then run down and out for the power tests, and before you know it you're up and away into the black sky. The sky really looks bad then. Really mean and black, black clouds. You fly and you think a lot. Then you wait for the first sign of sunlight. You see it. The sky is a welcome sight now. The clouds pink with a powder blue background and a few shafts of golden light flashing through. It makes you feel good then, secure. It makes you feel as though someone who really cares is watching.

I don't know if that's the way you felt but it's the way it is to me. It's scary when you first get up there, but when that great sun comes up it's a whole different day. I imagine things were different though with you. But the sky was still black and mean and the sun still came up.

Well dad, so long, if mom wants to read it go ahead, it was a bus. letter but I just got carried away a bit.

LOVE,
john

JAMES E. COOPER (1946–1993) grew up in Milwaukee and worked as a chemist before being drafted into the army in January, 1970. He served as a fire direction controller (HHB, 2–320th Arty., 1st Bde., 101st Abn. Div. [Airmobile]) near Phu Bai from June, 1970, to August, 1971. Cooper was discharged in August, 1971, and earned a nursing degree from the University of Wisconsin-Milwaukee. He worked as an infection control nurse at the Veterans Administration Hospital in Milwaukee until his death in November, 1993. In this letter to his family, Cooper assures them of his safety and highlights his reservations about media accuracy in reporting the war.

Eagle Country, July 13, 1970

Dear Mom, Dad, & D.J.,

. . . One other thing concerning the war action around us, judging from [what] I read in the newspapers and hear on the radio (Armed

Forces Radio not my radio here) the news is presented more or less out of proportion as to what really is happening. For example if we take 3 mortar rounds—all of which landed in the middle of one of our garbage dumps the radio the next morning usually says something to the effect that "Eagle was hit by mortars, rockets, V-2s, buzzbombs, Kamikazes, human wave attacks, and suicide squads last night but our gallant men fought on amidst all the terror." So when you hear this nonsense over the radio or TV or read about it in the Journal—take it with a grain of salt. I'll let you know from time to time what's been doing. I monitor the radio for my area of operations so I know pretty well what's been going on. It's not that we take this war with a grain of salt—we here are always prepared for anything and as far as that goes we expect anything at anytime so we're always on guard. So this deal about the news back in the "World" is one of the things that bugs us here—there's a lot of needless worry on the part of our families, if anything happens we'll let you know. Currently, we're at a lull right now—however with only a couple of months to go before the rains come in we're more alert than ever. So don't worry—I'll write and tell you when to start worrying. . . .

Love,
Jim

MIKE JEFFORDS served with the Marine Corps near Da Nang. In the first of the following two letters, Jeffords shares with his parents his newfound sense of the fragility of life. In the second letter, written to his younger brother, he dispels romantic myths about war. (For a biographical sketch of Jeffords, see chapter 1.)

Da Nang, [May, 1965]

Dear Folks,

First, I'm okay and in good health. No complaints. Second, I haven't written much because of a guilty conscience. I said I'd write and let you know what I'm doing, and I've done that up to a point. Mainly because I haven't wanted to worry you. All of what I've written has been true—we hadn't been doing much. Within the last few weeks things changed somewhat and I struggled with myself trying to decide whether to keep the same deleted parts of our activities in my letters or tell the entire truth. I was, and still am, concerned about whether you will blow the realistic facts out of proportion and go insane with worry or accept them, as I have, as part of my job and responsibility to the United States: the people and government. And my concern for your future in coming years. For these reasons I am glad to be here. But, I'm wandering off base.

This is the most difficult letter I've had to write, believe me.... It isn't because of any fore-doomed premonitions but because of some incidents I've had recently:

I thought you might get the wrong idea before but I think you would like to know that I've been at mass every chance I get when they can arrange services. Usually, every Sunday. I carry a rosary with me at all times too. Not out of fright or the fear of death, but, I imagine, the thought that you're not alone out there. That someone's with you. The old cliché fits, "There's no atheists in a foxhole." When we go out each man is with his own body, personality, and thoughts. No one can help him but himself and his beliefs.

On Easter Sunday morning the chaplain said, "You're now in a situation where all of the distractions of life, which used to be so important, are gone and only the harsh realities of this war are present in your minds. The thought that it can happen suddenly and quickly to 'you,' not the other guy."

I believed him then, but not completely. Until I thought of a few things, and realities. We've been engaged in combat action (company-size patrols) against the Viet Cong. And a number of times in the capacity of reinforcements to Marine patrols hit too hard by the Cong. I was in on one operation where the bullets came extremely close. We sustained one wounded man and we killed a VC. It occurred over a three hour period. The chaplain's words made me think of it. What drove the point home was another operation where the squad, (8 men), I was leading was ambushed in the jungle from a distance of 15–20 feet away by two VC with carbines. One second we were stumbling along in the stifling heat; the next second a round came very, very close to me again. I know because I heard it and literally felt the "breeze." When I turned to fire I saw a kid I had trained go down in a heap. I fired 19 rounds under approximately 12 seconds. The entire ambush lasted almost .... 30 *seconds* before the VC vanished in the brush. The kid, (19), the VC hit was saved by the barrel of his M-14—it deflected the round when it smashed into it. He was treated for minor shrapnel injuries to his neck, shoulder, chest, and arm. One second, he said, he had been thinking of sitting in a shady, cool spot; the next he was fighting for his life. He's earned a purple heart. Two more did that day, too. The chaplain's words made me realize how close that thin line of life is.

He also makes me realize how unfair I've been to you by not telling you the whole truth. If anything would have happened you would have been totally unprepared for it. I won't bother you with the "exploits" any more. What has been happening and will happen in the future is

*Mike Jeffords, Landing
Zone Dove, June 1, 1965.
Courtesy Mike Jeffords.*

better left forgotten. What I've almost done, will have to do, or have
already done is better forgotten, too.

If I've caused you more pain, I'm sorry, (that's a stupid word; it doesn't
say half of what you mean), I can only justify myself by saying I believe
in facing facts straight on—it takes some of the sting out.

I will have to close now. I have a lot to do. There's another operation
tomorrow.

Before, I beat you to death completely with too much. Remember,
two things: First—90% of my job here is boredom, the other 10% is
action. Don't be misled or overexaggerate. *Remember most of my previous
letters.* And Second—I believe in my job 100%. I wouldn't want to be
anywhere else, for either Tim would be here or Francis in five years—*I
wouldn't want that.* If President Johnson wouldn't have sent us in; I would
have found some way to get here. Even by volunteering or extending
my time. So, I'm not forced here. Happiness and war are not synonymous.
I'm no war-lover—I don't enjoy this. But it has to be done. Why not me???

Say hello to everyone. I hope everyone's well and happy. *I am in good health!*

See you soon!!

Sincerely,
Mike

Da Nang, [June 15–20, 1965]

Dear Francis,

. . . As for your question of the fighting—it is hard to tell you. Not because you are young; it would be just as hard to tell even an older person. You have to live with it every day. All you really learn is how very close you are to that thin line between life & death. How close God is to you. Your nun has told you this very often, out here you can see how true that is. You must be ready at all times to meet Him.

Fighting out here isn't like the movies, Francis. I wish there was some way I could make you understand that. When a man goes down it isn't "tricky" or exciting or "sharp" the way he looks. When he stops moving you realize that his soul has left his body and you caused it. It makes you wonder whether he had time to ask God for pardon for his sins. The area we're working in is made up mostly of Catholics. Many of the VCs are Catholic. I sometimes wonder if they want a priest or not. They die very, very alone, Joe. I've answered you man to man, Francis. I hope you realize "fighting" means someone will not see his family again. Someone has to win; someone lose. And in the end no one wins—so it isn't good to be proud of having to fight a war. You do it because of responsibility. . . .

Till the next time you write,
Mike
Marine-type GI Joe

To avoid worrying their parents, GIs sometimes omitted details that they included in letters to their brothers. HOWARD SHERPE, a field medic in the central highlands, wrote the following letter to his younger brother, David. Despite Howard's hopes, David was drafted two years later and was wounded while serving with the army in Vietnam. (For a biographical sketch of Sherpe, see chapter 4.)

[1966]

[Dear David,]

. . . It won't be long before you'll be back in school. Just wish I was back there too. As far as the draft is concerned, you can tell them your brother is giving the VC hell for you too, and that some other family can furnish a son. There are plenty of others around. Stay out of this place if you possibly can. Too many people are getting killed and maimed here and I'm not sure what it's all for. I've already seen more destruction of lives than I care to, and it's only just begun. Don't say anything to Ma and Dad about what I tell you in the letters I write to you. I'll try not to tell them things that will make them worry any more than they already do. I'll write to you when I need to get things off my chest. After seeing what I've already seen in this short time, I don't know how I'm ever going to survive this year. . . .

[Howard]

STEVEN A. HOVEL (b. 1947) was born in Red Wing, Minnesota, and was a student in Rochester, Minnesota, when he enlisted in the air force in January, 1969. During his tour of duty, he worked with target overlays (12th Recon. Intelligence Technology Sqdn.) at Tan Son Nhut from January through September, 1972, when he was discharged. He currently works as an artist and lives in DeForest. Hovel wrote after learning that his brother, Dan, had received a high number in the draft lottery and consequently would not have to serve in the military.

[February 4, 1972]

Notice How often I write when it's Free. Ha Ha Why not.

I'm ecstatic I really cried and my eyes still water when I think of all You don't have to go through. All the unnecessary shit that Uncle Sam's chief Sergeant Mickey Mouse tracks all over the Place. You are free. WOW! I've been looking in the Stars and Stripes waiting on nerve's edge. But today this Friday I'm oh wow what can you say? I'm So happy.

I had to let you know I found out. It is just great*!!!!!* I still don't really believe it.

Do you know what this means? I'm sure you don't know fully. It means you shouldn't have to see any of this crap. An experience yes but totally unnecessary, a toothpick of unnecessary experience in a Norwegian Forest. As remote as it seems I live on this last Summer's Memories alone. I can relax and give a Sigh. If I were to die it would be happily.

I'm a Skeptic with a new Skeptic view of my Skepticism. Maybe there is something just purely good. Well not really because think of the others who might not have fared so well. Pray they are OK. I'm going back to the orphanage downtown and give away a 25 pack of gum and tell them it's from you. All the little Half American Half Vietnamese Children who have been Abandoned. Why not collect some old clothes, anything, they surprisingly will use everything. . . .

Steve Hovel made this drawing after learning that his brother had drawn the number 315 in the 1972 draft lottery. Courtesy Steve Hovel.

Again Congrats! It couldn't have happened any better than this. When I come home this Fall we will all go out for a steak dinner & Wines the works to celebrate our part's end in the war!

love—Peace
Your Bro—Steve
SHovel

Girlfriends, Spouses, and Children

Many young Americans in Vietnam left girlfriends—and in some cases wives and children—behind in the United States. Draft boards considered married men among the last of possible draftees prior to August, 1965, when President Johnson revoked their deferment. In other cases, men and women met future spouses while in Vietnam and exchanged correspondence while separated.

ERHARD P. "ERIK" OPSAHL (b. 1943) was born in Port Washington and was living in Thiensville when he enlisted in the army in July, 1965. He received his commission in November, 1966, and served as a lieutenant with a mechanized infantry unit and as a scout platoon leader (A Co., 2-22d Inf. [Mech.], 3d Bde., 25th Inf. Div.) near Dau Tieng from September, 1967, until September, 1968, when he was discharged. Opsahl returned to active duty in February, 1975, and served until his retirement in July, 1991. He now lives in McFarland and works for the Wisconsin Department of Military Affairs. Lieutenant Opsahl met his first wife, Marta Reeves, while on R & R in Australia. Opsahl and Reeves corresponded while he was in Vietnam, and they married in December, 1968.

May 18, 1968

Hello, Lover (I think),

Enclosed please find: Engagement ring; 1 each; O[live] D[rab] (green); Cracker Jack-type; adjustable; made in Hong Kong; price: CLASSIFIED.

Really there has not been much time lately with rocket attacks, mortar attacks, ambushes, and the paperwork involved because of the wounded and killed.

I now live or sleep in a bunker that is underground. My nights are more peaceful now.

Last night we asked the cards many questions and came up with many answers. Some were pleasant for me like: I would marry you; three children, two boys and a girl; I would be wounded at the end of this month, and it would take five weeks to recover. I don't know about these cards.

I hope to write more later,

Love,
Erik

THRESSA D. "TERRI" SHAY (VINING) (b. 1947) grew up on a farm near Ettick and volunteered to serve in Vietnam in the fall, 1969, after completing a nursing program at Eau Claire State University. Lieutenant Shay was stationed at Pleiku (71st Evac. Hosp.) and at Qui Nhon (67th Evac. Hosp.) from June, 1970, to June, 1971. In early November, 1970, she met Sergeant Bill Vining, an operating room specialist serving in Quang Tri, on a blind date. The couple became engaged three days later and were married in Hawaii on January 15, 1971. Terri and Bill were separated for the next nine months, first at different locations in Vietnam and later when Terri returned to the United States to finish her service detail. During their time apart, they exchanged audiotaped letters, including the one from Terri transcribed here. The Vinings were discharged in 1972, and today they both work as nurses in Florida.

March, 1971

. . . Sure wish I could find a way to get up there, but I know we're kind of too short of nurses right now to do anything, and you're also too unpredictably busy as yet. You're not sure what's gonna happen, that either one of us can go the other direction. "Oh, tell me why, he's only a couple hundred miles away," and people just don't flat understand. And I say, "Hey, they're working up there, we're working down here, and it just can't be right now. And it don't make no difference if it's 300 or 3,000, 200 or 2,000 or 150." I'm not sure what it is, but they just quite don't understand that and [it] frustrates me sometimes! It's funny, though, you know most people think it's really a dirty deal that we're getting and I really do agree with them. And really it's the people in command who are pulling the stuff and not the general average person in the service.

Well, onto better subjects. I'm a little down. I guess I need to talk to you on the phone again, that brings me up more than anything does. And I know it's not your fault. You probably just haven't been able to get through. I tried last night and I couldn't even get Phu Bai let alone get any further than that. . . .

Home—I'm down to fifty-nine days, Love, and a little over thirty til I see you, thank God. Sure wish it were three or something, but I guess I'm gonna make it through this next month just like you are. Even though it doesn't seem like I will sometimes. I just love and miss you so much, darling, and you'd better believe it. You're the only guy for me, and I love you until the twelfth of never, and that is so. . . .

Love,
Terri

JOSEPH E. PILON (b. 1939) was born in Fond du Lac and was practicing as
a physician there when he enlisted in the Navy Reserve in February, 1967.
Dr. Pilon served as a general medical officer (1/5th Mar., 1st Mar. Div.) in
Que Son, Chu Lai, Da Nang, Phu Loc, and Dong Ha from May, 1967, until
May, 1968. He was discharged in February, 1969, and now lives in Menasha,
where he is an orthopedic surgeon. Pilon wrote the following letter to his
wife, Stephanie, about his daughters, one of whom he had never seen.

Hill 51, Que Son, August 23, 1967

Hi Honey,

Good morning. Looks like it's going to be a hot one today. It's only
7:30 and already we're cooking.

I was just thinking about "Birdseed" this morning and especially in
relationship to time and my knowledge of her.

F'rinstance, to me it seems she was born oh—about 2 weeks ago at
most. And yet she's more than 6 weeks old. I don't suppose you think
she's changed much but I imagine she occasionally grins and belches.

She'll probably be 11 mo old before I see her. I wonder if she'll like
me or whether she'll be mad at me because I haven't been there all along;
whether she'll accept me or crawl away into a corner until she figures
she can trust me; whether she'll become upset with me when I try to
steal her mother's attention or if she'll try to draw us closer together.

And Anne—will she forever have a mistrust of men because her daddy, who she thought loved her very much (and does) and for whom she
looked forward to interrupt her games at the end of the day and get her
ready for bed, suddenly walked out of her life for a year without even
telling her why.

And how could I have explained war to her so that she could understand why other little girls' daddies got together to fight other little girls'
daddies and after it was all over a lot of little girls would be without
daddies. Perhaps she would understand it if someone else wanted her
daddy more than she did—but no, that someone else is interested only
in destroying her daddy. Do you think you could explain "why" to Anne
and have it make sense—so that she won't think that God and the whole
world hate little girls and are forever trying to make them unhappy?

But that's what mothers must do—explain the impossible "why" while
men dream the impossible dream. I've never been so impressed with
how much is expected of "mommies"—and how much respect, love,
trust, hope, dependence, and responsibility is encased in that one little
word uttered by a child—"mommy." It must be terrifying. Perhaps if
men understood this more, if they were able to experience this same
terror day after day, minute after minute, there would be no need to

go seeking terror in battle. Ah yes—perhaps. Well, sweetheart, time for MEDCAP.

Love,
Joe

DONALD L. HEILIGER (b. 1937) grew up in Madison and began active duty in the air force in September, 1958. During the Vietnam War, Captain Heiliger was stationed at Takhli Air Base, Thailand, in 1966, and Korat Air Base, Thailand, in 1967 (469th TFS). On May 15, 1967, while on a bombing run thirty miles northeast of Hanoi, his F-105 Thunderchief was shot down. Heiliger remained a prisoner of war in North Vietnam for the next five years and nine months. After his release in February, 1973, he completed a master's degree in Latin American studies at George Washington University. Heiliger retired from the air force in August, 1985, as a colonel, and he currently lives in Stoughton.

Heiliger wrote the following brief communication to his family near the end of his captivity. The North Vietnamese largely did not allow communication between their prisoners and the outside world until late 1969 and then limited correspondence to a seven-line form on which the prisoners were to "write legibly and only on the lines." Heiliger conveyed his holiday greetings to his children under the strict conditions laid down by his captors.

November 22, 1972

Dear Children,

This letter sends warm Christmas greetings and Happy New Year. I truly was very elated when I received the picture of all of you sitting in your home. Have your Mother write to me soon and also send a nice picture of herself. Jim has very long hair, not too long however, and it presently must be the current style. You girls look very beautiful and all of you've grown so much since I left. I'm proud of each one of you. Happy Thanksgiving & Anniversary to my parents.

Love,
Dad

Vietnamese People

Even though Viet Cong guerrilla tactics made it difficult for servicemen to distinguish between friend and foe, many Americans nonetheless established relationships with the Vietnamese people. The children in particular captured the attention of American soldiers, many of whom were just barely adults themselves. The following letters illustrate the importance of these relationships.

TODD JACKSON served in the army as a LRRP member near Cu Chi prior to his death in January, 1968. In the following letter, Corporal Jackson explains to his parents the high price paid by Vietnamese children who attempted to help U.S. troops. (For a biographical sketch of Jackson, see chapter 3.)

September 9, [1967]

Dear Mom & Dad,

Hope everyone's fine at home. I sure miss it, a guy never realizes how good home & civilian life really are.

A couple little Vietnamese kids, about 9 or 10 years old, showed us where a mine was buried. It was located right outside our forward field base camp, right in our old tracks. The little kids saved about 6 or 7 lives by telling us. The same night after they told us, their parents and the rest of their family, including little babies, all had their throats slit, to set an example. This is the reason we can't win this war. The people can't help us, and without their help it's almost impossible to distinguish between an innocent villager and a Viet Cong. Charlie watches so close for security leaks, if a person helps us once, he never lives to do it again. At present, we're keeping the little kids inside the perimeter for safety reasons. The dreaded day has finally come, we're going to the Ho Bo woods in War Zone C, the day after tomorrow. It's located about 20 miles from here, on the Saigon river, it's a thick wall of jungle, right on Charlie's main resupply route. He frowns on us, disrupting his resupplies. I'm sure we'll see a lot of action there, but that's what makes life exciting.

I'm running out of things to say, so I guess I'll sign off.

Love
Todd

KRIS BLUMER served as an army rifleman near Di An prior to his death in June, 1969. Blumer was also taken by the Vietnamese children, who were equally fascinated by him, as he explains in the following letter to his family. (For a biographical sketch of Blumer, see chapter 3.)

[December 9, 1968]

Dear Mom & all,

. . . The Vietnamese people are much the same as any other people. The kids play & fight, laugh & cry, just the same as anyone else's kids do. The mothers love their kids & work hard to feed them. The fathers can't be of too much help because they are all in the army, one side or the other. Even the people who don't speak any English at all seem

Kris Blumer holding a Vietnamese orphan, spring, 1969.
Courtesy Virginia Blumer.

to understand the words please & thank you. I guess people are much the same everywhere. Most of the people I have met have been quite friendly. The children are shrewd & love to get the candy that the GIs pass out to them. If you stand still long enough, you will be surrounded by little people looking for a handout. The parents don't like to see them begging but it is one way to save on the ever so scarce food. They have to eat. Right now I have four of them sitting in front of me sharing a small can of peanut butter from a box of C-rations. They are all fascinated by my clip on sunglasses. A dog was killed by a booby trap last night. Now they have just finished butchering it. It will soon be their dinner. They don't waste anything. I hope to be able to take a dip in the river today to get cleaned up. Well I have to close now. It is about time for chow.

Love

Kris

TERRY F. MEZERA (1949–1971) was born in Prairie du Chien and was working as a carpet layer in Eau Claire when he enlisted in 1969. Mezera served in the army as a chief warrant officer (135th Avn. Co. [Assault Helicopter], 214th Avn. Bn. [Combat], 164th Avn. Grp.) piloting helicopters on combat and rescue missions near Vinh Long from April, 1970, until January 16, 1971, when he was killed in action. In the following

Terry Mezera. Courtesy Pam Nesbit.

letter to his girlfriend, Cathi, Mezera describes a little Vietnamese girl he just befriended.

[1970]

Dear Cath,

. . . So how's every thing going with you love? Are you being a good girl? I've finally got my self a girlfriend! She's about 2-3 years old—I found her in a little village we were at yesterday. She was standing along side the ship and I put my hands to her and she put her hands up. So I set her on my knee. I wish I would have had a picture of it. I set her down and we went walking up to this old French Church. She took a hold of my little finger and walked alongside of me—it was really cool.

We went in this church and was it cool—it was huge—an old Catholic church shot full of holes. . . .

Love
Terry

SCOTT ALWIN served with the army as a helicopter pilot in Bien Hoa. In the following letter, Alwin searches for a way to explain to his father that he had fallen in love with a young Vietnamese woman. Scott Alwin and Du Thi Duong (Teresa Alwin-Nguyen) married in 1969. (For a biographical sketch of Alwin, see chapter 3.)

Bien Hoa, November 27, 1968

Dear Dad,

. . . The subject of this whole thing is a young Vietnamese girl you may or may not already have heard something about from some of the other kids.

You can probably glean some good and bad stories and opinions from my brothers and sisters who speak through curtains of love and fear.

I did everyone a disservice when I was home and let a couple of letters she sent get opened by the others and then I didn't comment on it. Her letters are a poor reflection of the girl because I'm afraid they really only reflect the fact that she only had one year of formal English and was a young girl dealing with her first venture into the somewhat bewildering field of romantic love. I'm sure that it would be difficult to give in a few sentences a comprehensive insight into the difficulties surrounding any type of a relationship between a middle class *Vietnamese* girl and a GI.

I guess I will quit writing this because I will never be able to say anything worthwhile in a letter.

Why do I suddenly love some girl in a far away place? That is a difficult question. Maybe you only see so much death and destruction and do so much killing and that part of you that is kind and gentle cries out for some object to direct itself toward. I've thought of all the possible reasons and problems etc and finally let the whole thing lie at the point that there are some things that you do with your heart as well as your mind.

A couple of times while I was home I started to work toward talking with you about this but I never managed it. Now it'll have to keep until the end of March. . . .

Love
Scott

Comrades in Arms

Not surprisingly, some of the most intense relationships forged during the war were among those who fought together. Despite a rotation system that moved soldiers in and out of units with some regularity, the uncertainty of search-and-destroy-style warfare brought many men closer together as they depended upon one another. JEFF FIELDS served with the marines near Chu Lai and Da Nang early in the war. In this letter, Fields discusses the death of a friend. (For a biographical sketch of Fields, see chapter 3.)

April 19, 1966

Dear Family,

I'm sorry for not writing in such a long time but I've been pretty well under the sun for the past few days. I've never been really hurt as much as I am now in service. I don't know how to tell you this although it probably won't affect you as much as it does me. I've been running ambushes since April 17th and have finally finished with them. On the night of April 17th while heading towards our assigned ambush site my good buddy Lt. Smith was shot and killed while reconning our area out. He took [it] in the head. He was not killed by a gook but by the man next to me. It was dark out with no moon and heavy overcast skies and at the time he was on the high ground and we were still on the trail. I was in charge of the rear security. We had stopped not at that time knowing it was the designated site. I was not informed that Lynn was up there nor was I informed that any friendlies was in that area to our right flank. I heard noises advancing on us and aimed in on it. I could then see the object coming toward us, I was going to pull the trigger but then thought of yelling out or what we call challenging. If I would of done this it could of meant two things, I would of caused the killing of all three of us or whatever it was would of responded. I was about to yell out when this new boot opened up. . . . I then seen [Smith] fall and heard my squad leader Kwiatek yell out "Oh my God. No, please no." I then knew and ran up to where he was, he was still breathing when I got to him. Doc came up and started putting battle dressing over his head when Barnum (fire team leader) came up. I stood there for awhile crying and then finally pulled myself out of it. I was talking to Smith telling him that he's going to be okay and that we'd still be going home together etc, etc. He finally stopped breathing after fifteen minutes. Doc and I would take turns using mouth to mouth. He came around twice but after that it was no use. I honestly believe that he is in heaven now. I vowed that night that before I do anything on leave I'm going to his house to see his family only for an afternoon. I never have met his family but I know alot about them just as he knew of you in the same fashion. I first met Lynn when I reported into the FMF, 1st Mar. Division. We were friends ever since. I still can't believe its happened, I should think I'd be use to this by now but watching him go really tore me up. You probably think that is too detailed of a description to give about his death but who else can you tell things to? You can't tell them to anyone around here because they themselves have the same worries, troubles, and problems. Smith was a decent clean cut person—and I'd really enjoy fooling around with him. When the chips were down he was right there

with a smile on his face building them back up. I'll never forget him. . . .
Got to go

Love your Son & Brother
Jeff

BILL JUNG served two tours of duty in Vietnam with the Marine Corps. In
the following journal entry, Jung reflects on the death of a childhood friend.
(For a biographical sketch of Jung, see chapter 3.)

October 12, 1969

This war has cost me a lot of friends. Now it has taken another, Dale,
lost at sea. Many of my buddies fell around me from bullets, mines,
and mortars. I became cold toward death. After awhile it didn't bother
me much. This is different. This stuns me. Dale and I were raised
together. I sit here and all sorts of memories flash before me. It's hard
to believe he too is dead. But reality is a fact I face readily now. I'm
sure Dale won't be the last of my friends to die before the war is over.
But I'm alive, and until the time my number comes up, it's up to me
to not waste a single moment. I've been very lucky. Something tells me
the Lord has something else in store for me. We'll see. But Dale is at
the bottom of the South China Sea. Life is really so short and can be
snuffed out so fast. . . .

GREGG M. CARLSON (b. 1949) grew up in Milwaukee and enlisted in the
army in April, 1969. He served as a rifleman (A Co., 1–8th Cav., 1st Cav.
Div. [Airmobile]) near Bien Hoa, Tay Ninh, Quan Loi, and An Loc as well
as in Cambodia from September, 1969, to September, 1970. Carlson was
discharged in April, 1971, and returned to his job as a machine operator in
Milwaukee, where he still lives. He wrote the following letter after the
death of a friend, John Gmack, whose letters appear in chapter 4.

June 24, 1970

Mr. & Mrs. Gmack,

I'm one of the grunts from the second platoon of Alpha Company.
I've been either in Vietnam or Cambodia for nine months now. We're
in Cambodia right now. The last two days now the second platoon has
made contact while on patrols.

John and I got along quite well together and I considered him one
of my best friends. He was the only person in the platoon and one of
the three from Wisconsin. (One of the 3 in the company.) We went
through the bad times as well as the good times together.

Up until the time I got wounded in Bu Gia Map I had spent a lot of
time with him. I got out of the hospital a few weeks before we were

combat assaulted into Cambodia, for our first mission. Now we're 7 days into our second mission in Cambodia and I'm still going through the worst days of my life.

I really didn't know at first if I should tell you how he died because it was just an ironic accident; but who has a better right to know than you?

Here it is, exactly as it happened. That mission we were finding caches every day. On our seventh day we found an unusually large cache of NVA field gear. It took most of the day to uncover it and take an inventory of the items found. We were going to bring in engineers to blow a pad and extract the cache but it was too late to get them in that day.

To make sure the gooks didn't try taking it away before we got there the next morning the 1st platoon put an automatic ambush on the trail that led to it. An automatic ambush is several claymore mines on a trip wire. In the meantime the 3rd platoon moved about 150 meters out and found a suitable place to set up for the night.

They called the rest of the company but we had trouble finding them and walked (excuse the ink) 800 meters in a big circle before we found them. By that time it was dark and raining which just added to the confusion.

John's position was the next one to the left of mine. Two people from my squad went out to put out trip flares and John went out with one other man from his position.

To eliminate any gap a gook might walk through the trip flares had to be tied in.

Remember it was 8:00 o'clock and already dark when we got there. The 4 men were walking towards each other when a man from our squad tripped the ambush. The blast was about 25–30 feet away from me and it was absolutely deafening. Trees and bamboo were flying and 3 big balls of fire and smoke rose above the treetops.

Everyone was stunned at first and didn't know what it was for a while. I remembered they were out there putting out trips so I grabbed my weapon and about 8 other guys and a couple medics went running out there in the dark to see what happened.

This is the worst part, two of them we couldn't even find in the darkness. When the sun came up we did find what was left of them.

When we found John he wasn't in too bad a shape, at least not that any of us or the medics could see.

We called a medevac bird to take him out.

In the jungles of Cambodia we had aerial illumination and strobe lights going which is a bad thing to do in an enemy infested area but when a life is at stake the caution comes last.

That next morning word came over the radio that he had died in the early morning hours.

This was hard to take and it really hurt. I knew I had lost my best friend, but then I would think about it and find myself not believing it. Since I've been here I have trouble believing it. Almost as though it's all a bad dream and some day I'll wake up and it'll all be over. But when the AK-47s start singing and the B-40 rockets start coming in I know it's no dream.

Such is the life of the grunt. The people who are actually fighting this war; the people who search the dense jungles for the enemy and fight him face to face on his own ground. And what do we get for it? Quite a bit! We get our buddies killed and the chance to do it again tomorrow, and the next day for 364 days.

When I stop to think about it I wonder what's kept me alive and functioning all this time. But it's not over yet. At times I get so sick of seeing gooks, watching my buddies die, the mud and rain, the jungle and the bugs, that I feel like throwing down my weapon and quitting everything.

Almost forgot. If I remember correctly John did get to see the battalion surgeon about his jungle rot, but I can't recall if anything ever came of it.

I haven't even had the time to write for 6 weeks now—to anyone—but I figured I just had to do this.

I am *truly* sorry this had to happen and I'm sorry for you people too. I hope I never have to see this type of thing again.

Sincerely,
Gregg Carlson

R. PATRICK BOURGET (1949–1969) grew up in Cadott and enlisted in the army in the summer of 1967. He served as a radio telephone operator (C Btry., 2–4th Arty., 2d Bde., 9th Inf. Div.) in Tan An from June, 1968, to August, 1969, when he was discharged. Bourget died later that month in an auto accident. In this letter, Bourget writes to his family about the death of a man who took his place on a mission.

December 28, 1968

Dear All,

. . . Let me tell you a story: There once was a man named Cook. He was with me for 2 months as my recon sergeant while I was an Rto. After two months of carrying the radio they sent Cookie to B Company as forward observer, (a second Louie's job). The last letter you got from me was while I was at Thu Thua as a recon sergeant. Cookie came up to the thu thua because he was bored. He took my place as recon sarge so I said "I'm going to go to the Bob Hope Xmas show at Dong tam." Cookie said "No sweat, I'll go out with them till you get back." Cookie went out and now he is dead along with the company commander and his Rto and two tiger scouts. If Cookie wouldn't have come to thu thua and let me go to the Bob Hope show it would have been me instead of Cookie. God is on my side. I'll be out there three more months (I volunteered to even the score for Cookie). There's no reason why I shouldn't go out, me Pat, with no girl or children. I've got less to lose than Cookie with two children and a beautiful wife. Rather me than a guy with a couple of kids and a wife. Maybe I am taking a risk? But I've got to take care of my Rto. He's new and needs someone to break him in.

If I was sober I wouldn't write you this kind of letter but I'm not sober so here it is, that's the way things happen over here. . . .

My main man is on my side so don't worry about me. I'll make it home.

Give my love to the family and I'm waiting 'til the day we can be together again.

Robert Patrick Joseph Bourget

KEN M. ANDERSON served as an army A-Intel sergeant and a LRRP member during his two tours of duty in Vietnam. During his second tour of duty, Anderson worked near Phu Bai on a mission launch team, which had the responsibility of inserting, monitoring, and extracting recon teams. Anderson summarized information for the recon teams before they left and when they returned and had the responsibility of handling the dead when they arrived. In the following letter, Anderson describes his feelings on seeing the body of a man he had trained. (For a biographical sketch of Anderson, see chapter 4.)

August 27, 1971

Dear Mom Joe & Boys

. . . Since the last time I've written we've lost 7 Americans, 6 ARVN and 21 of our Commandos. I get so damn sick of seeing and stripping the dead and wounded. The last American I had to strip really got me sick. I had put the kid through weapons training at Fort Bragg in 69 and met him over here. He was only 21, married for a year and his wife was 8½ months pregnant. That's all he could talk about before he went out. I got so sick, I went on a 2 day drunk, but that doesn't help a thing. . . .

I've tried going back to Recon company, and the old man won't let me go. He says I'm getting too old for that kind of stuff. It's just that I get so tired of seeing these kids going out and getting blown away because most of them don't have the experience to know what they are doing out there. I like to think that if maybe I went out with them, I could probably save some lives. I know this much, that it's a rotten dirty stinking war out there and Charlie's playing for keeps. They keep sending us out in the same areas to determine if the enemy's there, and we know he's there especially when they send us into the A Shau valley. That's his home and we aren't going to take it from him. . . .

Your very loving Son
Ken

ED BEAUCHAMP served with the army on a reconnaissance team northwest of Chu Lai. Beauchamp wrote to his parents about his comrades' desire to free POWs from the temporary jungle prison camps located in South Vietnam. The Americans held in these camps endured even worse conditions than those in the established camps of North Vietnam. (For a biographical sketch of Beauchamp, see chapter 2.)

August 24, 1970

Mom & Dad

. . . Guess what? A Co was running eagle flights off siberia when they made contact with a NVA POW camp. Well A Co is under manned so they brought in part of B Co but had trouble with the birds so B Co got stranded on West. Anyways birds went in for A-Co who had 5 prisoners. From these prisoners they later found out that they were near a POW camp which had 3 GI & 4-ARVN officers. A Co got one of their men killed, a guy called mousey. It was their medic. I knew him well, this was to be his last mission. You see I got a buddy in Alpha & this guy was his best friend. My buddy is really upset about it.

Anyways what I wanted to say was since we learned there were GIs held prisoner, they're sending two companies & Recon in to find the camp. Alpha is one & all of them are more than willing to go back. It's strange what the love for a fellow GI is. All a fella needs here is a purpose like this, they'll fight! Here race doesn't mean any thing. All they need to know is they're GIs & any guy here is willing to risk his life to get these guys out!

Every GI here only exists here because they're all against this war & none of us want to be here. But let another GI's life be endangered, there's not one man here who'd refuse to go to aid him.

Well every one I'd like you to know I miss you all & I can hardly wait to come home.

So take care every one.
Love No 1 son
Ed

Ed Beauchamp. Courtesy Ed Beauchamp.

Men who held authority over others, whether as high-ranking officers or as noncommissioned squad leaders, bore heavy responsibilities for the safety of their men. The following letters from an army lieutenant, an army sergeant, and a navy captain illustrate the outlook of men whose leadership literally meant life or death for others.

TYRONE "TONY" PAULSON (b. 1948) grew up in Whitehall and was attending Eau Claire State University when he was drafted into the army in May, 1968. Paulson rose to the rank of first lieutenant and served as a platoon leader and company commander (B Co., 1–46th Inf., 196th Inf. Bde. [Light], 23d Inf. Div. [Americal]) near Chu Lai from October, 1969, until October, 1970. He was discharged in April, 1972, and now lives in Madison and works as a communications supervisor for the Wisconsin State Patrol. Paulson sent the following letter to Sue Mattison, whom he married in October, 1970, just a few weeks after he returned from Vietnam.

August 10, 1970

Dear Sue,

. . . I have been here 10 months and 1 week. I am not so physically beat but the mental anguish & turmoil is terrible. As you know I am very conscientious about people and everyday I have to decide will I get a guy killed if I send him that way or another way etc. I am always second guessing myself & checking on myself. And I know by the end of 12 months I will have had enough. It wouldn't be so bad if I wouldn't be in the field all the time and I wouldn't be responsible for lives all the time. Guys get hit, everybody feels bad and then it is my job to rally the men and get them going again so nobody else gets hurt. Well I can't show it or everybody will feel bad and nobody will work. When I get home I think I am going to let go with a whole year's worth of emotions. And I'll cry like a baby. Until then I really can't think short or anything. I am over here to help people come back alive. I have helped some. But for 55 more days I think I can help some more. I have been having bad dreams lately and am real nervous & jumpy a lot more than in Hawaii. I hope it will go away when I get back home. Honey you're going to have to take good care of me and be patient, and I'll come around. I love you very much and when I get back to a normal life I'll be o.k. Oh I hope I could go home tomorrow.

Love ya very much,
Tony

DAVID TERRENCE "TERRY" SMITH (1949–1974) was born in Madison and raised in Boscobel. He studied at the Madison campus of the University of Wisconsin before enlisting in the army in June, 1969. Sergeant Smith served as a mortar squad leader (E Co., 1–46 Inf., 196th Inf. Bde. [Light], 23d Inf. Div. [Americal]) near Chu Lai from June, 1970, to May, 1971, when he was discharged. He returned to the university and worked for a cable television company until his death on May 3, 1974.

LZ Mary Ann, November 11, 1970

Like hi, Mama Bear,

We're rained in again. I should have gone in on stand down two days ago, but now who knows? This damned hill is just too far out to be resupplied or reinforced during monsoon. You'd think higher higher would have realized that by now. You see Mary Ann is one of the farthest Fire Support Bases and it's in the middle of a mountain range to boot. Mary Ann is some big SNAFU, but I guess I've been in the Army long enough not to expect anything different. . . .

I'm afraid my men don't care too much for me. I guess they liked the old squad leader pretty well and resent my taking his place. Also there are the pot heads who used to come over to the Three Gun to "pass the bowl." I've brought an end to that. I'd like to be liked, but it's got to be on my terms. I have certain responsibilities as a squad leader.

As a matter of fact it's been such a hassle lately that I've been considering going back to the bush. Don't worry, I doubt if it will come to that, and if it does it wouldn't be until after monsoon. Impetuous yes— stupid no.

There is a new policy going into effect this month. If you have more than four months in country, and less than eight, you are eligible for a two week leave back to the world. The only catch is, you have to pay your own way. R & R is still possible with this leave. My only thought is I might not come back to this sorry place if I got back to the world. . . .

Some of the guys on the bunker line caught a mouse deer that was tangled in the wire last week. She (it was a doe) was only about twelve inches high. I remember reading about them in that Frank Buck book when I was a kid, so it was sort of cool to really see one.

Say, you know I could dig some tapes for Christmas. Tapes I'd like include: any thing of Clancy Bros. (I doubt if you can find anything); Rolling Stones—"High Tide & Green Grass"; Beatles "Abbey Road" or "Rubber Soul"; Anything of Crosby, Stills & Nash, or Creedence Clearwater Revival—just a thought. I wish Ron could make me up a tape of some of the old goodies from 1966–68. I know he's got some good stuff.

We've got rats in our hooch and the damn things are driving me crazy. I'm sorely tempted to open up on the little bastards with my .45, but I think the lifers might frown on that. Pity.

I really don't have much for news (do I ever?) but I know how much I look forward to letters so ...

Keep the faith baby.
Love,
Terry

WILBUR A. SUNDT (b. 1926) was raised in Fort Atkinson and enlisted in the navy in June, 1944. He fought in World War II and the Korean War and served three tours of duty in Vietnam. Commissioned in April, 1950, Sundt commanded the USS *Gunston Hall,* a dock landing ship, from September, 1966, to February, 1967, and January to September, 1968. From June, 1970, to June, 1971, Captain Sundt headed the Naval Advisory Department in Da Nang. Sundt retired from the navy in August, 1974, and taught in the Navy Junior ROTC program in Love's Park, Illinois until 1978. Since that time he has written Navy Junior ROTC textbooks. He lives in Fort Atkinson.

At sea, March 6, 1968

My dearest Jean, Eric, Scott, Lance, Silvia, & Dad,

Tomorrow morning we enter Vung Tau and proceed on up the river to Saigon to offload our cargo. Later in the day we will start down again, stopping at Nha Be to get the combat load for the Cua Viet [River].

My dear, this is the real thing this time, no drills involved. We will be at general quarters almost all day and will probably be within the sights of the enemy's guns much of the time. Whether he chooses to open up on us remains to be seen.

We have been preparing for this eventuality for a long time and now we may be given the opportunity to see if the right lessons were learned. I feel sure that we have done our best and, God willing, we will be all right. There is no question about our vulnerability, however, as it is largely the enemy's choice as we drive up the narrow river for over 40 miles through what is known as the Rung Sat Special Zone—the acknowledged hideout of the Viet Cong in the Delta of the Mekong.

The situation on the Cua Viet has deteriorated rapidly and the river to the HQ at Dong Ha is not safe for travel. What combat vessels we pick up at Nha Be are to rectify that situation. Those men on the monitors & A[rmored] T[roop] C[arrier]s do not have a picnic ahead. They lost 7 men and a YFU [a harbor utility craft] there last week as the result of direct hits by rockets on a cargo of powder.

We went into Cam Ranh Bay this morning to offload the PCF (Fast Patrol Craft) and then were on our way out again in one hour. It went very well and we are much more mobile by virtue of getting that boat off before the Saigon River trip.

I have caused small gun tubs to be made to protect my machine gunners today. We've also had a briefing of all officers and C[hief] P[etty] O[fficer]s, who in turn briefed their men at quarters. This afternoon I had a short G[eneral] Q[uarters] called to get all men on their stations and to ensure all had their flak-jackets and helmets and life jackets.

I will pray tonight that all will go well and that none of my crew are hurt tomorrow. My responsibility weighs heavily this evening—tomorrow

I won't have time to think about that as events will dictate the course of action we will be taking. It may well prove to be a ride up the river no more noteworthy than were our trips up and down the Columbia last summer.

When you receive this letter, of course, this whole episode will be history, and the letter may even appear a bit corny then. A lot goes thru the mind in circumstances like this though, and most of all one hopes he has done right by all concerned. All the 267 men aboard have the right to expect that I perform my duties in the proper manner. . . .

All my love,
Will & Dad

Coming Home

At the end of their tours of duty, servicemen went to brigade and division rear areas to complete paperwork that would allow them to return to the United States, a process that generally took one or two days. The soldiers next flew to the large replacement centers and waited for their names to appear on a flight manifest, which permitted them to board a civilian airliner headed for home. After arriving in the States, men went through processing centers where they would receive either a thirty-day leave (if their service was unfinished) or a discharge from the military. This abrupt transition gave Vietnam veterans much less time to reacclimate themselves to civilian life than the long ocean voyages of World War II veterans. Still, they were coming home.

LARRY BUETER served as a draftsman with the Marine Corps near Da Nang and wrote the following letter at the very end of his tour in Vietnam. (For a biographical sketch of Bueter, see chapter 1.)

May 16, 1969

Dear Mom, Dad & John,

. . . This is going to have to be sort of short and to the point—in other words—I'll be home *soon!!*

I'm up at the office right now at 1:30 in the morning and I'm writing my last batch of letters to everyone. I'm leaving at 6:00 in the morning to get in line down at the airport for that "freedom bird" to the world. I don't know if it's because I just said goodbye to all the guys, because I'm finally leaving after 23 months, or because I'm finally going home but I'm a little shaky and sentimental tonight. I just hope everything goes O.K., and I should be back there in about 15 days. It's all pretty uncertain as far as a definite date 'cause I'm not sure about how long it'll take to process me out. I'll try to write from Okinawa & California on the way, but I can't promise, 'cause I'll probably be quite busy. . . .

I guess that's going to be all from this part of the world until I join you on the other side. I'm all packed and over-anxious to get on my way. So I guess at last I can say see you soon,

Love,
your coming home son,
Larry

TONY PAULSON served as an army platoon leader and a company commander near Chu Lai. As he completed his tour, he reflected on his year in Vietnam in this last letter to his fiancée. (For a biographical sketch of Paulson, see earlier in this chapter.)

September 26, 1970

Dearest Sweetheart,

What do you say in the last letter from Vietnam? You have waited patiently for a year. Written 270 odd letters. Kept your spirits up and mine too. You kept your end of the bargain in that the wedding is ready—or just about. I have kept mine in that I'll be coming home. (Mine was a lot rougher to keep.) You've been patient in that I didn't always get a letter out every week etc. And you kept the faith. In April when we saw each other you hadn't changed. (—except for the hair.) I didn't think I had—maybe. I know I have changed in the last part of the year. I had rougher fighting and closer and more flirtations with death then ever before. I always believed in God—after this year I believe in him twice as much—if that is possible. I know too that some of the letters I sent sounded conceited but I shared the praise in that I told you. It was the only way I could justify it in my mind that I wasn't conceited. But I am still as proud of myself as I always was—maybe more. So what am I trying to say in this letter? Both of us went through the biggest changes of our lives. (at least for me.) We each did it by ourselves. In a few days we can share everything. Disappointments, successes, happiness, sadness and every little trial of a marriage. If you love me as much as you think you do and I love you as much as I know I do we are going to have the best marriage ever. Sue, I love you more than you'll ever realize. We have missed a lot in a year. But an engagement is a trial period. But only ours was twice as hard. But maybe it has made us each a little bit better. I am coming home, all I want to see initially is a smile and open arms. And later on I want to hear you say "till death do us part."

I love you,
Tony

*Tom McCabe. Courtesy
Marie McCabe.*

TOM MCCABE served as an army infantryman near An Duc. After being
wounded, McCabe returned to the United States and wrote the following
letter to his parents while he was recuperating. (For a biographical sketch of
McCabe, see chapter 1.)

Fort Lewis, Washington, June 30, 1969

Howdy—

What a marvelous feeling to be back in this glorious country of ours.
I am still awed every morning when I wake up & I can look out over
the plush countryside with its green grass, rolling forested hills & blue
skies overhead. It seems like I've been thru some sort of nightmare,
but dawn has come & the bad dream has vanished with the coming of
a new day. It is hard to believe that I was ever in the Nam, altho an
occasional sharp pain in my shoulder brings back the reality of that experience. . . .

I have a slight guilty feeling leaving my good friends back in Nam,
but I guess it wasn't done intentionally so I didn't exactly abandon them.
I hope that they will all survive their miserable year overseas & return

to resume natural & productive lives without a bitterness towards America. Even the short time that I was over in Nam I developed a bad taste for what our gov't. was doing & the way the people allowed it to continue. For those who are subjected to more killing & destruction that bad taste may turn into a permanent dislike & distrust of our American system, and then this country will really suffer. I was very happy when you said that you wanted to send my friends a care package; I know they will enjoy it & the thought behind it. It is a shame that we can only do so little for those men over there fighting a futile war. . . .

Your ever-so-happy-to-be-back son

T Mc

8

Costs of War

The names of more than 58,000 men and women cover the black granite walls of the Vietnam Veterans Memorial in Washington, D.C. Another 300,000 Americans were wounded in action. In addition to physical losses, Vietnam exacted other costs, including emotional strain, drug use, and a lack of public welcome following an unpopular war. The healing process persisted for many years, as veterans attempted to make sense of the war and their role in it.

Wounded in Action

The letters from the following two veterans discuss the physical costs of battle. Of those seriously wounded during the war, 82 percent lived, a testament to the air evacuation system referred to as Dust Off. Begun in Korea and perfected in Vietnam, Medevac helicopters allowed wounded servicemen to reach medical care facilities quickly, thus improving survival rates. In the following letter, DARREL LULLING, an army infantry squad leader in Quang Tri province, tells his girlfriend about a battle in which he and a number of his comrades were wounded. (For a biographical sketch of Lulling, see chapter 1.)

October 3, 1969

My Dearest Darling Jane,

Well my darling, I am going to write you this letter and then I am going to try to forget it all. October 1, the rest of our company joined us (first and third platoon) at A-4 early in the morning, we left mounted on tanks, there were also armored personnel carriers and various other armored vehicles, dusters, engineer vehicles etc. Anyhow we were mounted on tanks headed for a place called "Rocket Ridge" (a ridge line right on the DMZ), it took us the best part of a day because the tanks have trouble moving in the hilly terrain.

In the afternoon, we were moving up the hill. I was on the second or third tank in movement. Some of the tanks were up on the hill already, they sit in a circle formation so that they have firepower all around.

212

One tank was stopped just ahead of us so we moved up the hill off the tank trail because this tank was stopped in the tank trail. A tank trail is like a dirt road, the tanks try to stay off of old tank trails because they are mined. Well, we were about three feet off the tank trail moving up the hill when the tank upon which I was riding hit a mine. I was riding on the side of the tank, the right side, the mine went off right below me. It blew me from the side of the tank to the front. As usual it all happened so fast. I remember finding myself laying on the front of the tank and realizing that the tank had been hit, not knowing what hit us at the time I jumped over the main tank gun—off the tank—and ran over off the other side of the road. Needless to say I was shocked. Then I noticed a sharp pain in my ears. People were talking but I could hardly hear them. I checked the rest of my body, everything was alright. Pieces of dirt and rock had flew up into my face and I had some very small cuts. Needless to say I was very lucky. The tank had its track blown off and one road wheel was destroyed.

Well, the rest of the tanks moved the company to its destination. Since I was certainly in a rather bad way my company commander told me to stay with the downed tank and then when the rest of the tanks came back they would take me in. The tanks came back and it took a few hours to get [the] downed tank hooked on to another tank to be pulled back.

We were moving back to another hill where we left some tanks and APCs for security when movement was observed. I was riding on the tankers company commander's tank so naturally away we went investigating. To make a long story short our tank got stuck in the mud. It was stuck so bad that it was half tipped over in the mud (I was riding inside this time). They tried until dark to pull the tank out but gave up when it got too dark. So, we locked up the tank and stripped the outside. We got on another tank and started up the hill, the tanks with their lights on (a big mistake when you are this close to the DMZ).

We got to the hill with the rest of the tanks and pulled our tanks into a tight perimeter. They had no RPG screens and only a little barbed wire. They only set out a few claymores. But the tank commander was not dumb, he called for some ground troop support—so later on in the evening two platoons from C 1/11 company came and set up around us. The tanker CO found me a place to sleep under a little canvas pulled over the back of a tank so I went to sleep.

Now Jane, the real story starts. About 2 A.M. I was awakened by fire from the 50 caliber machine guns on the tanks. So I sat up, grabbed my M-16 which is always beside me and jumped out of the shelter. All kinds of shooting was going on. Then I saw explosions just in front of me. I knew what they were, I had studied all about them. They were RPGs, I could hear the ring of them when they were fired from the launcher and then the explosion. I was between two tanks. I fired about a magazine from my M-16. Then the tank to my left was hit with an RPG. I heard the guy in the T[ank] C[ommander] hatch scream "Oh my God Help." I ran over to the side of the tank and said "are you alright—is there anyone in the tank," he said "yes" and then I heard someone inside groaning. I looked at the man I was talking to, his arm was all blood. So I guess they all got out. I blanked out for seconds or minutes, I don't know. Well, anyway I was back between the two tanks. RPGs were hitting to my front. Then the tank to my right got hit by a RPG, more screaming. Then the tank to my left got hit again only this time it was on fire, the man on the TC hatch yelled she is on fire, he was hit and screaming. I saw that 50 just sitting there, no one using it. I wanted to get up there and fire away. But I was too scared. RPGs were nailing those tanks, she was bound to blow soon. So, I got up and got the hell out of there.

As I was running to the other side of the perimeter I saw someone drive that burning tank out away from the perimeter, whoever got into that tank deserves something. So, I went over directly to the other side of the perimeter. I was behind the tank that had been blown by the mine earlier, several other men were there, they were all wounded, blood all over and the medics working—Then there was an explosion on the other side of the tank, a RPG, or Chi Com Grenade or mortar I couldn't tell. But all of the men laying next to the tank screamed and moaned, all were hit again.

So, I figured this was no place to stay so I moved a few feet away between a tank and APC. I looked across our perimeter and saw a tank with no one in the TC hatch, its 50 caliber ammo burning. So, I laid between the tank and APC, there were some men coming in from an LP post and others, some men wounded, a platoon leader from "C" company, some ARVN scouts. I just laid there with my head down. Behind me I saw two men carrying someone in a poncho. They set him down and I had just a glimpse. He was blown in half, his legs were facing funny, he had no clothing on the bottom half of his body. I could see part of his insides laying on the ground. The upper half of his body was sort of resting on something. I looked at his face. There was no look of agony or pain. Just a look as if to say help me. I don't know if he was dead or alive yet. I was assuming he had died instantly or shortly after he took a direct hit with a RPG. I know the medics didn't even try to work on him, perhaps they gave him some morphine. So

Ground troops use colored smoke to guide the medevac choppers arriving to pick up wounded. Courtesy Tom Hounsell.

there I was laying, another explosion just in front of me, so I moved back farther. There was that awful screaming and the frightened yell for the medic. There was a smell, a distinct awful smell, it was frightening because it came from the explosive used in their explosives. Just about everyone was hit, some men were hit in the face, arms and legs. I saw something that looked like it moved so I threw a grenade. I fired—The time crept on.

I could hear the tanker CO yelling artillery coming in and it did but much too far away to be effective. They called in Puff and after about an hour it seems he came spraying our perimeter to the North with bullets. Then a dustoff medevac came, they filled it with the worst wounded and then another came later. I was helping with the wounded so I helped take some men to the helicopter, the crazy thing never did land, it was about five feet above ground and we had to throw the men on just about. So then it was around 5 so I went behind the tankers CO's tank, found me some poncho liners, one I laid in the mud to lay on and the other I covered myself with because it was cold, wet, and muddy. I stayed there resting and watching until daybreak. There were still wounded. Two medics were wounded. I saw one medic give himself morphine. The wounded weren't real serious. So at daybreak I heard someone yell gooks on the other end of the perimeter. So, I grabbed my M-16 and two hand grenades—I decided it was time for me to fight.

I went over there and there about ten feet from a APC laid a NVA with a RPG #7 and RPG Round still in the launcher. So I shot him again about six times. Then some more men came, we stayed low to the ground, we were going to sweep over the hill. But first I said—I will throw a grenade over in a clump of grass. So, I pulled the pin and let fly—the grenade exploded and up stood this NVA troop half covered with blood, his hands over his head trying to surrender. I had heard about how these NVA etc. trick you and too many GIs are dead because of it. So, I grabbed my other grenade and pulled the pin and threw that at him. He ducked a little and the grenade went off, lucky for him I threw it too far but it cut him up pretty bad.

Well, we had this ARVN scout, he came up and talked to the NVA. We told the scout to tell him to take off his shirt, pants and shoes and then we sent our medic out to him. He had a M-16 round through his side. And his legs were all split open no doubt due to me. The scout asked him questions and we found out that we had been hit by a NVA platoon and there were others out there. I had that poor prisoner so scared because I had my rifle pointed right at him, all he had to do was look wrong and he was dead. We got on line and started to sweep over the hill. There was a bomb crater and in the crater there was someone. So we crept up, I saw two more NVA laying there. The one nearest to me I pumped about eight rounds into.

They swept the whole hillside and found about 12 bodies in all. They had all kinds of RPG launchers #2s and #7s AK 47s. I only saw about three AK 47s, the rest had RPG launchers. There was a medic. These NVA were all shot up, badly deformed, it didn't even bother me to search them. They had all kinds of RPG rounds and even more Chi Comm grenades. It is good that they did not get close enough to use the grenades effectively or else we would of had more casualties. I walked up to this one NVA, I didn't like the way he was laying, he didn't look dead enough so I shot him in the top of the head and blew his brains out the back.

These NVA I believe were a new fresh unit. They had all new equipment, clean new uniforms, and all kinds of supplies, food, medical supplies, dope, ammo, even U.S. gear they had picked up. So I looked around the area, in mud around the Tanks & APCs were pools of blood here and there, ammo, old bloody bandages, sleeping gear, medical supplies, human intestines, it was a mess. The brass flew in their helicopters, looked around and said you fought one hell of a fight. That we did. We had one man killed as I mentioned earlier and about 20 wounded, so far I have not heard of any of the wounded dying.

We policed up the area, we took the enemy ammunition as well as our unusable ammo and placed it in a bomb crater to be blown up.

So, later that morning we left—leaving some other company on the hill to police up. We got back late that day. They sent me to the aid station at C-2 and I stayed there overnight, both of my ear drums have been blown away. Then they sent me to "B" 75th support Battalion hospital. They are sending me to the hospital ship out in the gulf of Tonkin tomorrow.

Actually I am fine—I can hear perhaps not quite as well but I can hear. I am thankful that I am in one piece. Here at 75th Spt Bn are some of the men who were on the hill, they all have holes in their body. The worst ones are on the hospital ship. You just can't realize how lucky I am, I think I was hit by some shrapnel but I couldn't find anything to complain about. There is only a few who got off that hill in good a shape as me.

Never again will I regret having to shoot the enemy. I will blow them away as quick as I can and I don't think that it will even bother me. I have seen too much and if I don't kill them they are going to kill me.

Don't mention any of this to my Mother because it would worry her to death. I am really fine and quite well—I am telling you because some-one has to know. I have been in a sort of a daze—I am still shaky. . . .

Love Always,
Darrel

GARY G. WETZEL (b. 1947) was born in South Milwaukee and was living in Oak Creek when he enlisted in the army in February, 1966. He served as a helicopter door gunner (173d Assault Helicopter Co., 11th Avn. Bn. [Combat], 12th Avn. Grp.) near Lai Khe from October, 1966, until January, 1968. On January 8, 1968, intense enemy fire trapped Wetzel's helicopter and the troops it was carrying on a landing zone. While attempting to aid his wounded aircraft commander, Wetzel was hit when two rockets exploded near him. He suffered the loss of his left arm and sustained severe wounds to his right arm, chest, and left leg. Despite a great loss of blood, Wetzel returned to his machine gun and subdued the automatic gun emplacements that had pinned down the American troops. Ignoring his own injuries, Wetzel helped his injured aircraft commander to safety, losing consciousness twice in the process. For his heroism, Wetzel was awarded the Congressional Medal of Honor. He was discharged from the army in August, 1968, and now lives in Oak Creek. The first letter was dictated to a Red Cross worker from his hospital bed in the 93d Evacuation Hospital in Vietnam just five days after he sustained his injuries. The second letter was written while he was a patient at Fitzsimons General Hospital in Denver, Colorado.

*President Lyndon B. Johnson awards Gary Wetzel the Medal of Honor,
November, 1968. Courtesy UPI/Bettman.*

January 13, 1968

Dear Mom & Dad,

While reading this letter I hope that you are in the best of health—I hope that everything is fine.

On Jan 8 at approximately 6:45 we had a CA down in the Delta. When we were coming in the LZ, as soon as we touched down the left front side of the helicopter was blown apart—I got out from behind my machine gun to help the pilot out—In doing this, there was a grenade thrown by a VC and that's how I got wounded.

I might as well tell you now, I lost my left arm about 2 inches below my elbow. I should be coming home shortly—I don't know yet just when—but I'm in the hospital and I'm O.K.

God bless & take care—

Love, Your son
Gary

I'll write again in a couple days.

February 15, 1968

Hi Dad.

. . . Today they took the bandage off of my leg where they took the skin to put on my back & arm. Of course it hurt, but in a couple of days it'll be all right. I also took a walk with Mom over to the hospital. And I really did good. Before you know it I'll be home, then we can really celebrate.

Also I will be getting married in September. Yep I finally will be getting HOOKED. *WOW!!* Bonnie set the date for Sept. 28th and then the next day I'll be 21. Before you know it, I'll be passing you up in age. *HA! HA!*

This Saturday they will be taking the bandages off of my arm and back. Before you know it I'll be running around.

You know Dad, at first when I lost my arm I really felt kind of guilty. I mean about not being married and then facing the world. To tell you the truth that's why I wanted to go back over to Vietnam. But when I had a long talk with the Doctor and when I talked to Bonnie I changed my mind. I guess for a person to really be a man he really has to face a lot of things. So I guess after giving it alot of thought I'm ready to face the world and humanity. But don't worry, things are just beginning and I've already faced a few things. . . .

God Bless & Take Care
Your oldest Son
Love
Gary.

Caring for the Wounded

When a U.S. serviceman suffered a wound in combat, he entered the
advanced medical support system, which consisted of army, navy, and air
force personnel assigned to base camp hospitals, MASH units, field units,
evacuation hospitals, navy hospital vessels, and air ambulances. The letter
that follows depicts the rigorous duties of the navy corpsmen or army
medic. Often assigned to combat units, these men administered to the
immediate needs of wounded in battle, exposing themselves to danger in the
process. With minimal formal medical training, they learned many
procedures on the job, trying to keep men alive until a Dust Off arrived.

   BRIAN P. MURRAY (b. 1948) was born in Waupaca and enlisted in the
navy in March, 1967. He served as a corpsman (F Co., 2/1st Mar., 1st Mar.
Div.) south of Da Nang from December, 1968, to April, 1969. Discharged
in August, 1969, Murray worked as a paramedic and currently is a student
in computer science at Lakeland College in Sheboygan.

December 24, 1968

Dear Mom & Dad, Bruce, Susie & Oscar;

   Merry x-mas, around here that's a standing joke right now. We're out
from the battalion in a spot we call the Riviera. We'll be here for 30
days (18 now), then another company will replace us & we'll go to the
POW compound which is supposed to be easy duty. Every 3 days my
platoon goes out from here & sets up an area called a P.P.B. (platoon
Patrol Base). We set up one P.P.B. & run a couple of patrols from there
in the morning [&] afternoon and then about dark we move to another
area & set up a nighttime P.P.B. & run patrols from there. Well yesterday we were at our Daytime P.P.B. & after security was set up we took
off our equipment & flak jackets & Helmets & most of us went to sleep
because we had been up all night the night before digging up the compound because somebody had heard tunneling under us. Anyway towards
evening a bunch of us (the 2 corpsmen, squad leaders & etc.) were
gathered around the Leut., getting the scoop about our night activities,
we didn't have any gear with us because we thought we were secure.
All of a sudden we heard the click of an AK-47 (gook weapon) opening
up so we scattered & hugged the dirt. We were surrounded on 3 sides
by gooks [&] boy were they giving it to us. The first shot must have
been fired by a sniper because it caught the leut right in the throat. I
heard the sgt. call for a corpsman & turned my head that way & saw
the other corpsman going for his gear so I just laid still because there
was nothing I could do and besides I was too scared to move at first
because I saw a round go into the ground about 2 inches from my elbow.
The other Corpsman started working on the leut. & after the firing had

died down some he called me over. We did everything we could to save
his life but the round had severed the carotid and there just wasn't any
way to save his life unless we would have had a suction machine & that
might not have worked. It's a weird feeling to be talking to a man one
minute & two minutes later be trying like hell to save what little bit of
life is left in him. The worst part about it is he was married for about
a year & had a young daughter he had never seen. According to the
other corpsman this was the first KIA in his own platoon & he's been
in the bush for 6 months. He said that he's only treated about 6 actual
wounds so it looks like it may be easier than I thought. Dad you'll be
glad to know I've learned how to keep my head & ass down. I don't
think there's anybody who can do better than I can.

Tet should be starting soon & the shit will really be hitting the fan.
I'm scared to death but I don't think anything will happen to me because
I've had good teachers. But if anything should happen remember I love
you all more than words can say.

Well I'd better sign off now,

Love & Merry Christmas
Brian

Chaplains in the armed forces in Vietnam filled a variety of roles
throughout the war. Their ministries included providing religious services
and sacraments on bases and in the field, counseling in a morally complex
war situation, assisting with social welfare programs for the Vietnamese
people, and serving as a spiritual leader for fellow troops. As RAY STUBBE,
a navy chaplain at Khe Sahn, noted, they were also drawn into one of the
grimmest aspects of the war—aiding the wounded and dying. (For a
biographical sketch of Stubbe, see chapter 5.)

September 19, [1967]

Dear folks:

. . . By now you should have received my letters that we haven't been
hit. We still haven't. But there's always some young man dying here—
malaria, snipers, drowning. Sunday morning I was walking to chow when
the ambulance came to the medical area in which I live. I helped carry
in the stretcher. The man had blood all over his mouth and nose. I helped
cut away his shirt. The doctor put a tube in his chest cavity to drain
off the internal bleeding, and then operated on his neck and chest to
restore breathing. The man was unconscious all the time. They sent him
away on a helicopter to our nearest hospital at Phu Bai; he died on the
way. Another man was brought in, fully conscious. Since we have no
way of putting people "under" here, he remained fully conscious as the

doctor cut into his side to insert the tube to drain the blood. He screamed; I cried. I guess he's all right now. Ten others were brought in with
broken legs and backs. A bunker they were in collapsed. After looking
at it, it's a wonder more didn't die. The men were all "short-timers"—
only a week or two yet to do. The man who died was 20 years old,
and married. . . .

Love,
Ray

Medical doctors in all branches of the military provided preventive and
emergency care for soldiers in Vietnam and health care to the Vietnamese
when feasible. LARRY KAMMHOLZ, commander of the 736th Medical
Detachment at Moc Hoa, reflects in this journal entry on the problems of
doctors in a war without fronts—civilian casualties, losing young men they
knew, and the fear of assault on the medical compound. (For a biographical
sketch of Kammholz, see chapter 2.)

November 14, [1966]
. . . Last night at 12 P.M. we heard mortar rounds begin to fall about
1½ miles away & much machine gun fire. One of the 4 bridges down
the road was being hit. Those are usually protected by 10 Regional Forces
soldiers who live there with their families. The alert was sounded at
our compound & I was quite concerned that we were going to be hit.
There was intermittent machine gun fire from close by—just a few blocks
away. At 5 A.M. we began to receive the casualties. Two infants were
brought in each of whose parents were killed. There were two women
with bullet wounds of the abdomen & 4–5 soldiers with various wounds.
These were taken care of by 10 A.M. when they began to fly in helicopter
loads of wounded Viet soldiers from the A camp 414 who were on an
operation near Cambodia. They ran into VC who were in well prepared
positions & the company was hit with heavy casualties. Throughout the
afternoon 7 dead were brought in & 20 or so others with wounds, many
of which were chest & abdominal injuries. Two Americans from the
A camp were killed (there are only 7 Americans there). My men had
known those men well. One had been shot through the forehead. Another
American had been wounded in the leg and the helicopter pilot I mentioned before also came in at that time. We were able to do several abdominal cases but then were overwhelmed & had to evacuate the rest
of the severely injured to Can Tho.

Women made up the great majority of the thousands of military nurses who
served during the Vietnam War. They assisted wounded soldiers and sailors

in hospitals and aboard patient transport flights and worked long hours at medical facilities. Although nurses did not participate in actual combat missions, they confronted pain, suffering, and death on a daily basis.

MARY ANN LEMIEUX (HARTL) (b. 1944) was finishing nursing school in Rochester, Minnesota, when she enlisted in the Army Nurse Corps in 1964. She served as a operating room nurse in Bien Hoa, Cu Chi, Saigon, and Long Binh from June, 1966, to July, 1967 (7th MASH, 3d Fld. Hosp., and 24th Evac. Hosp.). Lemieux was discharged in March, 1969, and subsequently moved to the Milwaukee area, where she completed nursing and education degrees at Marquette University and the University of Wisconsin-Milwaukee. She later worked as an operating room nurse and currently resides in Racine, where she instructs student surgical technicians.

[November 7, 1966]

Dear Mom and Dad:

. . . I went to work at 11:00 Thursday morning and didn't get off until 9:00 *this* morning except for about 3 hours one day to get some rest. We started out with a Vietnamese woman in labor who delivered a beautiful baby girl. During the delivery, we were notified to expect some casualties. We did too. Dust Off couldn't get to them so slick ships and gun ships went in to bring out the casualties. The casualties came from two sources—a brigade of our men were ambushed by a *whole division* of VC and couldn't fight them off. Also, Tay Ninh, where we were supposed to move, was mortared. They hit the hospital there and killed the C.O. which I'm sure you've read all about—not to mention what else they hit. We had close to 300 casualties sent to us in these few days. The wounds were ugly—really ugly. We did more major surgery in these few days than we've done since we've been here—total! Of all the patients brought to us, we only had one death. That was the 1st day and I was scrubbed on it. It was a chest wound and they brought him right off the chopper into surgery where we worked like dogs to save him, but just couldn't. I left at 9:00 Friday morning and slept til 11:00 and then back to it. Went on like this all weekend. They flew us in supplies from Guam and the States as we ran out of everything. When I could I took pictures as it was unbelievable. What was really unbelievable was the chopper loads of KIAs—stacked high. Eighty-three of our guys killed Thursday. Yesterday, they brought in 6 more KIAs who were killed Thursday. The whole thing was unreal. They had them packed in a chopper and then unloaded them in front of pre-op on stretchers as there was no place else for them. They had to identify them and get records straight. I took pictures of this whole thing because it was so unbelievable. You could smell them if you were anywhere near the area. What they looked like, I could never tell you. These slides I won't send you—at least

Medical personnel unload a casualty from a helicopter.
Courtesy Anthony Hamelink.

not while I'm still here. I'm sure you can tell it left quite an impression
on me. It is something I never want to see again. . . .

Love,
Mary

The Strain of War

Survival for servicemen in Vietnam required burying the fear, pain, and
anguish about what they witnessed and felt during the war. Journal entries
and letters home sometimes served as outlets for disclosing the psychological
strain of war. In the following letter, MIKE JEFFORDS, an infantryman and
squad leader in the Marine Corps, wrote to his parents explaining the
stresses of line duty. (For a biographical sketch of Jeffords, see chapter 1.)

Da Nang, [June 30–31, 1965]

Dear Folks—

I'm writing to let you know I'm still active and kicking. I'm feeling
O.K. As much as can be expected. In ma's last letter she asked about
some marines leaving here.—They are. It isn't my Battalion, though.
I never kidded you; I'm not going to start now. I figure I'll have at least
six months on the line before they pull us out. You had better plan on

that. If we go; we are "supposed" to be the next after this other Battalion leaves. I'm ready to go. Three months of line duty—on the front is a hell of a long time for these guys. Three more will make it worse for them. As a unit they'll be O.K., but I think some of them are going to crack pretty soon. Not go nuts—understand—but turn pretty rowdy. I can't explain it to you—I probably never will. You have to see it. Pictures help but not much. It's in their faces and actions. They are old men before their time. I feel ten years older myself. It will pass after we leave, I know, but now it is very real. . . .

This sounds stupid but many of us, myself included, I'm not ashamed to admit, are tensing at strange sounds at night and hitting the deck at loud noises. It may be silly—I feel that way afterward—but maybe it isn't in the long run. I figure it is one of the reasons there's no holes in my hide yet. You are either quick or dead. . . . I'm safe to be around. I'm not crazy. (I think—or is that what they all say—HA! HA! HA!) I guess I'm just tired. Tired of constantly being on edge. . . .

Sincerely,
Mike

HOWARD SHERPE, an army field medic near Pleiku, reflected in his journal on the premature aging of young men in Vietnam. (For a biographical sketch of Sherpe, see chapter 4.)

[1966]

It doesn't take long to age a boy in Vietnam. Young, in both age and spirit, they arrive in this war torn land, full of the ideals and bright dreams of youth. Life has been good. There have been more flowers than thorns along our path. We have a child's confidence that all will be well and as the fairy tales always end, And they lived happily ever after.

Suddenly these young bodies and hearts are thrown into war. Death stalks among them, plucking at random, the life and spirit from a chosen few, leaving the rest saddened, bewildered, and frightened. You see bodies torn and ripped, voices that only a short time ago had been filled with hope and joy, now screamed in pain.

Rain pours, mud envelops the land, mud that seems to reach out and pull your feet out from under you, that captures you and pulls you in. You struggle, you fall in the mud. Bullets fly and you try to bury yourself in it. You crawl through the mud and filth. This mud of war seems to cover everything. Your eyes, your mouth, even your mind.

Where only a few short weeks ago a young boy full of dreams and hopes stood, now a dirty, bedraggled, old man crawls on his belly through

It doesn't take long to age a boy in Vietnam. Young, in both age and spirit, they arrive in this war torn land, full of the ideals and bright dreams of youth. Life has been good, there have been more flowers than thorns along our path.

88

"It doesn't take long to age a boy in Vietnam."
Sketch from Howard Sherpe's journal. Courtesy Howard Sherpe.

the mud. His hopes have turned to fear and frustration. His dreams to nightmares. His joy to hate. Light has turned to dark and life will never be the same for him again. Survival is all that matters now. Life seems to have lost its sense and meaning. The youthful zest is gone, replaced by sobering thoughts. Life has been stripped of all its superficial coatings, of its many centuries of civilizing, and we are thrust again into the evolution of our past and I see man as the animal he is, fighting for his survival. It is when this stage is reached, that men are changed and they can never see things in the same light again.

I was no longer the same person that landed on that shore such a short time ago.

It doesn't take long to age a boy in Vietnam.

After 1968, an increasing number of American soldiers in Vietnam began to use drugs to help ease the stresses of combat or cope with declining morale. Marijuana, which was inexpensive and readily available, became the drug of choice. Following a military crackdown on marijuana use in 1969, heroin's popularity soared because of its odorless nature and accelerated "high." In the letter that follows, infantryman STEVE PLUE, situated in Cu Chi, discusses the availability of drugs for soldiers and the potentially destructive consequences of regular drug use. (For a biographical sketch of Plue, see chapter 1.)

September 11, 1970
Dear Mom & Dad:

. . . I figured the drug issue was rising in Fort [Atkinson, Wisconsin]. You wouldn't believe how out of proportion it's gotten over here and it's not surprising. A person can buy a bag of marijuana for a dollar that a person would spend $20–$30 for in the United States. So because of the inexpense and easy access the problem is growing rapidly.

It would make you sick to see how messed up some of these guys are. They literally go crazy, especially those who smoke every day and it's impossible to communicate with them and they inflate everything out of proportion, especially problems and they can't hardly bear the everyday little things. I can't say for a fact that it's marijuana alone but it's not helping them. Marijuana's the big drug but they also can get the harder drugs just as easily and that's what's really killing these guys. . . .

Love
Steve

DOUGLAS J. BRADLEY (b. 1947) was born in Philadelphia and was drafted into the army in March, 1970. He served as a journalist for the *Army Reporter* at the U.S. Army headquarters in Long Binh from November,

1970, to November, 1971, when he was discharged. Bradley currently resides in Madison, where he is a public information officer for the University of Wisconsin Extension. He wrote the following entry in his journal.

May 8, 1971

. . . Many brief pictures can be drawn of the decay of Vietnam—and they are brief only because time is brief—for they will reappear tomorrow although perhaps in a different guise. The dislike & in some cases the intense hatred that exists between the ARVN & U.S. forces is unbelievable. In some cases the hatred is made hostile, but oftentimes it is not. But it can be seen in the eyes of the GI & the ARVN. The reasons behind this on either side are numerous—but unnecessary to relate. Let it suffice to say that there is no love lost between allies ... For that matter there is a good bit of anti-Amer. feelings here—and they become more prevalent every day. Perhaps if we can't bring ourselves home the Vietnamese will someday tell us to leave.

Apart from the regular Army assholes that dig on this sort of thing, the effect Vietnam has had on our youth has been most devastating. It is they that have lost their spirits & their souls. I've never seen as much bitterness & despair as I've seen here. So many young men strung-out on heroin—sacrificing their lives to escape from Vietnam's unreality. So many young men strung-out on hatred—despising any & all systems, institutions & leaders, bent-on getting-even at any costs. And so many young men just strung-out—bitter, despairing & destroyed—giving-up on any & all they might have done & simply checking-out. We have denied our sons the laughter of their youth—a youth that is not confined to the adolescent years—but an aura of youth—of a brightness & a glow— that remains with a man until his own children take it up for him. We have denied them the leisure of peace. And we have not given them love—just pure & simple love without any strings attached ...

As I pause to reflect on Vietnam at perhaps another time & another place, I feel empty. There is a vast emptiness here—no love, no compassion, no peace, no brotherhood, no beauty—& no tomorrow. . . .

Beginning in 1969, unpopular officers became targets of an increasing number of fragging incidents in which their own troops tried to kill or injure them. (The term "fragging" came from the practice of rolling a fragmentation grenade under another soldier's tent.) The number of such intentional casualties rose from an estimate of 126 in 1969 to 333 in 1971, coinciding with the breakdown in discipline and morale during the final years of the war. DENNIS BOYER, serving at the Combined Intelligence Center (MACV) in the tactical scale studies area based in Saigon, commented on the problem in the following letter. (For a biographical sketch of Boyer, see chapter 4.)

Bien Hoa Air Base, December 30, 1970

Pete:

. . . That brings me to your question about fraggings. I don't think they have solid numbers on that stuff. There was a rash of them in 1st Inf Div. in late 1969. There may have been a dozen or so in Americal Div. And now we're working close with 1st Cav. and they had several incidents that look suspicious recently. There were even more back during the Cambodian mess. But that's when the mutinies happened too. People tend to think that 101st ABN DIV and 173 ABN BDG didn't have these problems. With the pulled out Marine divisions I hear totally opposite stories. Some say nothing like that happened among Marines. Others say that Marines were just more likely to do it in the field and do it with NVA weapons and get away with it.

There's a clearer picture on the drug deaths. The O.D. [overdose] figures I saw had over 70 dead between January and the end of October of this year. So it should go over 100 for the year.

What's not clear is whether fraggings, O.D.s, truck accidents, etc are included in the KIA figures. That may apply to later deaths of medevaced wounded. So casualty figures may be under-reported. I'll send you the O.D. sheet in a package.

Give them hell,
Dutch

RICHARD J. SHAFEL (b. 1951) lived in Antigo and Madison prior to enlisting in the army in March, 1971. He drove armored personnel carriers and operated a mortar (A Troop, 3–5th Cav., 101st Abn. Div. [Airmobile]; A Co., 3–187th Inf., 3d Bde., 101st Abn. Div. [Airmobile]) near Dong Ha and Quang Tri from March through December, 1971. Shafel was discharged in February, 1972, and now lives in Madison, where he manages a restaurant. In this letter to his mother, Shafel mentions a fragging incident in his unit.

April 9, [1971]

Dear Mom,

. . . We leave for the bush on Easter Sunday. We're going up to Camp A4 right on the DMZ. I man a 50 caliber machine gun on the top of an APC. There's five of us on the APC and for the past couple of days, we've been getting them ready. I haven't been too lucky for the last few days, so I didn't do much. We're going out for two weeks to whenever we come back. I heard today that it probably won't be longer than a month or two. It seems kinda strange that I'm really going into it now. This isn't a game anymore Mom. A couple of nights ago some guy got mad at a guy and threw a grenade under his hooch at night. Instead of hurting the one intended for, it killed a different guy and it was only two hooches away from mine. There really are some crazy people over here. . . .

Love
Rick

HELEN WEIDNER, an Army Special Services worker in Phu Loi, wrote to her parents about the impact of the war on one GI. (For a biographical sketch of Weidner, see chapter 2.)

March 14, 1972

[Dear Mom and Dad,]

. . . I think in most of life we can label everything that happens as good or bad or boring or exciting or "at least I learned something," and so we cut life up into experiences and digest them into our personalities and our own approach to life.

War is different. Too much happens that can't be digested, yet not discarded & forgotten either. . . . Over here we talk about the war all the time. Back home, no. People who live in a normal world can't understand this anyway. A reporter remarked recently that almost no literature has come out of this war, unlike the other wars. . . .

[Sam] was talking about his tour in Vietnam. He got so he hated everyone. He would shoot at anything that moved, woman, child, water-buffalo, he didn't care. They pulled a raid on a VC village & killed almost everyone, but when [Sam] and his company went hooch to hooch, he heard a baby cry. Its mother was dead. [Sam] said that baby just tore his heart. He picked up the little girl and put her in his pack, and carried her for 4 days to civilization. That changed him. Now he sees the Vietnamese as hardworking people trying to build good homes for their families. He is planning to marry a Vietnamese girl. He is a gentle man, kind and understanding. I would never have guessed a history of hate so strong his CO tried to get him transferred out, lest he crack up completely. Some men are destroyed by Vietnam. And some become new and better people than they ever were. Hardly anyone can go thru a war and come out unchanged, but the question is, changed which way? That's one reason I'm here, to try to control the direction of the change. . . .

The Ultimate Price

More than 58,000 Americans died during the Vietnam War. The following letters serve as a somber reminder of the precious cost of war. RICHARD P. WOLFF (b. 1947) grew up in Watertown and enlisted in the Marine Corps in

March, 1966. He served as an administrative clerk, driver, and combat engineer (Spt. Co. [Hq.], 1st Eng. Bn., 1st Mar. Div.) near Chu Lai and Da Nang from September, 1966, until September, 1967. Wolff was discharged in January, 1968. He now teaches sixth-grade science in Watertown.

November 23, [1966]

Dear Mom,

. . . I don't know if you've heard of the operation going on south of here or not. I was down there for the first day & a half driving a dump. The dump is always right behind the autos in a convoy. We were driving down there, I was the third, two autos were in front of me, when the front one hit a anti-tank mine. It blew the autos apart. The driver had both his legs blown off above the knees. They laid him on the ground and wouldn't let him sit up. He said it wasn't too bad if only his legs didn't hurt so. He didn't know they were gone. He talked alot before he died. He had only 29 days left and he was going home to get married. He said this would delay things a little and then he died without even knowing he was going to. War sure isn't a very pretty thing. I hope Paul never has to go into the service. . . .

Love
Richard

DENNIS BELONGER, a LRRP member in the central highlands northeast of An Khe, wrote this letter to his parents the day before he was killed in action. (For a biographical sketch of Belonger, see chapter 2.)

July 18, [1969]

Dear Folks,

Well, I'm a team leader now whether I wanted to be or not. They say I'm qualified and needed, so ... Price has a team now too. He came in today—was shot out of his AO; Denny got his first dink. His point man heard the dink coming but his weapon jammed so he moved to the side and Denny pumped 5 rounds into the guy. Captured an AK47—they might get a medal for some other stuff too. Just a couple hours ago another team was shot out. They had to be extracted by ladder at night; the team leader was hurt. They killed a mess of dinks too and may also get some medals out of it. *LRRPs are good* and we do a tough job.

Now get ready: I'll be back on Rat's team for a special mission—going out tomorrow. We'll be inserted into an area in which several battalions have been observed. They believe the headquarters for a regiment is there: 1200 dinks. I'm not making up a story; this is from intelligence reports. We volunteered to go in and try to find the HQ and

Dennis Belonger. Courtesy Mrs. V. Ehlinger.

pull out at least one POW. If we pull this off I guarantee you I'll get a Silver Star. Say some prayers, OK? They're needed!

I'm damned scared and I had to tell somebody. Kestell doesn't know anything about what I've been doing or am about to do. Don't want her to worry. I was put in for promotion but it hasn't come through yet. I can use the extra money.

By the way, check & see if Wisconsin pays Vietnam vets anything for returning, purple hearts, or medals, OK?

I'll be OK, I'm good.

Love,
Dennis

JOHN K. MARSHALL (1949–1968) was born in Green Bay and enlisted in the Marine Corps in December, 1967, while still a senior in high school. He served with the military police (27th Mar., 1st Mar. Div.) and as a fire team leader (C Co., 1/5th Mar., 1st Mar. Div.) near Da Nang from May, 1968, until November 17, 1968, when he was killed in action.

August 29, [1968]

Dear Mom & Dad & Family

Well I got here to the 5th Marines yesterday. We came over by heli-

John K. Marshall.
Courtesy John E. and
Helen Marshall.

copter. Guess what I'm getting. Now don't panic. I'm getting a "Purple Heart." At 8:30 P.M. on Aug 27 I was coming back from the bathroom and we started getting mortared. I started to run to the bunker but the second round came in and I got shrapnel in the left high part of the leg and in the forehead right above the eye. When I was running the mortar hit and I fell to the ground. I felt the piece of metal hit my head. I then made it to a bunker and took off my T-shirt and put it on my head. After that I went to the doctor and they took the metal out. I then got a penicillin shot. I got a little piece in the arm too. So I guess I was lucky I wasn't nearer to it when it hit. There was about 6 that hit. There were about 3 other guys that got hit too. I thought at first that was the end of me. Cause I felt it hit my head & blood started coming out fast. I didn't know I was hit in the leg till later. Well I get a Purple Heart out of it anyway. . . . You know if you get three purple hearts you get out of Vietnam. . . .

love
John

September 2, [1968]

Dear Mom & Dad & Family

Well this isn't such a quiet unit as the 27th. We got into a fight with the VC. We killed a bunch of em but they killed & wounded more than enough of our guys. Our squad leader was killed. He got shot in the back in the spinal cord. The guy next to me was shot right in the shoulder. Those bullets make some big holes in people. I seen a couple of VC with bullets in their heads. It's enough to get you all shook up. I'm getting another purple heart cause this morning I was scraped by a bullet. It was on the right side. I had my flak jacket on laying on the ground. I was crawling when I was hit. The flak jacket isn't bulletproof but it helps against mortars & grenades some. Your novenas are helping me. That's 2 purple hearts in 6 days. Those wounds I had could of turned out real serious if I wasn't lucky. It rained out hard the last 2 nights. I get wounded 1 more time, and I come back to the U.S. Well I pray everyday so I can make it back. I'll write soon as I can again. So keep praying and I'll make it back.

love always
John

Marshall wrote the following letter three days before he was killed in action. His third Purple Heart was awarded posthumously to his parents.

November 14, [1968]

Dear Mom & Dad & Family

Hi again. Everything is pretty okay here. Been having quite a bit of rain the last few days but today has been pretty hot. Been getting all your letters. . . .

I had a dream last night that some VC were coming towards me and I got shot pretty bad but lived & got a third purple heart. Before I was wounded I had a dream I was shot. So who knows. We been back on C-rats the last 2 weeks. Your last letter I got was dated Nov. 4th. Did you get my check from Nov. 1st for 120.00. I should have close to 600.00 in the bank now. Well that's about all I have to say for now so I'll close.

Love always
John

While stationed south of Saigon near Vung Tau, STEVE PLUE, an infantryman, wrote to his parents regarding the death of a comrade and the raw pain of war. (For a biographical sketch of Plue, see chapter 1.)

February 11, 1970

Dear Mom & Dad:

I wanted to write yesterday but I was too sick to even try. I wasn't ill because of a bug or any other Asian disease but it's a sickness that will bother me the rest of my tour in Vietnam.

What's the worse way a man can die or rather what's the most frightening death to watch? Is it by bullet? Is it by slaughter?

What I saw and heard yesterday is so horrid perhaps I shouldn't even be writing the memory.

We went out yesterday pulling security for the team of men putting up the mechanical ambush traps.

Remember I described one of these traps once before. It's a combination of four or five claymore mines connected by an electrical wire set off by a trip wire which creates an electrical impulse setting off these mines, enough force to blow half of our house away.

We left the road near a stream and headed into the thick traveling parallel to the stream. It took all morning to move 2,000 meters to the location where we were to set up the traps.

At about 1:00 in the afternoon the sites had been picked and the three man team proceeded across the stream. The security element stayed on the other side guarding the trails while the three man team started setting up the mines.

After about 10 minutes came this enormous explosion from across the stream and several screams.

We heard someone screaming, what we thought [was] "We're under fire," thinking that they had made contact with the enemy.

We smelled smoke and heard the crackling of flames. We crossed the stream feeling we were to be fired upon any moment. After crossing the stream one of the members of the team screamed for the Radio Operator to call a dust off. He was too hysterical to talk and myself and my friend Jeff Vicker followed him running into a wall of fire. The flames were at tree top level and made a perimeter with at least a 40 meter diameter.

And God, I couldn't believe my eyes. There in the middle of this fire was a member of this three man team. Lying on the charred ground all ablaze and twitching.

It was so horrid I felt like passing out. I was so afraid and I've never felt fear like I did at that moment. We tried to get through the perimeter but to no avail and the fire advanced toward us and spread quickly because it was in a marsh area with tall dried elephant grass, ten feet tall.

We were so damn helpless. We couldn't get in to help. We were watching our friend being burned mother. How could we cope with reality?

We finally found a break in the fire and could get to him but he was dead. Burned so badly all facial features were gone. It was so ungodly terrible. Seeing his naked, charred body lying on the smoldering ground. It wasn't as if it were a death by bullet but he was so mutilated from the blaze.

Seeing Jeff and I were of the lowest rank we were ordered to take his body from the area and all we could do was roll the body onto the litter. I'll never forget the feel of his flesh on my fingertips and we had to cover his face because it was too unbearable to see.

I felt so much like crying but could only curse the multiple reasons for what had happened.

His wallet was strewn on the ground. Pictures of little children, probably his family and they gave me the ungodly honor of carrying his helmet filled with letters from probably his girl because they were pink color and stained with blood.

I couldn't sleep without visualizing what had happened. How can I forget mother? I keep thinking that it could be my turn next.

This is the fifth accidental death by these damn traps. They're dangerous as hell but still they insist we risk our life putting up these fool things.

How can they ask us to continue these things after witnessing such a horrible death.

It wasn't as if we had come across such a body but we watched him dying and we couldn't do a damn thing to help. I keep remembering him living and finding it so hard to realize that it was his charred body we had rolled onto that litter.

I'll never forget. It's the first time I've seen a man die and [I] feel so hopeless of ever coming home. I've got so much time and the risks are so high we pay each day. It could have been myself or Jeff and who knows that tomorrow will not repeat yesterday.

For once I'm afraid of dying and wish I could find that helping hand like a little child being shielded by his parents.

The society asks too much of us. Where will we find the courage or faith. Finally I'm beginning to realize there'll never be any hope for peace. Damn this war and everything that's put us here. If I'm to die here, I only wish it were for something I believed in.

Your son
Steven

Courtesy 101st Airborne Division Association.

Epilogue

BOB ROCK, an infantry platoon leader, wrote this poem in the late afternoon of January 19, 1970, after attending the memorial service (pictured on the facing page) for Robert G. Mitcheltree of Longview, Texas, who was killed in an enemy ambush earlier that day. (For a biographical sketch of Rock, see chapter 1.)

VIETNAM

The sand I kick belongs to unwonted beaches.
The air I breathe to a frightened and hopeful people.
The earth I move belongs to unsown seeds and
the miles behind me seem wasted.

Threads of life are woven together by yesterday's songs and
tomorrow's dreams. The unity of forgotten legions conceived for
the purpose of a not so unified end.

    ... a delusive effort for those who will
    never see tomorrow ... and, possibly, for
    those that survive.

As it grows on, boys become men. Men become older,
each knowing that until men become something more, some will
continue to die in vain.

    I will fight and may die in the blind
    hope that the generations to come will
    evolve beyond the ignorance of today's
    peoples—a tomorrow that brings a
    brotherhood of man that is not built
    on the shoulders of its dying brethren.

4 Deuce: 4.2-inch heavy mortar.

11B: Military occupational specialty (MOS) code number designating an infantryman. Additional numbers following 11B indicate special training a soldier has received. The designation 11B10 indicates an infantryman.

81: M-29 81 mm mortar.

Abn.: Airborne.

A/C: Aircraft commander.

ACR: Armored Cavalry Regiment.

Admin.: Administration.

AFB: Air force base.

AIT: Advanced individual training or advanced infantry training.

AK-47: Soviet-designed assault rifle widely used by the Viet Cong and North Vietnamese army.

AO: Area of operation.

APC: Armored personnel carrier; often called a track.

Arty.: Artillery.

ARVN: Army of the Republic of Vietnam (the South Vietnamese army).

Avn.: Aviation.

AWOL: Absent without official leave. To leave a military base or post without official orders, an offense punishable by a court-martial.

B-40: Rocket-propelled grenade launcher used by the North Vietnamese army and the Viet Cong.

BAR: Browning automatic rifle. There were several different Browning rifles, all of which were modified versions of the long-barreled, heavy, gas-operated weapon with a twenty-round clip originally designed for use by the U.S. Army in World War I.

Base Camp: Semipermanent brigade or division headquarters. Artillery batteries and airfields, as well as supply dumps and facilities such as offices, showers, mess halls, hospitals, and clubs, were located in base camps.

Battalion (Bn.): Two or more companies (approximately 500 men) under the command of a major or lieutenant colonel.

Bird: Airplane or helicopter.

Bivouac: Short-term encampment in the field.

Body Count: Number of North Vietnamese and Viet Cong soldiers captured, killed, or wounded in combat. Government and military leaders used the body count as a way to measure the combat success of U.S. and ARVN units during the war.

Boonies: The field, especially the jungle. Any place in the Vietnamese countryside outside the security of a military base.

Brigade (Bde.): One or more battalions with support units, under the command of a colonel or a brigadier general.

Bru: A tribal people of the mountains of Vietnam.

Btry.: Battery.

Burp Gun: A light, portable submachine gun.

Bush: *See* Boonies.

C-4: Plastic explosives that were also used in the field as a cooking fuel.

C-123 (Caribou): A light aircraft designed to operate from small airfields.

C-141 (Starlifter): A large jet aircraft used for transport.

CA: *See* Charlie Alpha.

Casual Company: Soldiers waiting for a new duty assignment or soldiers on R & R.

Cav.: Cavalry.

CBU: Cluster bomb unit or canistered bomblet unit. A bomb that releases numerous smaller bombs when dropped from the air. Most CBUs were antipersonnel weapons.

Charlie or **Charlie Cong:** Short for Victor Charlie, the military phonetic form of VC, or Viet Cong. Used to mean both the Viet Cong and North Vietnamese soldiers.

Charlie Alpha (CA): Combat assault. To fly soldiers by helicopter into combat situations.

Charliemed: C Co., 3d Medical Battalion, 3d Marine Division.

Chi-Com: Chinese communist. Used to designate items made in the People's Republic of China.

CICV: Combined Intelligence Center of Vietnam, part of the Military Assistance Command of Vietnam (MACV). An agency that shared intelligence on Vietnam among the United States and its allies.

Claymore: An antipersonnel mine that fired hundreds of small steel projectiles in a fan-shaped pattern.

Click: One kilometer.

CO: Commanding officer.

Cobra: A small, high-speed Huey attack helicopter.

Company (Co.): Two or more platoons commanded by a captain.

Corpsman: *See* Medic.

C-Rations: Prepackaged food carried and eaten by troops in the field. Often called Cs or c-rats.

DI: Drill instructor.

Dink: Derogatory term for an Asian.

Division (Div.): Three army brigades.

"D" Med: Company D, 4th Medical Battalion. "D" Med provided medical support for the 4th Infantry Division, 3d Brigade, in the northern sector of South Vietnam (I Corps).

DMZ: Demilitarized zone. The buffer area between the borders of North and South Vietnam.

Domino Theory: Cold War theory holding that if communists took over one nation, its neighbors would also succumb.

Dove: Opponent of U.S. participation in the war.

Dust Off: A medevac helicopter or the act of being transported by a medevac helicopter.

Duster: A self-propelled antiaircraft weapon that ran on caterpillar treads and was used against low-flying aircraft and for ground support.

EM Club: Enlisted men's club.

Engr.: Engineers.

Evac.: Evacuation.

Firefight: Exchange of small-arms fire between units.

Fire Support Base: Temporary installation established to provide mortar and artillery support to units in the field.

Fire Team: Four-man marine unit.

Flak Jacket: Fiberglass-filled vest worn for protection against shrapnel.

Fld.: Field.

FMF: Fleet Marine Force. An administrative subdivision of a U.S. Navy fleet consisting of Marine Corps land, air, and support elements.

FOB: Forward operating base. A headquarters located in the field.

Four-Party Joint Military Supervision Commission: A group including representatives of the United States, South Vietnam, North Vietnam, and the Viet Cong that attempted to establish a cease fire and supervised the withdrawal of U.S. troops and the exchange of prisoners of war between January and March, 1973.

Frag: To kill or attempt to kill one's own officers, often with a fragmentation grenade.

Gen.: General.

Gook: Derogatory term for an Asian.

Grp.: Group.

Grunt: A foot soldier.

Gunship: Armed combat helicopter.

Hawk: Supporter of U.S. participation in the war.

HHB: Headquarters and Headquarters Battery.

HHC: Headquarters and Headquarters Company.

Ho Chi Minh Trail: Network of roads, paths, and trails running from North Vietnam, through Laos and Cambodia, to South Vietnam; used extensively by the north to transport troops and supplies into the south.

Hooch or **hootch:** A hut or other small dwelling, such as a tent, in which U.S. military personnel in Vietnam or Vietnamese civilians lived.

Hosp.: Hospital.

Hot: A dangerous place or an area experiencing combat, as in "a hot LZ."

Hq.: Headquarters.

Huey: The Bell UH utility helicopter, originally named the Bell HU helicopter.

Hump: To carry gear or to be on patrol out in the field, as in "humping the boonies."

ICC (International Control Commission): Three-nation group including Canada, Hungary, and Indonesia that investigated violations of the Paris Peace Accords of 1973. Also known as the International Commission for Control and Supervision.

Illumination: A light-producing flare. Also, a type of small hand grenade.

In Country: In Vietnam.

Inf.: Infantry.

Jungle Rot: Severe skin affliction caused by extended exposure to moisture; generally developed on the feet and in the crotch.

Khmer Rouge: Leftists who gained control of the Cambodian government in 1975 and slaughtered millions of the country's citizens.

KIA: Killed in action.

Klick or **K:** One kilometer.

L/C: Lieutenant colonel.

Lifer: Career military personnel.

Line: Field infantry units.

Line Doggy: Foot soldier.

Log: Aerial logistical resupply of troops in the field.

Louie: Lieutenant.

LP: Listening post. A group of men stationed outside a night perimeter to provide the main body of troops with an early warning in case of attack.

LRRP or **Lurp:** Long-range reconnaissance patrol; after 1969 called Rangers. Also the special food rations issued to units going on long-range patrol missions.

LST: Landing Ship Tank. A large cargo ship capable of discharging vehicles and supplies directly onto a beachhead. The vulnerability of LSTs earned them the nickname "large slow targets."

LZ: Landing zone. The names of specific landing zones usually followed the letters LZ, such as LZ Dolly.

M-1: The M-1 Garand rifle, a long-barreled, heavy weapon with an eight-round clip. The U.S. Army used the M-1 as the standard infantry rifle from 1936 until 1957, when the M-14 rifle replaced it.

M-14: Rifle adopted by the army in 1957 to replace the M-1 as the standard infantry weapon. The M-14 followed the basic design of the M-1 but was easier to load and more accurate.

M-16: A light, plastic and steel short-barreled rifle first issued to the air force in 1962 and then to the Army Special Forces in Vietnam. Though the M-16 was less accurate than the M-14, its superior firepower made it preferable for jungle combat.

M-60 MG: General-purpose machine gun used by U.S. forces in Vietnam.

M-79: A shoulder-fired, single-shot grenade launcher used by the U.S. Army from 1961 until the early 1970s.

MACV: Military Assistance Command, Vietnam. Headquarters of the U.S. military in Vietnam, located on the Tan Son Nhut air base.

Mar.: Marine.

MASH: Mobile army surgical hospital

Mech.: Mechanized.

MEDCAP: Medical civil action program. A program in which volunteer doctors provided medical service and health instruction to Vietnamese civilians.

Medevac or **Medevac Bird:** Helicopter ambulances designed to pick up injured or wounded soldiers in the field.

Medic (Corpsman): Enlisted man trained in basic medical skills who offered medical care to wounded soldiers in the field to stabilize them for transport to the rear. Medics also provided basic medical services under the direction of nurses at hospitals.

MiG-17: Soviet-designed fighter jet.

Military Occupational Specialty (MOS): An alphanumeric rating system used by the army and marines to classify the rank and training of military personnel.

Monitor: An armored gunboat used for transporting equipment and personnel along shallow rivers and shorelines. Monitors were equipped with both 40 mm and 80 mm guns and mortars.

Montagnards: A tribal people of the mountains of Vietnam.

MOS: *See* Military Occupational Specialty.

MP: Military police.

Napalm: Sticky, flammable, jellied gasoline compound used as a weapon and defoliant. Napalm could be dropped in bombs or fired from flame throwers.

NCO: Noncommissioned officer.

NDP: Night defense perimeter. Precautions taken by units in the field to protect them from enemy attack, usually consisting of sentry posts and claymore mines.

New Boot: Recently arrived soldier.

Nguyens: Derogatory term for the Vietnamese.

NVA: North Vietnamese army.

NVN, N.VN or **No. VN:** North Vietnam.

PF: *See* Popular Forces.

Platoon (Plt.): Military unit commanded by a lieutenant, usually consisting of two or more squads of eight to ten men.

Point or **Point Man:** Soldier who would walk ahead of units on patrol. The point man would try to spot dangerous situations before they could affect the unit.

Popular Forces (PF): Militia units organized in South Vietnamese villages that were supposed to protect them and assist regular army units operating in the area.

Port Arms: Position for carrying a rifle; barrel up and near the left shoulder, rifle butt down and near the right hip.

POW: Prisoner of war.

PT: Physical training.

Puff (AC-47 Skytrain): Military version of the DC-3 transport plane, also called Puff the Magic Dragon, typically equipped with three 7.62 mm electric Gatling guns that could be fired as the aircraft circled its target.

PX: Post exchange; military store that sold goods only to American military personnel.

Quiz (Qz.): Interrogation.

Rack: Bunk.

Rangers: Highly trained U.S. commando troops specialized in combat and reconnaissance. *See also* LRRP.

RC: Red Cross.

Recon, Recondo, or **Reconnaissance:** Act of locating, observing, and identifying enemy positions or activity.

Regiment (Regt.): Three infantry battalions. Only the marines and armored cavalry units divided themselves into regiments.

ROTC: Reserve Officers Training Corps. A program offered at colleges and universities through which soldiers could enter the military with the rank of second lieutenant.

RPG: Rocket-propelled grenade.

R & R: Rest and recuperation, rest and relaxation, or rest and recreation. A three- to seven-day vacation from the war, taken at locales such as Thailand, Australia, Japan, and Hawaii.

RTO: Radio-telephone operator. The person responsible for carrying and operating a unit's radio in the field, often a prime target for the enemy.

RVN: Republic of Vietnam; South Vietnam.

Sampan: Small Vietnamese boat.

Satchel Charges: Canvas bag containing explosives that the VC threw or dropped onto targets.

Seabee: U.S. Navy Construction Battalion (CB). The Seabees constructed most of the U.S. military installations in Vietnam.

SFG: Special Forces Group.

Short or Short-Timer: Soldier whose tour of duty in Vietnam was almost over.

Slick: Unarmed helicopter.

Soul Brother: African American male.

Special Forces: U.S. troops trained in counterinsurgency and guerrilla warfare techniques.

Spiderhole: Small hole, usually connected to a tunnel system, used by the Viet Cong to ambush U.S. troops.

Spt.: Support.

Squad: Unit of eight to ten men.

Squadron (Sqdn.): Army cavalry unit of between 400 and 600 men under the command of a lieutenant colonel.

Standdown: Movement of a unit from the field to a base for a period of noncombat duty or to be sent home.

Sweep: To thoroughly search an area or village for enemy soldiers or supplies.

Tet: Seven-day celebration of the Vietnamese lunar new year. On January 30, 1968, the first day of Tet, the North Vietnamese and Viet Cong launched a massive offensive against U.S. and ARVN positions in South Vietnam, especially urban areas.

TFS: Tactical Fighter Squadron.

TFW: Tactical Fighter Wing.

Tiger Scouts: Members of the Capital Division of the South Korean army, which arrived in Vietnam in 1965.

Tracer: Ammunition that leaves a trail when fired.

Track: Vehicles that ran on treads, especially armored personnel carriers.

Trans.: Transportation.

USO (United Service Organizations): Group that provided entertainment, refreshments, and care packages for military personnel.

VC or Viet Cong: South Vietnamese leftist guerrillas in revolt against the government of the Republic of Vietnam.

WAC: Member of the Women's Army Corps.

WIA: Wounded in action.

The World: Western civilization, especially the United States.

Wpns.: Weapons.

Suggestions for Further Reading

There are numerous accounts of America's experience in Vietnam, and more are published with each passing year. Thus, the following represents a highly selective list of suggestions for further reading. George C. Herring, *America's Longest War: The United States and Vietnam, 1950–1975* (3d ed., New York: McGraw-Hill, 1996) offers a concise overview of the history of the war. Two lengthier but more detailed surveys are Phillip B. Davidson, *Vietnam at War: The History, 1946–1975* (Novato, Calif.: Presidio, 1988) and Stanley Karnow, *Vietnam: A History* (New York: Viking, 1983). Karnow's book accompanies the Public Broadcasting System series *Vietnam: A Television History* (New York: Sony, 1987), which is available on videotape.

Hundreds of Vietnam veterans have published their memoirs. Tobias Wolff, *Pharaoh's Army: Memories of the Lost War* (New York: Knopf, 1994), and Philip Caputo, *A Rumor of War* (New York: Holt, Rinehart, and Winston, 1977), are among the best. Michael Herr, a journalist who visited Vietnam in 1967 and 1968, wrote about the experiences of American soldiers in *Dispatches* (New York: Knopf, 1977). General histories of the experience of combat soldiers that cover the entire war are harder to find. Two superb books that have proved useful in preparing this volume are Christian G. Appy, *Working-Class War: American Combat Soldiers and Vietnam* (Chapel Hill: University of North Carolina Press, 1993), and James B. Ebert, *A Life in a Year: The American Infantryman in Vietnam, 1965–1972* (Novato, Calif.: Presidio, 1993). Both books offer vivid accounts of the day-to-day lives of enlisted men in Vietnam, and Ebert's work draws heavily on interviews with Wisconsin Vietnam veterans. Linda Reinberg, *In the Field: The Language of the Vietnam War* (New York: Facts on File, 1991) is a helpful and interesting sourcebook on the slang developed by American soldiers.

The New York Vietnam Veterans Memorial Commission gathered letters from veterans from that state and published them in Bernard Edelman, ed., *Dear America: Letters Home from Vietnam* (New York: Norton, 1985). Elizabeth M. Norman, *Women at War: The Story of Fifty Military Nurses Who Served in Vietnam* (Philadelphia: University of Pennsylvania Press, 1990), is based heavily on oral histories, as is Wallace Terry, *Bloods: An Oral History of the Vietnam War by Black Veterans* (New York: Random House, 1984). John G. Hubbell tells the story of American prisoners of war in *P.O.W.: A Definitive History of the American Prisoner-of-War Experience in Vietnam, 1964–1973* (New York: Reader's

Digest Press, 1976). Craig Howes, *Voices of the Vietnam POWs: Witnesses to Their Fight* (New York: Oxford University Press, 1993), reviews the memoirs, biographies, and collective histories of POWs published in the twenty years after their release. Wilbur J. Scott, a Vietnam veteran and sociologist, examines veterans' postwar experiences in *The Politics of Readjustment: Vietnam Veterans since the War* (New York: Aldine De Gruyter, 1993).

Lance Sijan, Wisconsin Medal of Honor winner and one of those whose letters are contained in this book, is the subject of Malcolm McConnell's *Into the Mouth of the Cat: The Story of Lance Sijan, Hero of Vietnam* (New York: Norton, 1985). Ray W. Stubbe, whose letters also appear here, was at Khe Sanh during the siege and is the author, with John Prados, of *Valley of Decision: The Siege of Khe Sanh* (Boston: Houghton Mifflin, 1991).

Index

251